Nadiia Koval, Denys Tereshchenko (eds.)

RUSSIAN CULTURAL DIPLOMACY UNDER PUTIN
Rossotrudnichestvo, the "Russkiy Mir" Foundation, and the Gorchakov Fund in 2007–2022

Bibliografische Information der Deutschen Nationalbibliothek
Die Deutsche Nationalbibliothek verzeichnet diese Publikation in der Deutschen Nationalbibliografie; detaillierte bibliografische Daten sind im Internet über http://dnb.d-nb.de abrufbar.

Bibliographic information published by the Deutsche Nationalbibliothek
Die Deutsche Nationalbibliothek lists this publication in the Deutsche Nationalbibliografie; detailed bibliographic data are available in the Internet at http://dnb.d-nb.de.

Cover picture: "Soon the Whole World Will Be Ours" by Leonid Sayansky (1889–1945). Lithography, 1920. Source: Russian State Library, https://search.rsl.ru/ru/record/0100670

ISBN-13: 978-3-8382-1801-4
© *ibidem*-Verlag, Stuttgart 2023
Alle Rechte vorbehalten

Das Werk einschließlich aller seiner Teile ist urheberrechtlich geschützt. Jede Verwertung außerhalb der engen Grenzen des Urheberrechtsgesetzes ist ohne Zustimmung des Verlages unzulässig und strafbar. Dies gilt insbesondere für Vervielfältigungen, Übersetzungen, Mikroverfilmungen und elektronische Speicherformen sowie die Einspeicherung und Verarbeitung in elektronischen Systemen.

All rights reserved. No part of this publication may be reproduced, stored in or introduced into a retrieval system, or transmitted, in any form, or by any means (electronical, mechanical, photocopying, recording or otherwise) without the prior written permission of the publisher. Any person who does any unauthorized act in relation to this publication may be liable to criminal prosecution and civil claims for damages.

Printed in the EU

Soviet and Post-Soviet Politics and Society (SPPS) Vol. 268
ISSN 1614-3515

General Editor: Andreas Umland,
Stockholm Centre for Eastern European Studies, andreas.umland@ui.se

Commissioning Editor: Max Jakob Horstmann,
London, mjh@ibidem.eu

EDITORIAL COMMITTEE*

DOMESTIC & COMPARATIVE POLITICS
Prof. **Ellen Bos**, *Andrássy University of Budapest*
Dr. **Gergana Dimova**, *Florida State University*
Prof. **Heiko Pleines**, *University of Bremen*
Dr. **Sarah Whitmore**, *Oxford Brookes University*
Dr. **Harald Wydra**, *University of Cambridge*

SOCIETY, CLASS & ETHNICITY
Col. **David Glantz**, *"Journal of Slavic Military Studies"*
Dr. **Marlène Laruelle**, *George Washington University*
Dr. **Stephen Shulman**, *Southern Illinois University*
Prof. **Stefan Troebst**, *University of Leipzig*

POLITICAL ECONOMY & PUBLIC POLICY
Prof. **Andreas Goldthau**, *University of Erfurt*
Dr. **Robert Kravchuk**, *University of North Carolina*
Dr. **David Lane**, *University of Cambridge*
Dr. **Carol Leonard**, *University of Oxford*
Dr. **Maria Popova**, *McGill University, Montreal*

FOREIGN POLICY & INTERNATIONAL AFFAIRS
Dr. **Peter Duncan**, *University College London*
Prof. **Andreas Heinemann-Grüder**, *University of Bonn*
Prof. **Gerhard Mangott**, *University of Innsbruck*
Dr. **Diana Schmidt-Pfister**, *University of Konstanz*
Dr. **Lisbeth Tarlow**, *Harvard University, Cambridge*
Dr. **Christian Wipperfürth**, *N-Ost Network, Berlin*
Dr. **William Zimmerman**, *University of Michigan*

HISTORY, CULTURE & THOUGHT
Dr. **Catherine Andreyev**, *University of Oxford*
Prof. **Mark Bassin**, *Södertörn University*
Prof. **Karsten Brüggemann**, *Tallinn University*
Prof. **Alexander Etkind**, *Central European University*
Prof. **Gasan Gusejnov**, *Free University of Berlin*
Prof. **Leonid Luks**, *Catholic University of Eichstaett*
Dr. **Olga Malinova**, *Russian Academy of Sciences*
Dr. **Richard Mole**, *University College London*
Prof. **Andrei Rogatchevski**, *University of Tromsø*
Dr. **Mark Tauger**, *West Virginia University*

ADVISORY BOARD*

Prof. **Dominique Arel**, *University of Ottawa*
Prof. **Jörg Baberowski**, *Humboldt University of Berlin*
Prof. **Margarita Balmaceda**, *Seton Hall University*
Dr. **John Barber**, *University of Cambridge*
Prof. **Timm Beichelt**, *European University Viadrina*
Dr. **Katrin Boeckh**, *University of Munich*
Prof. em. **Archie Brown**, *University of Oxford*
Dr. **Vyacheslav Bryukhovetsky**, *Kyiv-Mohyla Academy*
Prof. **Timothy Colton**, *Harvard University, Cambridge*
Prof. **Paul D'Anieri**, *University of California*
Dr. **Heike Dörrenbächer**, *Friedrich Naumann Foundation*
Dr. **John Dunlop**, *Hoover Institution, Stanford, California*
Dr. **Sabine Fischer**, *SWP, Berlin*
Dr. **Geir Flikke**, *NUPI, Oslo*
Prof. **David Galbreath**, *University of Aberdeen*
Prof. **Frank Golczewski**, *University of Hamburg*
Dr. **Nikolas Gvosdev**, *Naval War College, Newport, RI*
Prof. **Mark von Hagen**, *Arizona State University*
Prof. **Guido Hausmann**, *University of Regensburg*
Prof. **Dale Herspring**, *Kansas State University*
Dr. **Stefani Hoffman**, *Hebrew University of Jerusalem*
Prof. em. **Andrzej Korbonski**, *University of California*
Dr. **Iris Kempe**, *"Caucasus Analytical Digest"*
Prof. **Herbert Küpper**, *Institut für Ostrecht Regensburg*
Prof. **Rainer Lindner**, *University of Konstanz*

Dr. **Luke March**, *University of Edinburgh*
Prof. **Michael McFaul**, *Stanford University, Palo Alto*
Prof. **Birgit Menzel**, *University of Mainz-Germersheim*
Dr. **Alex Pravda**, *University of Oxford*
Dr. **Erik van Ree**, *University of Amsterdam*
Dr. **Joachim Rogall**, *Robert Bosch Foundation Stuttgart*
Prof. **Peter Rutland**, *Wesleyan University, Middletown*
Prof. **Gwendolyn Sasse**, *University of Oxford*
Prof. **Jutta Scherrer**, *EHESS, Paris*
Prof. **Robert Service**, *University of Oxford*
Mr. **James Sherr**, *RIIA Chatham House London*
Dr. **Oxana Shevel**, *Tufts University, Medford*
Prof. **Eberhard Schneider**, *University of Siegen*
Prof. **Olexander Shnyrkov**, *Shevchenko University, Kyiv*
Prof. **Hans-Henning Schröder**, *SWP, Berlin*
Prof. **Yuri Shapoval**, *Ukrainian Academy of Sciences*
Dr. **Lisa Sundstrom**, *University of British Columbia*
Dr. **Philip Walters**, *"Religion, State and Society", Oxford*
Prof. **Zenon Wasyliw**, *Ithaca College, New York State*
Dr. **Lucan Way**, *University of Toronto*
Dr. **Markus Wehner**, *"Frankfurter Allgemeine Zeitung"*
Dr. **Andrew Wilson**, *University College London*
Prof. **Jan Zielonka**, *University of Oxford*
Prof. **Andrei Zorin**, *University of Oxford*

* While the Editorial Committee and Advisory Board support the General Editor in the choice and improvement of manuscripts for publication, responsibility for remaining errors and misinterpretations in the series' volumes lies with the books' authors.

Soviet and Post-Soviet Politics and Society (SPPS)
ISSN 1614-3515

Founded in 2004 and refereed since 2007, SPPS makes available affordable English-, German-, and Russian-language studies on the history of the countries of the former Soviet bloc from the late Tsarist period to today. It publishes between 5 and 20 volumes per year and focuses on issues in transitions to and from democracy such as economic crisis, identity formation, civil society development, and constitutional reform in CEE and the NIS. SPPS also aims to highlight so far understudied themes in East European studies such as right-wing radicalism, religious life, higher education, or human rights protection. The authors and titles of all previously published volumes are listed at the end of this book. For a full description of the series and reviews of its books, see www.ibidem-verlag.de/red/spps.

Editorial correspondence & manuscripts should be sent to: Dr. Andreas Umland, Department of Political Science, Kyiv-Mohyla Academy, vul. Voloska 8/5, UA-04070 Kyiv, UKRAINE; andreas.umland@cantab.net

Business correspondence & review copy requests should be sent to: *ibidem* Press, Leuschnerstr. 40, 30457 Hannover, Germany; tel.: +49 511 2622200; fax: +49 511 2622201; spps@ibidem.eu.

Authors, reviewers, referees, and editors for (as well as all other persons sympathetic to) SPPS are invited to join its networks at www.facebook.com/group.php?gid=52638198614
www.linkedin.com/groups?about=&gid=103012
www.xing.com/net/spps-ibidem-verlag/

Recent Volumes

259 *Mykhailo Minakov (Ed.)*
Philosophy Unchained
Developments in Post-Soviet Philosophical Thought
With a foreword by Christopher Donohue
ISBN 978-3-8382-1768-0

260 *David Dalton*
The Ukrainian Oligarchy After the Euromaidan
How Ukraine's Political Economy Regime Survived the Crisis
With a foreword by Andrew Wilson
ISBN 978-3-8382-1740-6

261 *Andreas Heinemann-Grüder (Ed.)*
Who are the Fighters?
Irregular Armed Groups in the Russian-Ukrainian War in 2014–2015
ISBN 978-3-8382-1777-2

262 *Taras Kuzio (Ed.)*
Russian Disinformation and Western Scholarship
Bias and Prejudice in Journalistic, Expert, and Academic Analyses of East European, Russian and Eurasian Affairs
ISBN 978-3-8382-1685-0

263 *Darius Furmonavicius*
LithuaniaTransforms the West
Lithuania's Liberation from Soviet Occupation and the Enlargement of NATO (1988–2022)
With a foreword by Vytautas Landsbergis
ISBN 978-3-8382-1779-6

264 *Dirk Dalberg*
Politisches Denken im tschechoslowakischen Dissens
Egon Bondy, Miroslav Kusý, Milan Šimečka und Petr Uhl (1968-1989)
ISBN 978-3-8382-1318-7

265 *Леонид Люкс*
К столетию «философского парохода»
Мыслители «первой» русской эмиграции о русской революции и о тоталитарных соблазнах XX века
ISBN 978-3-8382-1735-2

266 *Daviti Mtchedlishvili*
The EU and the South Caucasus
European Neighborhood Policies between Eclecticism and Pragmatism, 1991-2021
With a foreword by Nicholas Ross Smith
ISBN 978-3-8382-1735-2

267 *Bohdan Harasymiw*
Post-Euromaidan Ukraine
Domestic Power Struggles and War of National Survival in 2014–2022
ISBN 978-3-8382-1798-7

Contents

List of Tables 7

List of Figures 8

Introduction
Nadiia Koval, Denys Tereshchenko 11

Rossotrudnichestvo: The Unbearable Harshness of Soft Power
Nadiia Koval, Maryna Irysova, Serhiy Tytiuk, Denys Tereshchenko 23

"The Russian flag will be flown wherever Russian is spoken":
The "Russkiy Mir" Foundation
Yulia Masiyenko, Kateryna Zahryvenko, Nadiia Koval,
Denys Tereshchenko 99

First Roubles, Then Guns: The Alexander Gorchakov Public
Diplomacy Fund
Denys Tereshchenko, Nadiia Koval 161

Conclusions: Russian Cultural Diplomacy after 2022
Nadiia Koval, Denys Tereshchenko 199

Bibliography 205

List of Tables

Table 1. Predecessors of Rossotrudnichestvo 29
Table 2. Host countries for foreign offices of Rossotrudnichestvo 52
Table 3. Core values of the "Russian world" according to A. Gromyko 110
Table 4. Social networks of the "Russkiy Mir" Foundation 134
Table 5. Number of Centres, Cabinets and friendly organisations of the "Russkiy Mir" Foundation per 1 million population (as of March 2022) 144
Table 6. Russian Centres that were closed down after the Russian full-scale invasion of Ukraine 147
Table 7. Distribution of grants provided by the "Russkiy Mir" Foundation by areas of activity 151

List of Figures

Figure 1. Publicly funded cultural diplomacy institutions in Western countries and Russia.................. 45

Figure 2. Rossotrudnichestvo's offices abroad (as of April 2023) 54

Figure 3. Frequency of mentions of the word "compatriot" on Russkiy Dom Telegram channel within a week, 2021-2022.................. 74

Figure 4. Countries with organisations of Russian compatriots and Rossotrudnichestvo offices (as of April 2023)....... 78

Figure 5. Frequency of publications at Russkiy Dom Telegram channel, 2021-2022.................. 85

Figure 6. Revenues of the "Russkiy Mir" Foundation, 2013-2021.................. 123

Figure 7. Expenditures of the "Russkiy Mir" Foundation, 2013-2021.................. 124

Figure 8. "Russkiy Mir" website attendance in February-April 2022.................. 129

Figure 9. "Russkiy Mir" website attendance in February-April 2023.................. 130

Figure 10. Distribution of "Russkiy Mir" website visitors by Country.................. 130

Figure 11. Distribution of "Russkiy Mir" website visitors by Source, February 2022.................. 131

Figure 12. Distribution of "Russkiy Mir" website visitors by Source, March 2023.................. 132

Figure 13. Key geographical clusters of the "Russkiy Mir" Foundation's network (as of March 2022).................. 141

Figure 14. The number of Centres and Cabinets of the "Russkiy Mir" Foundation in different countries of the world (as of March 2022).................. 142

Figure 15. The number of Centres, Cabinets, and friendly organisations of the "Russkiy Mir" Foundation in different countries of the world (as of March 2022)... 143

Figure 16. Annual amounts of funds allocated as grants by the "Russkiy Mir" Foundation, 2016-2020......................... 150

Introduction

Nadiia Koval, Denys Tereshchenko

In June 2022, the La Scala Theatre in Milan announced that its new season should begin in December 2022 with the Russian XIXth century "Boris Godunov" opera by Modest Mussorgsky. The decision sparked protests from Ukrainian community in Italy and the Consul General of Ukraine in Milan has urged the theatre to reconsider, citing the full-scale Russian aggression that raged for four months now and the role of the Russian culture in supporting Russian political aims. Still, the theatre stuck to its decision, differentiating bloodthirsty Russian regime and allegedly benign universal Russian culture, and reminding that it has already severed ties with pro-Putin conductor Valery Gergiev, provided humanitarian aid to the refugees, and employed some Ukrainian artists, albeit together with the Russian ones, in this opera. Moreover, the premiere on December 7 was visited by the president of the European Commission Ursula von der Leien, prime minister of Italy Giorgia Melloni and the president of Italy Sergio Mattarella, all of whom emphasized that while they resolutely support Ukraine, they harbour no bad feelings against Russian culture and Russian people. That decision raised high hopes in Russian elites that had just began to feel first consequences of cultural isolation. The head of key Russian soft power institution, Rossotrudnichestvo, Evgeny Primakov Jr., referred to the La Scala case with a conjecture "we are seeing very cautious positive signals that this psychosis will wind down" (Laru 2022). And the spokesperson of the Russian MFA, Mariya Zakharova, has noted that this decision "testifies to the cultural sovereignty, wisdom and far-sightedness of Italians" and "lays the foundation for the continuation of fruitful exchanges between our countries in the cultural and humanitarian sphere."[1]

On the second year of the invasion, the question of the role of culture in the war remains contentious. Is Russian culture a repository of values that upholds the regime and its policies while preserving and spreading colonial attitudes to other peoples? Or is it a universal good that benefits all humanity and transcends war and conflict? We do not seek to answer such lofty questions in this book; rather, we focus on a narrower and far more practical topic: Russia's intended political and war-related instrumentalization of its culture, as seen through the lens of analysing the key institutions involved in cultural and public diplomacy.

Russia's proactive use of soft power and the network of soft power institutions have been repeatedly addressed by scholars and analysts, first and foremost in the context of hybrid information warfare tools (Meister 2016; Surowiec 2017, 21–27; Horbulin 2017). Most of these publications attempt to grasp the phenomenon as a comprehensive and multifaceted system that contains many different actors and strategies, thus providing a rather general overview of the major players (Van Herpen 2015). The situation is very similar with narrower, thematic studies, like those that try to show how think tanks spread propaganda (Smagliy, 2018) or more geographically focused studies of Russian "soft power" in specific countries (Foxall, 2015) or of their proxy agents or local collaborators (Lutsevych, 2016, Vendil Pallin, and Oxenstierna, 2017), where institutional analysis is more of a background to the main research questions. Most of the research, even with separate sections on one or a few major Russian soft-power organisations, tends to focus on a generalised analysis of their structure and goals, history and background, funding, etc. For instance, there is an important tradition of research on the Russkiy Mir ideology and its ideologues, but far fewer studies are available on the key organisations established to

---

1   Ministry of Foreign Affairs of the Russian Federation. "Brifing oficial'nogo predstavitelja MID Rossii M.V.Zaharovoj" [Briefing of M.V. Zakharova, the officcial representative of the MFA of Russia}. Moscow, November 30, 2022. https://mid.ru/tv/?id=1841096&lang=ru#11

promote it (Van Herpen 2015; Laruelle 2015; Lutsevych 2016; Smagliy 2018; Suslov 2018; Popovic, Jenne, and Medzihorsky 2020). Thus, what was still missing and what inspired us to start this book project was the need for an in-depth approach to key Russian soft-power organisations, especially after Russia's war against Ukraine has entered its most bloody phase and these soft-power organisations became fully aligned with Russian state war propaganda and its coverage for international audiences.

This book covers Russia's three most important "soft power" organisations: the Russian MFA-dependent state agency, Rossotrudnichestvo, and two government-organised non-governmental organizations, the "Russkiy Mir" Foundation and the Gorchakov Fund. While the initial idea was to research Russian cultural diplomacy and its political instrumentalization, we decided to widen our scope to the more general topic of "soft power." The reason is that in the Russian language and political tradition, there is a clear preference to include cultural diplomacy in "international humanitarian cooperation," which covers a whole number of different fields related to establishing relations with the citizens of foreign countries directly, be it cultural diplomacy, public diplomacy, or even humanitarian assistance. In other words, both in theory and in practice, from the typical Russian vantage point, cultural diplomacy is only one manifestation of the broader policy of influence operations aimed at the outside world. Limiting our research to cultural diplomacy sensu stricto would have omitted the essential parts of the aims and activities of the respective organisations and would have produced a rather distorted picture of Russian efforts in this direction.

This research first originated as a series of policy papers conducted by the Ukrainian Institute in 2022 (Koval et al. 2022; Masiyenko et al. 2022; Tereshchenko and Koval 2022). In this series, we studied Rossotrudnichestvo, the "Russkiy Mir" Foundation, and the Gorchakov Fund in detail. In particular, we focused on their history, structure, and purpose; their exact place within the Russian authoritarian regime; the ideological underpinnings of their activities; their principal activities, projects, and target audiences. All the papers were enlarged and re-edited for this book into three chapters: we updated them with the most recent developments as of spring 2023. We added the introduction and the conclusion chapters, tackling the current state and the perspectives of Russian cultural and public diplomacy development after the war.

All the Russian soft power institutions under scrutiny were established or comprehensively reformed in the late 2000s. The colour revolutions in Georgia and Ukraine provided the impetus for change. Following the regime shifts in the neighbouring states, Russia decided that soft power was crucial to furthering its political goals and eventually sought to develop its means of influence through the institutionalisation and investment of additional financial resources into respective institutions. Rossotrudnichestvo, having the most extended institutional history and the most expansive geography, also covers the broadest portfolio, including cultural diplomacy, humanitarian assistance, and cooperation with compatriots, which is unparalleled with any Western cultural diplomacy institutions but remains characteristic for the Russian understanding of "international humanitarian cooperation." The "Russkiy Mir" Foundation concentrates on promoting the Russian language and culture abroad, nurturing ties and cooperation with foreign universities and libraries, often focusing on provincial cities typically not covered by the Rossotrudnichestvo representations. As for the Gorchakov Fund, it specialises in direct support and promotion of Russian foreign policy visions in the foreign expert and academic community, mainly aiming at its younger cohort. Moreover, since the latter two institutions, in addition to organising their own projects, function as funds, they tend to directly finance foreign entities by providing (micro)grants. Finally, they extensively cooperate with the state media and boast an impressive social media presence, including, in the case of the "Russkiy Mir" Foundation, a whole set of own media designed for Russian speakers worldwide.

We scrutinise the most significant, most visible, and even system-forming players in the field of Russian soft-power institutions responsible for creating constellations of lesser players around themselves. Thus, a whole array of other state and private players fall outside the scope of this research. In order to have a broader and more representative depiction of Russian cultural diplomacy, this should be further researched, and here we will only use this introduction to outline the field and its internal complexities. To mark the prospective itineraries, we try to name and categorise all the partners involved in projects or the governance of the key institutions in the respective chapters. In addition, some researchers have already attempted to map the links and role-sharing between different players, which could be elaborated upon (see, for instance, Smagliy 2018).

A paradoxical situation in Russia's cultural and public diplomacy field is that it is simultaneously very hierarchical and highly dispersed. This provides soft power institutions with notable flexibility but does not deprive the regime of the opportunity for thorough oversight and control. A significant drawback of this organisational approach is the lack of order and the coexistence of often overlapping functions and initiatives.

The vertical organisation has two different dimensions. The first is the ever-tightening state control over each emanation of soft power, inspired by the personal interest of Vladimir Putin, as would be typical of personalistic authoritarian regimes. As of 2023, Putin personally appoints and dismisses the head and deputy heads of Rossotrudnichestvo and the heads of the "Russkiy Mir" Foundation's governing bodies, appoints his close collaborators from the Presidential Administration to the key posts in all three organisations, and attempts to execute direct control through creating his own institutions, like the Presidential Fund of Cultural Initiatives or the Presidential Grant Fund, both of which at least partially finance cultural diplomacy-related and highly political events.[2]

Besides, on the governmental level, the Ministry of Foreign Affairs hosts at least three different departments dealing with soft power (in addition to Rossotrudnichestvo, a separate agency under the auspices of the MFA). The latest such department was founded

---

2   For instance, Russian Presidential Fund of Cultural Initiatives spent over a billion roubles on cultural initiatives for promotion of the war against Ukraine. See Sirena (2022a, 2022b).

in 2022 to coordinate the cultural policy, a role it still shares with other institutions. The MFA and the Ministry of Education are co-founders of the "independent" "Russkiy Mir" Foundation, whereas Minister Lavrov heads the Board of Trustees of the Gorchakov Fund, effectively controlling the organisation.

Still, the all-encompassing description of "international humanitarian cooperation" implies all-government involvement. As Rossotrudnichestvo's functionaries describe it, the key players of Russian soft power encompass the Ministry of Science and Higher Education, which develops academic diplomacy and accommodates foreign students in Russian universities; the Ministry of Education, responsible for supporting the schools and Russian language learning abroad, including spreading the manuals and organising training for foreign teachers, building brand new schools on Russian programmes, Ministry of Defence and Ministry of Emergency Situations, in addition to death and destruction, also provide humanitarian assistance, including that related to the Russian language and schooling, Ministry of Culture controls and operates sizeable portions of cultural events abroad, for instance, "Russian seasons" in different countries and "Roskino" (Russian cinema) events (Polikanov 2023). The Ministry of Economic Development and the Ministry of Finance have an essential say in providing actual funds for the organisations and particular projects and financing Russian participation in multilateral international projects or organisations. The Ministry of Internal Affairs has a voice in the compatriots' resettlement, the Ministry of Digitalization supports translation and book publishing, and so on (Ibid.). Such an overlapping of multiple ministries and other state entities, starting from the Presidential Administration and Security Council, indicates not only the importance but also numerous organisational hurdles, so there is a visible trend towards centralization either through presidential or MFA vertical control, through creating state-level programmes, "International development assistance" and "Support and promotion of Russian language abroad," and the Federal Project "Russia as an attractive country for education and work," fusing some organisations, etc. At least three other state-created funds cover the related questions, "Fund for Support and Protection of the Rights of Compatriots Living Abroad,"[3] as well as the Presidential Grant Foundation and the Presidential Foundation for Cultural Initiatives, which were mentioned above. In addition, the will to control all the humanitarian initiatives led to the situation where, for instance, the director of the Foreign Intelligence Service, Sergey Naryshkin, chairs the Russian Historical Society and the Minister of Defence, Sergey Shoigu, leads the Russian Geographical Society.

However, when considered horizontally, the three institutions are the primary nodes of the state-controlled ecosystem of organisations devoted to expanding Russia's influence abroad. These include universities and their departments, research centres and think tanks, oligarch-sponsored foundations, GONGOs, state media broadcasting abroad, state culture-related institutions (e.g., libraries, museums), religious organisations (first and foremost, the Russian Orthodox Church), etc. Their leadership, members, and individual representatives serve on one another's supervisory, trustee, and executive boards, conduct multiple joint activities, post on each other's websites, and coordinate activities in general. Still, as an ultimate solution, after another change of the Rossotrudnichestvo management in 2020, the idea of reforming Russia's soft power by establishing a single state corporation that would consolidate all resources and operate projects of influence on foreign audiences was voiced (Atasuntsev, Galimova, and Khimshiashvili 2020). This corporation will likely be based on Rossotrudnichestvo since its operations are more diverse, and its infrastructure is more developed than those of Russia's other state soft power institutions.

Finally, the utmost importance of "humanitarian policy abroad" for Russian foreign policy is underlined by its growing presence in strategic documents. Thus, the first foreign policy strategy document publicised since the start of the all-out invasion on

---

3   Sanctioned by Ukraine for its support for the war. War & Sanctions. n. d. "Nonprofit organization 'Fund for Support and Protection of the Rights of Compatriots Living Abroad." https://sanctions.nazk.gov.ua/en/sanction-company/4344/.

February 24, 2022, was the Concept for Russia's Humanitarian Policy Abroad, adopted on September 5, 2022. It directly defines culture to be the instrument of foreign policy:

> Russian culture is an essential, integral part of global culture. As an instrument of "soft power," it contributes to strengthening Russia's international standing, forming its objective perception abroad, and neutralising anti-Russian sentiments of political and ideological origin. International cultural and humanitarian cooperation is required to foster favourable conditions for implementing foreign policy tasks and simultaneously contribute to establishing a constructive dialogue and overcoming disagreements with foreign partners.[4]

While summarising already proven strategies and activities in the field rather than introducing innovations, this concept underlines, inter alia, that a distinct culture makes Russia a separate civilization based on conservative values whose mission is to support all the conservative countries worldwide against Western (neo)liberalism and its values. It importantly introduces the Russkiy Mir ideology as a reference point and the source of foundational values in Russian culture. It keeps the traditional focus of Russia's "humanitarian policy" on the CIS and former USSR but extends geographical interest well into the Global South, especially Asia, the Middle East, and Latin America.[5]

In a similar vein, Russia's new Foreign Policy Concept, adopted on March 31, 2023, further reinforces the classical foreign policy doctrine of Putin's regime, promoting multipolarity and further curbing Western influence wherever possible, seeking new

---

[4] Russian Federation. President. Ukaz [Decree] #611 "Ob utverzhdenii Kontseptsii gumanitarnoi politiki Rossiiskoi Federatsii za rubezhom" [On approving the Concept of Humanitarian Policy of the Russian Federation]. Adopted 5 September 2022. http://static.kremlin.ru/media/events/files/ru/G3CkAuMhZXio8AzNaweT3wTGTaEA16OU.pdf.

[5] Priority countries from the 2022 Concept of Russian Humanitarian Policy Abroad include CIS states, Moldova, Baltic states, and unilaterally recognized occupied territories of Georgia and Ukraine ("Republic of Abkhazia," "Republic of South Ossetia," "Donetsk People's Republic," "Luhansk People's Republic"). Second, these are East-Asian countries: China, India, Japan, Vietnam, Laos, Mongolia. Also, Middle East and Maghreb Algeria, Egypt, Israel, Jordan, Iraq, Lebanon, Libya, UAE, Saudi Arabia, Syria, Iran, Afghanistan, Palestinian state. Finally, Latin America: Argentina, Brazil, Venezuela, Cuba, Mexico, Nicaragua, Paraguay, Uruguay, Chile.

partners in the East, starting with China, India, and Iran, and strengthening itself through the reintegration of the former Soviet republics. It also underlines the cultural and even civilizational uniqueness of Russia, claiming it to be a country-civilization with a natural, cultural, and value-defined sphere of influence:

> More than a thousand years of independent statehood, the cultural legacies of bygone eras, strong historical ties to traditional European culture and other cultures of Eurasia, and the capacity developed over many centuries to ensure the peaceful coexistence of various peoples, ethnic, religious, and linguistic groups on a common territory determine Russia's unique position as a distinctive state-civilization, a vast Eurasian and Euro-Pacific power that united the Russian people and other peoples who comprise the Russian world's cultural and civilizational community.[6]

The Russkiy Mir ideology is vital in building and consolidating this "country-civilization" as a foreign policy goal. While we will discuss the Russkiy Mir ideology in more detail in the respective chapter about the "Russkiy Mir" Foundation, it is important to note that this revanchist conservative ideology is designed with the purpose of symbolically re-integrating the former Soviet space as a specific Russian civilization through supporting and promoting the Russian language, Orthodoxy, and a set of conservative social and political values. Remarkably, there is an innate contradiction between the nativist and exclusivist ideology of the Russian world idea and the multinational nature of the Russian Federation itself, coupled with the incredible heterogeneity of all those considered to be part of the Russian world beyond the Russian borders. According to the Concept for Russia's Humanitarian Policy Abroad, adopted on September 5, 2022:

> The primary objectives of multilateral humanitarian cooperation with the CIS member states are the formation of a single cultural, educational, and informational space; the preservation of centuries-old cultural ties with the peoples of these states; the comprehensive development of such relations; the search for new effective forms of cooperation; and the strengthening of the historically established positions of the Russian language in these states. The objectives of the humanitarian policy of the Russian Federation abroad

---

6   Russian Federation. President. "Kontseptsiia vneshnei politiki Rossiiskoi Federatsii" [Concept of Foreign Policy of the Russian Federation]. Approved on 31 March 2023. https://www.mid.ru/ru/detail-material-page/1860586/

are: ...protection, preservation, and promotion of traditions and ideals inherent in the Russian world.[7]

Considering all the features mentioned, it is no surprise that all three organisations have supported the Russian war against Ukraine. The extreme case is Rossotrudnichestvo, implicated in many war-related activities. First, it provides, facilitates, and promotes extensive "humanitarian aid" from the Rossotrudnichestvo and its partners, including the Ministry of Defence, to the Ukrainians residing in the occupied territories or those evacuated or deported to Russia. Second, it produces and spreads war-related narratives as to the reasons, responsibility, and war crimes, driving parallels with the WWII/Great Patriotic War, promoting war symbolics, organising manifestations and rallies in support of Russia, organising and disseminating supportive videos from celebrities and ordinary citizens in foreign countries, and finally investing enormous resources into combating "Russophobia" and "Russia cancelling," first and foremost in the sphere of culture. Likewise, the "Russkiy Mir" Foundation is actively involved in streamlining and supporting the russification of the occupied regions, primarily through school education. It also extensively promotes war-related narratives through the Foundation's media and by the Foundation leader, Vyacheslav Nikonov, personally. The Gorchakov Fund keeps a comparatively low profile in war promotion but follows the key narratives and approaches.

An important role of Russian soft power organisations in Russian foreign policy theory and practise up to spreading propaganda and subversion was first noticed back in 2016, when Rossotrudnichestvo and the "Russkiy Mir" Foundation, together with the multilingual Russia Today (RT) TV platform and the Sputnik multimedia service, were identified as Kremlin-funded instruments of disinformation and propaganda in a resolution passed by the European Parliament on November 23, 2016. After the start of the full-scale

---

[7] Russian Federation. President. Ukaz [Decree] #611 "Ob utverzhdenii Kontseptsii gumanitarnoi politiki Rossiiskoi Federatsii za rubezhom" [On approving the Concept of Humanitarian Policy of the Russian Federation]. Adopted 5 September 2022. http://static.kremlin.ru/media/events/files/ru/G3CkAuMhZXio8AzNaweT3wTGTaEA16OU.pdf.

war in February 2022, the cultural diplomacy institutions' involvement in the war effort became so apparent that all three organisations and their leaders were sanctioned.[8] Specifically, in July 2022, the Rossotrudnichestvo was sanctioned by the EU as "the main state agency projecting the Kremlin's soft power and hybrid influence," "an umbrella organisation for a network of Russian compatriots and agents of influence, and it funds various public diplomacy and propaganda projects, consolidating the activities of pro-Russian players and disseminating the Kremlin's narratives, including historical revisionism," "and the Foundation has been used as an important influence tool by the Kremlin that is strongly promoting a Russia centric-agenda in the post-USSR states, rejecting Ukraine's legitimacy as a sovereign nation, and advocating for its unification with Russia." [...] "The 'Russkiy Mir' Foundation has disseminated pro-Kremlin and anti-Ukrainian propaganda and justified Russia's unprovoked and unjustified military aggression against Ukraine" (EU Council Regulation 2022/1269 of 21.07.2022). There are also personal sanctions against Evgeny Primakov Jr., Vyacheslav Nikonov, and Dmitry Syty, a former Wagner PVC combatant, who established a Rossotrudnichestvo representative office, Russkiy Dom, in the Democratic Republic of Congo.

All in all, given the role that Russia's soft-power organisations and culture instrumentalization as a foreign policy instrument have been playing in promoting and facilitating the war and the attempts

---

8 Rossotrudnichestvo, "Russkiy Mir" Foundation and Gorchakov Fund are sanctioned by the EU, Canada, Switzerland, and Ukraine. Voina & sanktsiii [War & Sanctions]. n. d. "Fond podderzhki publichnoi diplomatii imeni A.M.Gorchakova" [The Alexander Gorchakov Public Diplomacy Fund]. https://sanctions.nazk.gov.ua/ru/sanction-company/6079/. Voina & sanktsiii [War & Sanctions]. n. d. "Fond 'Russkiy Mir'" ['Russkiy Mir' Foundation]. https://sanctions.nazk.gov.ua/ru/sanction-company/6080/. Voina & sanktsiii [War & Sanctions]. n. d. "Federal'noe agentstvo po delam Sodruzhestva Nezavisimykh Gosudarstv, sootechestvennikov, prozhyvaiushchikh za rubezhom, i po mezhdunarodnomu gumanitarnomu sotrudnichestvu (Rossotrudnichestvo)" [Federal Agency for the Commonwealth of Independent States Affairs, Compatriots Living Abroad, and International Humanitarian Cooperation]. https://sanctions.nazk.gov.ua/ru/sanction-company/3977/. Ukraine, President, Ukaz Prezydenta Ukrainy #726/2022 'Pro rishennia Rady natsionalnoi bezpeky i oborony Ukrainy vid 19 zhovtnia 2022 roku "Pro zastosuvannia ta vnesennia zmin do personalnykh spetsialnykh ekonomichnykh ta inshykh obmezhuvalnykh zakhodiv (sanktsiy)."' Issued 19 October 2022. https://www.president.gov.ua/documents/7262022-44481.

to absorb the captured Ukrainian territories while trying in parallel to speculate on culture as being a reconciliatory, universal phenomenon beyond borders and politics, it is necessary to study what these organisations are and how they act to ensure an adequate response. We hope this study will contribute to a better understanding of culture's political use and abuse, especially in a war situation.

Rossotrudnichestvo
The Unbearable Harshness of Soft Power

Nadiia Koval, Maryna Irysova, Serhiy Tytiuk,
Denys Tereshchenko

Introduction

> For Russian leaders, soft power is not about attraction; it instead refers to non-military instruments for manipulating, undermining, and weakening opponents, a supplement to Moscow's military power.
> —Stefan Meister, *Isolation and Propaganda.*
> *The Roots and Instruments of Russia's Disinformation Campaign*

Rossotrudnichestvo, or, in its full name, the Federal Agency for the Commonwealth of Independent State Affairs, Compatriots Living Abroad, and International Humanitarian Cooperation, is an unusual case of a government agency that embraces multiple functions that in the West are typically distributed among numerous institutions. The analysis of its declared objectives, audiences, projects, and topics points to a comparison with internationally recognised cultural diplomacy institutions, such as the British Council, Goethe-Institut, or Institut français, and with international development agencies, such as the United States Agency for International Development (USAID)[9] or the German Gesellschaft für Internationale Zusammenarbeit (GIZ).

The first area Rossotrudnichestvo covers is "shaping an objective perception of contemporary Russia, its role and place in global history among the international community" (Rossotrudnichestvo 2021, 4). It is formally similar to the objectives of most cultural diplomacy institutions worldwide. However, as we will demonstrate in this chapter, it seeks to influence countries through cultural events in a way that creates a favourable ground for Russia's ex-

---

9   Rossotrudnichestvo's representatives often refer to this parallel. See, for instance, Solovyov 2012.

pansionist policy and ideological visions, which in the most extreme cases turns into the use of soft power to justify or relativise the use of hard power.

The second area is "strengthening the humanitarian influence of Russia in the world."[10] It reveals Russia's aspiration to present itself as a global donor of humanitarian assistance and expand its influence in certain regions through international development aid, providing economic and financial assistance to developing countries. This is a nationally mandated field of foreign policy work guided by Russia's Policy Concept for international development aid and supervised by the Ministry of Foreign Affairs.[11] Providing humanitarian assistance is also a way for Rossotrudnichestvo to avoid the limitations of traditional cultural diplomacy and to find more modern and effective ways to project the country's power and influence. Thus, Yevgeny Primakov Jr., Head of Rossotrudnichestvo, claimed in 2019:

> "Russia's investment in humanitarian policy should pay off. It should promote our companies in new markets, keep our companies busy and bring them contracts, guarantee that the recipient countries pay their debt, and ensure that the lands surrounding our borders are secure and will never become a base for open or covert aggression." (Novyie izvestiia 2019)

The third area of Rossotrudnichestvo is the loosely defined work with the audience that Russia refers to as "compatriots," primarily ethnic Russians or Russian speakers in the countries of the former Soviet Union and beyond. This work comprises meeting their informational and cultural needs, assisting in their resettlement to Russia, reinforcing Russian identity, and supporting Russia's political objectives, such as protecting the monuments and cemeteries abroad that are significant to Russia (Zakem, Saunders, and Antoun 2015, 39).

---

10 Rossiia s mirom [Russian with peace]. n. d. "Agentstvo" [Agency]. http://web.archive.org/web/20220425212752/https://rwp.agency/agency/.
11 Russian Federation. President. Ukaz [Decree] #259 "Ob utverzhdenii Kontseptsii gosudarstvennoi politiki Rossiiskoi Federatsii v sfere sodeistviia mezhdunarodnomu razvitiiu" [On the adopting of the Concept of the state policy of the Russian Federaion in the field of promoting of international development]. Adopted 20 April 2014. http://www.kremlin.ru/acts/bank/38334.

Such a combination of work areas is uncommon for soft power institutions in Western countries, but it is deeply related to the history and changing priorities of the organisation (see the section below). In addition, they often overlap with the activities of other bigger or lesser Russian organisations working in a similar direction. For instance, the "Russkiy Mir" ("Russian World") Foundation, another Russian cultural diplomacy institution, also engages in promoting the Russian language, organising cultural events abroad and providing (micro)grants projects thematically related to Russia or Russian culture. Both Rossotrudnichestvo and "Russkiy Mir" Foundation pay significant attention to the needs of "compatriots" in their activities.

In addition to working in the three mentioned areas, Rossotrudnichestvo has a slew of other organisational, functional, operational, and ethical differences from its Western equivalents. Rossotrudnichestvo, along with a number of other Russian organisations, was identified as a Kremlin-funded instrument of disinformation and propaganda in a resolution passed by the European Parliament on November 23, 2016,[12] and sanctioned by several countries in 2022.[13] On top of that, and long before that, Rossotrudnichestvo and its foreign offices have a long legacy of accusations of espionage, provocations, and other scandals, including instances in the United States,[14] the Czech Republic,[15] and Ukraine.

This chapter aims to develop a comprehensive institutional profile of Rossotrudnichestvo, outlining its areas of operations and

---

12 European Union. European Parliament. Resolution of 23 November 2016 on EU strategic communication to counteract propaganda against it by third parties (2016/2030(INI)). https://www.europarl.europa.eu/doceo/document/TA-8-2016-0441_EN.pdf.
13 See Introduction in this book.
14 Horwitz, Sari. "Head of D.C.-based Russian cultural center being investigated as possible spy" *The Washington Post*. October 23, 2013. https://www.washingtonpost.com/world/national-security/head-of-dc-based-russian-cultural-center-being-investigated-as-possible-spy/2013/10/23/63a0bb54-3c02-11e3-a94f-b58017bfee6c_story.html.
15 Higgins, Andrew. "Prague Says Ricin Plot Was a Hoax, and Moves to Expel 2 Russians." *The New York Times*. June 5, 2020. https://www.nytimes.com/2020/06/05/world/europe/czech-republic-russia-ricin.html.

target audiences and the scope and nature of its influence in Russia's information war. By looking at the propaganda element of Rossotrudnichestvo's operations, this research focuses specifically on Rossotrudnichestvo's information policy and influence campaigns since the beginning of the full-scale war against Ukraine on February 24, 2022. This research examined the official website of Rossotrudnichestvo and its social media accounts, in addition to the official documents governing Rossotrudnichestvo's operations, such as decrees, resolutions, and other documents. It also uses secondary sources, i.e., relevant policy papers and media reports by Ukrainian and foreign authors.

1. Noms de Plume: Predecessors of Rossotrudnichestvo

Rossotrudnichestvo was officially founded on September 6, 2008, by Decree No. 1315 of the President of the Russian Federation, Dmitriy Medvedev. In contrast to other agencies established within the same period to promote Russia's cultural influence abroad, Rossotrudnichestvo did not begin from scratch. Its predecessor agencies are nearly a century old. Each of the previous iterations of Rossotrudnichestvo was established and restructured amidst historical transformations and challenges posed to the international image of the Soviet Union and later Russia. Although they had different legal statuses (some were founded as civic organisations or associations), they were government-controlled and promoted pro-Soviet and pro-Russian propaganda (Svystovych 2011; Ditkovska 2014).

The first predecessor of Rossotrudnichestvo was the All-Union Society for Cultural Relations with Foreign Countries (VOKS), established in 1925. The primary objective of VOKS was to whitewash the image of the Soviet Union and the Bolshevik government following the Civil War and its early years in power. This essentially state-run agency was in charge of organising cultural events with representatives of the Soviet Union abroad and bringing regime sympathisers to the Soviet Union.

It was rebranded for the first time in 1958 as part of the effort to combat the detrimental effect that Stalin's regime had on the international image of the Soviet Union. While VOKS primarily targeted Western countries, the Soviet Union has sought to expand its global influence since the beginning of the Cold War. Consequently, VOKS became the Union of Soviet Societies of Friendship and Cultural Relations with Foreign Countries (SRTD). It began establishing contacts with countries in Africa, Asia, the Middle East, and Latin America that were friendly to the Soviet Union. Until 1991, the SRTD oversaw 98 societies and associations of friendship with the peoples of foreign countries and 600,000 students enrolled in Russian language courses abroad.[16]

After the Soviet Union collapsed and the Cold War ended, Russia inherited a vast network of cultural and research centres in 41 countries. The first female astronaut, Valentina Tereshkova, led the organisation from 1987 until 2004. The SRTD was transformed into the Russian Agency for International Cooperation and Development in 1992, and in 1994, its name was changed to the Russian Centre for International Science and Culture Cooperation (RosZarubezhCentr). These changes were likely not reflected in the SRTD's work for a long time. RosZarubezhCentr expanded its operations in 2002, when it was resubordinated from the Government of Russia to the Ministry of Foreign Affairs. Eleonora Mitrofanova, a former Russian envoy to UNESCO, chaired it in 2004. Under Mitrofanova, RosZarubezhCentr shifted to prioritising work in the Baltic States and CIS countries, particularly with civic organisations (both organisations of "compatriots," and local organisations). It also analysed and collected data about the Russian diaspora in the post-Soviet space.[17]

---

16   Ruski dom. "O Rossotrudnichestve" [About Rossotrudnichestvo]. n. d. https://ruskidom.rs/россотрудничество-ру/о-россотрудничестве/.
17   RIA Novosti. 2005. "Mitrofanova vydelila prioritety raboty Roszarubezhtsentra" [Mitrofanova highlights the priorities of RosZarubezhCentr]. January 18, 2005. https://ria.ru/20050118/1741088.html.

Notably, the predecessors of Rossotrudnichestvo, starting with VOKS, served to mask the intelligence work with a facade of cultural propaganda and the establishment of international cultural contacts.[18] The intelligence function was an integral part of all successors of VOKS, and many of their employees were KGB or FSB agents or Soviet and Russian foreign intelligence. According to the Dossier Center, at least 17 out of RosZarubezhCentr's 546 employees between 1994 and 2008 were agents of Russia's Foreign Intelligence Service (Dosie 2021).

---

18 See, for example, Nevezhyn (1993); Dosie (2021). VOKS maintained ties with the intelligence community down to the personnel level. See the story of Grigoriy Heifetz, Soviet intelligence agent and deputy head of VOKS in Laamanen (2017).

Table 1. Predecessors of Rossotrudnichestvo

Title	Years	Subordination	Declared goals
All-Union Society for Cultural Relations with Foreign Countries (VOKS)	1925 – 1958 (established in the early years of the Soviet Union's existence)	Held the status of a civic organisation	Establishing and fostering academic and cultural ties between institutions, civic organisations and individuals engaged in culture and arts from the Soviet Union and foreign countries.
Union of Soviet Societies of Friendship and Cultural Relations with Foreign Countries (SRTD)	1958 – 1992 (Cold War period)	Officially an international all-union association (Tereshkova 1991) – association of civic organisations, including societies, associations, friendship committees, and republican associations for cultural relations with foreign countries, their industry sections). Funded by the state	Assisting the autonomous republics, oblasts, krais and cities of the Russian Soviet Federative Socialist Republic to establish commercial and cultural ties with foreign countries, thereby facilitating the receipt of humanitarian aid from abroad.
Russian Agency for International Cooperation and Development	1992 – 1994 (first years after the USSR disintegration)	It was a federal state agency subordinated to the Government of RF (i.e., belonging to its	Implementing state policy in international financial and invest-

		executive branch).[19] As the SRTD's successor, the Russian Agency for International Cooperation and Development received the SRTD's facilities and other assets.	ment cooperation and coordinating advisory, technical, humanitarian and cultural cooperation with foreign governmental and non-governmental organisations.[20]
Russian Centre for International Science and Culture Cooperation under the Ministry of Foreign Affairs (RosZarubezhCentr)	1994 – 2008	The successor of the Russian Agency for International Cooperation and Development. Received the premises and other property of the SRTD. From 1994 to 2002, RosZarubezhCentr was a state agency subordinated to the Government of the Russian Federation.[21] It has	Humanitarian, cultural, research and technical, and information relations of Russia with foreign countries through the established network of Russian research and cultural centres abroad. Assistance to Russian and foreign NGOs in fostering these relations.

19 Russian Federation. President. Ukaz [Decree] #889 "O Rossiisskom agentstve mezhdunarodnogo sotrudnichestva i razvitiia" [Russian Agency for International Cooperation and Development]. Adopted 14 August 1992. http://www.kremlin.ru/acts/bank/1830.
20 Russian Federation. President. Ukaz [Decree] #995 "Ob utverzhdenii Polozhenia o Rossiiskom agentstve mezhdunarodnogo sotrudnichestva" [On approving the Statute on the Russian Agency for International Cooperation and Development]. Adopted 12 December 1992. http://webcache.googleusercontent.com/search?q=cache:https://docs.cntd.ru/document/9003489.
21 Russian Federation. Pravitelsvto Rossiiskoi Federatsii [The Government of the Russian Federation]. Postanovleniie [Resolution] #311 „Ob obrazovanii Rossiiskogo tsentra mezhdunarodnogo nauchnogo i kulturnogo sotrudnichestva (s izmeneniiami na 17 noiabria 1997 goda)" [On Establishing the Russian Centre for International Science and Culture Cooperation (with the changes as of November 17, 1997)]. Adopted 8 April, 1994. http://web.archive.org/web/20170915142528/https://docs.cntd.ru/document/9005507.

Federal Agency for the Commonwealth of Independent State Affairs, Compatriots Living Abroad, and International Humanitarian Cooperation (Rossotrudnichestvo)	2008 – till now (revision of Russia's foreign policy doctrine, incorporation of soft power into its foreign policy strategy)	been under Russia's Ministry of Foreign Affairs since 2002. The successor of RosZarubezhCentr. A central federal state agency of the government's executive branch. Reports to the President of Russia and operates under the Ministry of Foreign Affairs of Russia.[22]	Providing state services and managing public property in developing Russia's international relations with CIS and other countries. Providing international humanitarian cooperation and international development aid.

---

22 Russian Federation. President. Ukaz [Decree] #1315 "O nekotorykh voprosakh gosudarstvennogo upravleniia v oblasti mezhdunarodnogo sotrudnichestva" [On Some Aspects of Governance in the Field of International Cooperation]. Adopted 6 September 2008. http://www.kremlin.ru/acts/bank/28020.

RosZarubezhCentr was reformed into Rossotrudnichestvo in 2008 because of Russia's realisation that it needed to reconsider its approach to the use of soft power and re-evaluate its weight in light of the 2003-2004 colour revolutions in Eastern Europe and the deterioration of attitudes toward Russia in the aftermath of its 2008 attack on Georgia. By the mid-2010s, Russia had a considerably lower soft power ranking than the United States, Canada, EU countries, Japan, China, and India. This period, however, witnessed the strengthening of Russia's economy, political modernisation and other transformations that may have contributed to making Russia more attractive internationally and restoring its influence in the post-Soviet space (Iliuk 2016).

A former head of Rossotrudnichestvo, Konstantin Kosachev, stated that as a result of the war with Georgia, Russia "became somewhat isolated and was portrayed as an aggressor in international media, that is, in the eyes of the international community. Essentially, we learned the most important lesson about the effects of information and image manipulation" (Kosachev 2021). This led to the conclusion that Russia had to focus more on soft power to promote its positive image abroad. The Russian President signed a decree establishing Rossotrudnichestvo on September 6, 2008, less than a month after Russia's troops invaded the territory of Georgia. The decree's objective was to "increase the effectiveness of governance in the field of international cooperation."[23] Apart from the failure to accomplish massive geopolitical goals, organisational inefficiency and internal corruption at RosZarubezhCentr could have been a less apparent reason for that rebranding.[24]

---

23 Russian Federation. President. Ukaz [Decree] #1315 "O nekotorykh voprosakh gosudarstvennogo upravleniia v oblasti mezhdunarodnogo sotrudnichestva" [On Some Aspects of Governance in the Field of International Cooperation]. Adopted 6 September 2008. http://www.kremlin.ru/acts/bank/28020.
24 In one fragment of her unpublished book, Tatiana Poloskova, a former member of the expert council at Rossotrudnichestvo, described the idleness of RosZarubezhCentr employees in the departments of the Baltic States and CIS countries, their total ignorance of the local context in the countries where they worked, the pursuit of business trips to distant countries, corruption, and the

Complaints of inefficiency have accompanied the present-day Rossotrudnichestvo since its first days and have been the primary impetus for numerous reform initiatives.[25] They focus primarily on its shortage of funding compared to its foreign competitors and other Russian public agencies engaged in "international development aid." In 2013, Rossotrudnichestvo expanded its role as a soft power agent with plans to increase its budget significantly and transform into the Russian version of USAID (Chernenko 2013). Rossotrudnichestvo reform discussions resumed in 2018 when Eleonora Mitrofanova returned to her position as head of the organisation, followed by Yevgeny Primakov Jr. in 2020. The current plan is to establish a state soft power corporation based on Rossotrudnichestvo. And another change of name for the international audience is imminent, as its leaders have spent a decade complaining that the current title is too complicated for foreigners (Fediakina 2014).

---

receipt of residence certificates for NATO member-states. See Poloskova, Tatiana. "Rossiiskaiia diplomatiia i ee zarubezhzhie: Kak kadry reshali vsyo" [Russian diplomacy and its representation abroad: How staff decided everything]. *Iarex* (Livejournal blog). 24 February, 2014. https://marss2.livejournal.com/899015.html.

25 One indirect evidence of the continuing complaints and ensuing discussions is the recurring responses to such criticism on the part of Rossotrudnichestvo's leadership. In one of such responses, Primakov objected that "[t]he better Rossotrudnichestvo becomes, the better the Agency works, [...] the more is the yelling, the louder is the scream of pain," apparently implying that the criticism of Rossotrudnichestvo was becoming more frequent (https://t.me/evgenyprimakov/2487). Once, Primakov even obviously felt obliged to address the concerns being spread on the internet about the hypothetical closing down of the Agency (https://t.me/evgenyprimakov/2871). Among the recurring criticisms of Rossotrudnichestvo are the complaints about its alleged negligence of compatriots (https://t.me/evgenyprimakov/2902) and "Russian" schools abroad (https://t.me/evgenyprimakov/2633). One of the typical explanations used by its leadership to justify what others identify as its failures is the lack of resources, always in comparison to the budgets of the biggest analogous Western institutions. Primakov regularly complains about the Agency's budget constraints as well as about legal restrictions on its use, as well as other restrictions, for instance, to establish legal entities such as non-commercial organisations or funds, to fund foreign organisations (https://t.me/evgenyprimakov/2529), or even to make its own website without extensive bureaucratic complications (https://t.me/evgenyprimakov/2530).

2. Staff, Budgets, Networks: Institutional Profile

Reporting to the President of Russia and operating under the Russian Ministry of Foreign Affairs, Rossotrudnichestvo enjoys the best funding and geographic coverage out of all of Russia's soft power institutions. How precisely it is integrated into the existing institutional infrastructure of Russia's soft power could be clarified by describing where its leaders are recruited, whom it collaborates with, where its funding comes from, how it spends the funds, and what its geographic priorities are.

2.1 Chained by "United Russia:" Rossotrudnichestvo's leadership and partners

The ultimate authority to appoint and dismiss the head and deputy heads of Rossotrudnichestvo belongs to the President of Russia.[26] Throughout its existence of fifteen years, Rossotrudnichestvo had six heads. This reflects the political turbulence surrounding Rossotrudnichestvo and starkly contrasts the "Russkiy Mir" Foundation and the Gorchakov Fund, whose current heads have been in place since establishing both organisations. Except for Eleonora Mitrofanova, all heads of Rossotrudnichestvo were MPs in the State Duma or Federation Council, the two chambers of the Russian Federal Assembly, before or after they led Rossotrudnichestvo, which implies that they belonged to the highest echelons of Russian elites. In other words, the key representatives of the main soft power institution of Russia were unlikely to be career diplomats, cultural managers, or international cooperation experts. Yevgeny Primakov Jr., the current head, for instance was a journalist from loyalist *nomenclatura* circles. Before being appointed to Rossotrudnichestvo, he hosted the *International Digest* (*Международное обозрение*) show on Rossiya 24, a state television channel. He continued to host the show for some time after taking office.

---

26 Russian Federation. President. Ukaz [Decree] #1315 "O nekotorykh voprosakh gosudarstvennogo upravleniia v oblasti mezhdunarodnogo sotrudnichestva" [On Some Aspects of Governance in the Field of International Cooperation]. Adopted 6 September 2008. http://www.kremlin.ru/acts/bank/28020.

 Yevgeny Primakov Jr. is the grandson of Yevgeny Primakov Sr., the former Minister of Foreign Affairs of Russia. Primakov Jr. has chaired Rossotrudnichestvo since June 25, 2020.

He is a former member of parliament, advisor on foreign policy and humanitarian projects to Vyacheslav Volodin, the seventh speaker of the State Duma; member of the praesidium of the Council for Foreign and Defence Policy; co-founder and board chair of the Russian Humanitarian Mission (RHM), a key partner for Rossotrudnichestvo.

As a descendant of a Soviet elite family, Primakov Jr., within a year after the launch of the all-out Russian invasion of Ukraine, turned into a devoted supporter of Russia's war effort, posting numerous comments on his Telegram channel (@evgenyprimakov) that, among other things, made appeals for a nuclear strike in the centre of Kyiv,[27] which he elsewhere called "a Russian city." He alleges the "Kyiv regime" to be "cannibal and criminal."[28] He suggests that "the Ukrainian state must be declared the enemy and be eliminated."[29] His Ukrainophobia proved to be quite eccentric when he called the Ukrainian state a "*salo*-devouring caliphate."[30] He also praised Evgeniy Prigozhin and his private military company "Wagner" as they rose to public prominence in Russia, extensively used freshly mobilised Russian prisoners for indiscriminate mass fighting with a high fatality rate, and performed at least a few

---

27 Primakov (@evgenyprimakov). 2023. "Mne, kak chastnomu litsu, khotelos by uvidet v tsentre Kieva…" [As a private person, I would like to see in the centre of Kyiv…]. Telegram, March 2, 2023. https://t.me/evgenyprimakov/3055.
28 Primakov (@evgenyprimakov). 2022. "Kievskiy rezhim—ludoiedskii i prestupnyi" [The Kyiv regime is cannibalistic and criminal]. Telegram, September 29, 2022. https://t.me/evgenyprimakov/2767.
29 Primakov (@evgenyprimakov). 2022. "Vpervyie s Velikoi Otechestvennoi Voiny my otdali rossiiskii gorod vragu" [For the first time since the Great Patriotic War have we surrendered a Russian city to the enemy]. Telegram, October 1, 2022. https://t.me/evgenyprimakov/2777.
30 Primakov (@evgenyprimakov). 2022. "Budet primechatelno, esli v khode sledstviia vyiasnitsia, chto podryv mosta…" [It will be remarkable if, during the investigation, it will become clear that the demolition of the bridge…]. Telegram October 10, 2022. https://t.me/evgenyprimakov/2808. *Salo* (pork lard) is stereotypic Ukrainian food in the Russian imagery, hence it is referred in quite a derogatory manner.

documented violent tortures of Ukrainian and Russian prisoners of war, one of them including the squashing of a man's head with a sledgehammer, all captured on video.[31] In another instance, Primakov boasted of an edition of Alexander Solzhenitsyn's writings on Ukraine, compiled and published in 2022 and signed by Solzhenitsyn's wife. Among the pictures posted was one of the book's pages saying that "the vast realms of Ukraine, such as Novorossiya, Crimea, and the whole Southwestern province, which had never belonged to historical Ukraine, were violently squeezed into the contemporary Ukrainian state and into his policy of greedily craved NATO accession."[32] Primakov did not shun demonstrating outright loyalty to the regime: he congratulated Putin on his birthday at his Telegram channel, praising him for restoring Russia's potence after "the abyss of the 90s," for the peace which "came to the North Caucasus," and claiming that under him the population of Russia witnessed unseen levels of wealth and affluence.[33]

Primakov's series of two programmatic articles from October 2022 was even more remarkable. There, in yet another historical lesson, he portrayed an extravagant representation of world history and international politics, according to which the predatory West has acquired its wealth exclusively due to centuries of extortion and "piracy," while the comparatively disadvantaged, and hence offended, Russia, allegedly not allowed to join the post-1991 world security architecture on equal footing, and suffering infringements on its sovereignty from the West, including the economic one, was

---

31 Primakov (@evgenyprimakov). 2023. "Prigozhin—rezkii i pravilnyi chelovek iz piterskikh opasnykh let" [Prigozhin is a straightforward person from Petersburg's dangerous years]. Telegram, February 22, 2023. https://t.me/evgeny primakov/3038.
32 Primakov (@evgenyprimakov). 2023. "Spasibo uvazhaiemoi Natalie Dmitrievne za knigu A.I. Solzhenitsyna" [Thanks to dear Nataliia Dmitriievna for the book by A.I. Solzhenitsyn]. Telegram, January 17, 2023. https://t.me/evgenyprimakov/2979. Primakov (@evgenyprimakov). 2022. "Vot k etoi rabote Nadany—28 minut 12 sekund 'propagandy Vagnera'—para bezpristrastnykh myslei" [To this work by Nadana, 28 minures and 2 seconds of "Wagner propaganda," a couple of impartial thoughts]. Telegram, October 6, 2022. https://t.me/evgenyprimakov/2793.
33 Primakov (@evgenyprimakov). 2022. "Vladimir Vladimirovich, s dnem rozhdeniia" [Happy birthday, Vladimir Vladimirovich]. Telegram, October 7, 2022. https://t.me/evgenyprimakov/2802.

forced to defend itself with an assault on Ukraine. Ukraine, in Primakov's opinion, was "a historically Russian land, populated [...] with Russians, and Russian-speaking people," and was used as a "battering ram" against Russia, specifically in a row of "colour revolutions" that swept across the region of former Soviet republics in the 2000s, and, of course, during Maidan.[34] It never occurred to him that Ukrainian identities could be "native" and not necessarily instrumentalised by outsiders to vex or cripple Russia. He perceives Ukraine as the West's weapon against Russia, whose "unity" with Russia must be "restored." Outstanding is Primakov's "realization" that one of Russia's foreign policy failures was an overreliance on foreign elites without reaching out to the population. This observation additionally underlined his perception of the importance of soft power, humanitarian policy, and Rossotrudnichestvo for Russia's influence operations abroad.[35]

As to the other Rossotrudnichestvo functionaries, nearly all of its deputy heads previously held important offices in Russian state agencies, often in institutions closely linked to the President's administration. Some of them possess multiple state decorations. Dmitriy Polikanov has recently been the most visible and media-present deputy head, typically representing Rossotrudnichestvo at its own events or those organised by Rossotrudnichestvo's partners.

It is helpful to consider Polikanov in more detail due to the innovative and modernising effort he aimed to bring to the activities of Rossotrudnichestvo. Appointed deputy head only in 2021 and possessing rich experience working for non-governmental organisations, he appeared to be a new type of manager determined to override this institution's long-established and obsolete bureaucratic practices. In fact, in his public appearances, be they interviews for the media, programmatic articles, or even Telegram posts,

---

34 @evgenyprimakov. 2022. "Chto zhe proiskhodit i pochemu" [What is happening and why]. Telegra.ph, October 17, 2022. https://telegra.ph/CHto-zhe-proishodit-i-pochemu-10-17.

35 @evgenyprimakov. 2022. "Chto zhe proiskhodit i pochemu, chast 2" [What is happening and why, part 2]. Telegra.ph, October 17, 2022. https://telegra.ph/CHto-zhe-proishodit-i-pochemu-chast-2-10-17.

he exercised open criticism of the inflexibilities and lack of creativity in Russian cultural diplomacy. He began to argue in favour of introducing new KPIs of Rossotrudnichestvo's activities, which would be tailored to assess not the input and direct output but rather the outcomes of its cultural diplomacy offensive, for instance, in the language policy.[36] These would replace old Soviet and post-Soviet indicators of efficiency. Despite having received training in African studies, he critically assessed Russia's capacity to develop active cultural diplomacy in Africa, saying that Russian society was still negatively perceiving Africans and that there was a lack of human and material resources for the cause. Instead, Polikanov defended the need to concentrate on the countries and regions with long-established connections and developed capacities, such as the "near abroad," including former Soviet Union states. Donning a soft-liner and reformist persona, Polikanov advocated a more conciliatory approach to the Russians who left the country after February 24, 2022, especially after the mobilisation in September of the same year. The idea was to accept that some might still return as long as these people did not openly criticise the Russian state. Still, as they organised in their host countries, especially in defence of their language rights or even for some leisure activities, this could be, in Polikanov's view, a valuable resource for Russia's cultural diplomacy. However, despite a seemingly liberal, Western-like, and modern approach, Polikanov still claimed that the tasks of Russia's cultural diplomacy included promoting Russian spiritual and moral values, as defined in various governmental documents and strategies. According to him, this led to Rossotrudnichestvo's cooperation with more conservative segments of society. One example of this peculiar stance is that African parents would instead bring their children to Russian schools, where they would allegedly be taught traditional values, instead of French schools.[37] However, this client-oriented approach of Rossotrudnichestvo's leadership might

---

36 Polikanov govorit (@polikanovgovorit). "Na vcherashnem Dne Obshchestvennogo soveta govorili o roli russkogo iazyka v mire" [At yesterday's Public Council Day, we talked about the role of the Russian language in the world]. Telegram, April 29, 2022. https://t.me/polikanovgovorit/132.
37 For these and other his ideas see Polikanov (2023), Dergachev et al. (2022).

mean more efficiency when compared to more conventional patterns, and this new approach received more sway in 2022, as Polikanov boasted that some of the innovations could eventually be introduced despite the resistance of conservatists.

Another interesting case was Natalia Poklonskaya's appointment as Rossotrudnichestvo's deputy head mere weeks before the launch of the all-out Russian invasion on February 2, 2022, and her dismissal just months later, on June 13, 2022. After her appointment, Poklonskaya claimed she intended, in her new position, to defend the rights of "Russian-speaking compatriots" in Ukraine. In the following months, she primarily appeared in connection with Rossotrudnichestvo's activities focused on what it presents as humanitarian development aid. In a comment on her appointment to KrymInform, an outlet controlled by the Russian occupation authorities, Poklonskaya said that "protecting the rights of compatriots abroad, including in Ukraine, will be her priority" in the new office. To support this statement, she claimed to have relevant expertise in "human rights protection, the world and security" and said that her "...Russian-Ukrainian experience will serve her well."[38] Born in Luhansk oblast, Ukraine, she served as a prosecutor of the Russian occupation administration in the temporarily occupied Autonomous Republic of Crimea. It was Poklonskaya who initiated the prohibition of the Mejlis, the representative body of the Crimean Tatar people, in 2016 while being a prosecutor in the occupied Crimea. Poklonskaya has been sanctioned by Ukraine (charged with high treason, among other things), the EU, the US, Canada, and Japan. It is unclear what she was sacked for; Moscow's military ineffectiveness in Ukraine and her ambiguous comments about the war are among the hypothetical reasons.

---

38 See Ukrainska Pravda. "Poklonska na novii posadi zibralasia 'zakhyshchaty prava rosiian v Ukraini'" [Poklonskaya plans to "protect the rights of Russians in Ukraine" at her new position]. February 3, 2022. https://www.pravda.com.ua/news/2022/02/3/7322690/.

Dmitriy Polikanov, formerly a high-ranking official at the United Russia party, the first deputy executive director at the Russian Geographical Society, and the former head of other state agencies.[39]

Kirill Bogomolov, standing 3d class state councillor of the Russian Federation (a bureaucratic rank within Russia's public service system), was formerly an official who had made a decade-long career within the Ministry of Finance.

Aleksei Polkovnikov, standing 3rd class state councillor of the Russian Federation, formerly director general at the Russian Humanitarian Mission.

Pavel Shevtsov, former deputy director of the Department for Economic Cooperation with CIS Countries and Development of Eurasian Integration in the Russian Ministry of Economic Development.

---

39 The photographs of Rossotrudnichestvo's deputy heads as of 2023 were borrowed from the Agency's website at https://rs.gov.ru/about-foiv/.

Since late 2020, Rossotrudnichestvo has had a Public Council, supposed to represent the public's interests in overseeing the organisation's operations. However, the membership of the Public Council suggests a close connection between Rossotrudnichestvo and key state educational institutions (for instance, Viktor Sadovnichiy, Rector of Moscow State University, is both an Honorary Director of this Public Council and a member of the Academic Board of the Russian Security Council), other public and cultural diplomacy organisations, such as the "Russkiy Mir" Foundation and Valdai Club, and its membership includes representatives from the most prominent state corporations, including Gazprom Neft and Rostech. Virtually all Public Council members hold multiple state decorations and are engaged in other Russian state agencies, and some have experience of working in Russian-occupied territories, including those in Moldova. Thus, the Public Council membership rather reflects horizontal connections inside a state-led network of players, than genuine public oversight.[40]

In addition, Rossotrudnichestvo systematically collaborates with other Russian organisations that operate in similar areas, including the Presidential Grants Foundation, Alexander Gorchakov Public Diplomacy Fund, the Russian Geographical Society, the Russian International Affairs Council, and others. Rossotrudnichestvo collaborates, supports, and participates in the following partner projects by other Russian organisations:

- *InteRussia* research and academic internships for foreign specialists implemented by the Gorchakov Fund and the Moscow State Institute of International Relations.[41]
- *SPUTNIKPRO workshops* for international journalists, media managers, and press service personnel, an international project of Russia Today, the Russian state propaganda me-

---

40 Rossotrudnichestvo. n. d. "Obshchestvennyi sovet pri Rossotrudnichestve" [Members of the Public Council at Rossotrudnichestvo]. https://rs.gov.ru/app/uploads/2023/01/avtobigrafii-chlenov-soveta-3.pdf.
41 MGIMO University. "Internship programme InteRussia: call for applications is open." January 31, 2022. https://english.mgimo.ru/announce/interussia-03-22.

dia company. Since 2015, over 250 people from eighty countries have participated in Rossotrudnichestvo's *New Generation programme* workshops.[42]

- *School of Real Journalism* by the Russian Reporters organisation with support from the "Russkiy Mir" Foundation and Rossotrudnichestvo. RIA Novosti, the Russian Union of Journalists, the Presidential Grants Foundation, and the Yandex technology company are also involved in this project.[43]
- *Leaders of Russia*, an open competition for education grants of 1 million roubles (around $16,000) for Russian and non-Russian executives. It was declared the flagship project of the presidential platform, *Russia – Land of Opportunity*. The competition's International Track's supervisory board is chaired by Foreign Minister Sergei Lavrov and includes Rossotrudnichestvo head Yevgeny Primakov.[44] Dmitriy Polikanov, the deputy head of Rossotrudnichestvo, has expressed interest in and plans to collaborate with the winners of this track.[45] In a broader sense, this competition appears to be a means for the Russian regime to select qualified and loyal executives for regional and federal positions. In the context of Russia's full-scale invasion of Ukraine, it is interesting to note that the 2022 Leaders of Russia winners include ministerial appointees in the self-proclaimed "Donetsk People's Republic" and "Luhansk People's Republic"

---

42 Rossiia s mirom [Russia with peace]. "'Novoie pokoleniie' inostrannykh zhurnalistov proshli master-klass 'Sputnikpro'" ["A New Generation" of foreign journalists attend "Sputnikpro" workshop]. October 29, 2021. http://web.archive.org/web/20220524222721/https://rwp.agency/news/637/.

43 Rossiia s mirom [Russia with peace]. "Shkola realnoi zhurnalistiki v Belarusi" [The School of Real Journalism in Belarus]. February 4, 2022. https://www.rwp.agency/news/1035/.

44 Lidery Rossii [Leaders of Russia]. "Lidery Rossii. Mezhdunarodnyi trek" [Leaders of Russia. International Track]. n. d. http://web.archive.org/web/20210827002010/https://www.лидерыроссии.рф/international2021.

45 Russkii dom [Russian House]. 2022. "18 marta v Rossotrudnichestve proshla vstrecha finalistov treka 'Mehdunarodnyi' konkursa 'Lidery Rossii'" [On March 18, "Leaders of Russia" (track "International") finalists' meeting was held at Rossotrudnichestvo]. Facebook, March 19, 2022. https://www.facebook.com/rsgov/posts/pfbid0337LguQPuLT7Vrp3pTYQgjrrejTJc5Ei8H81wcuhgPhADsV8FzdBDRpyNWtbaLF7Ll.

(Russia-occupied territories). Examples include Ivan Kusov, vice-president of the Sevastopol State University, who was invited to become minister of education in the self-proclaimed "LPR." At the same time, Oleg Trofimov received the same position in the self-proclaimed "DPR." Vladimir Putin endorsed both appointments in a personal meeting with Kusov and Trofimov.[46]
- International development aid with the Association of Volunteer Centres and Russian Humanitarian Mission *(see "Russia with peace/world?" International development aid below for more details about international development aid partners).*

Rossotrudnichestvo, therefore, is deeply integrated into the state apparatus of the Russian Federation, as evidenced by its management, Public Council, and list of partners. Moreover, since many of its leaders are also members of the United Russia ruling party, political expediency and favouritism are prioritised over efficiency. Cultural diplomacy and international development specialists are less favoured than performers who could propagate narratives compatible with the other government agencies in Russia. Lyubov Glebova, the head of Rossotrudnichestvo in 2015-2017, is an illustrative case in point: she never held any international relations-related positions. She was a senator from two regions of the Russian Federation in the Federation Council before and after her tenure at Rossotrudnichestvo. This approach differs significantly from the selection of managers for comparable Western organisations, such as the British Council or Goethe-Institut, where leaders typically hail from academia, non-governmental organisations, or charitable organisations. Lacking any organisational autonomy, Rossotrudnichestvo follows the foreign policy course the Russian regime is pursuing at any given time and serves as the platform for disseminating Kremlin narratives.

---

46 Prezident Rossii. "Vstrecha s pobediteliami konkursa 'Lidery Rossii'" [Meeting with the winners of the competition "Leaders of Russia"]. July 7, 2022. http://kremlin.ru/events/president/news/68835.

2.2 Catching up with USAID: The funding challenges

According to Rossotrudnichestvo's Statute, it is funded from Russia's state budget and the revenues from the activities it is allowed to conduct.[47] This method is typical of financing the West's public and cultural diplomacy institutions. Unlike them, however, Rossotrudnichestvo's funding is far from transparent. Its standard financial statement provides very limited details on its revenues and expenditures, offering little insight into how exactly Rossotrudnichestvo is funded. It has an annual statements section on its website, which, similar to such organisations in other countries, should provide more details on its activities in a way that is not strictly bureaucratic. But almost all links to annual statements lead to empty pages. As of 2022, only the 2020 annual statement was available, which, despite providing no insight into the funding's dynamics, permits comparisons with soft power institutions from other countries.

Rossotrudnichestvo earned 455 million roubles in revenue in 2020, equivalent to € 5.5 million at the average annual exchange rate.[48] Nearly 83% of this revenue came from using Russian property abroad and providing paid services, most likely Russian language classes. Its expenditures were tenfold higher, at 4.538 billion roubles, or € 54.8 million. The Russian budget made up the difference. This demonstrates that 90% of Rossotrudnichestvo's expenditures are subsidised. The unknown is the spending section of its budget structure. However, interviews with the organisation's leaders reveal that approximately 70% of its budget is spent on staff salaries and property maintenance (Khimshiashvili 2018). This funding is significantly less than comparable soft power institutions in Germany and the United Kingdom. The Goethe-Institut, for instance, generated € 388 million in revenue in 2020 and spent € 393

---

47 Russian Federation. President. Ukaz [Decree] #1315 "O nekotorykh voprosakh gosudarstvennogo upravleniia v oblasti mezhdunarodnogo sotrudnichestva" [On Some Aspects of Governance in the Field of International Cooperation]. Adopted 6 September 2008. http://www.kremlin.ru/acts/bank/28020.
48 Rossotrudnichestvo. 2021. "Otchetnost ob ispolnenii budzheta ot 01.01.2021" [Report on the implementation of budget as of 01.01.2021]. January 1, 2021. https://rs.gov.ru/app/uploads/2022/12/095_01.01.2021_0503127.pdf.

million (Goethe Institut 2021, 128). The British Council generated £925 million in revenue and spent £1,008 million in 2020-2021 over the financial year from April 1, 2020, to March 31, 2021 (British Council n. d., 68–71). In addition, Rossotrudnichestvo differs in terms of its revenue structure, as most of its income comes from the state, not from its activities. Rossotrudnichestvo's expenditures are moderately comparable to those of the Institut français, which generated € 42.1 million in revenue in 2020, 72% of which was subsidised by the French government, and spent € 35 million (Institut français 2020, 61).

Figure 1. Publicly funded cultural diplomacy institutions in Western countries and Russia

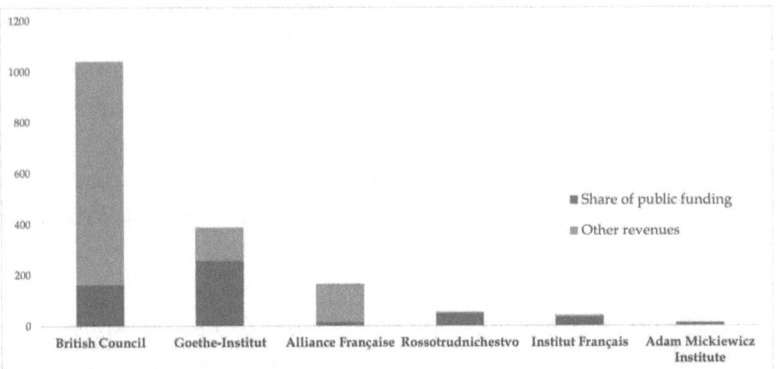

Note. Data is derived from the 2020 annual reports of these entities. The amount was converted to EUR for the British Council and Rossotrudnichestvo using the yearly average exchange rate of the pound and rouble in 2020.

In addition to apparent funding disparities with comparable institutions, the current funding for Rossotrudnichestvo is also significantly less than envisaged at the beginning of the 2010s. A presidential decree from 2013 mandated an increase in the 2020 budget from 0.03% to 0.1% of the Russian GDP (Tafuro 2014, 4). Initially, things were moving in this direction. As the 2014 Concept of the State Policy of Russia in International Development Aid granted Rossotrudnichestvo the leading role in developing Russia's soft power, it was expected to administer much more money in the context of providing international aid. 2014 compared to 2013, its budget increased by a third, from 2 billion roubles to nearly 2.74 billion roubles, or € 61 million, at the beginning of the year's exchange rate. From then on, all international development aid would be administered by Rossotrudnichestvo rather than the Ministry of Finance (Lutsevych 2016).

But the initial drive was sapped quickly. Rossotrudnichestvo receives 25 times less than the 0.1% planned in 2013, ending up with 0.004% of the Russian GDP in 2020.[49] Despite retaining these functions, Rossotrudnichestvo never received large budgets to provide international aid. Its most recent public statement on this topic dates to 2015 (Burlinova et al. 2018, 17). In 2016, Leonid Slutskiy, chairman of the State Duma Committee on International Affairs, criticised Rossotrudnichestvo's inadequate funding. He compared it to a "good brand automobile that knows how and where to go but has an empty tank."[50] According to Slutskiy, Rossotrudnichestvo's foreign offices were forced to relocate from prestigious and symbolic buildings to the suburbs of capitals because of a lack of funding. Even in 2023, as the Russian full-scale invasion reached its first anniversary, Rossotrudnichestvo's Head, Yevgeny Primakov Jr., complained on his Telegram channel that the funding for culture in Russia is insufficient, especially in times of war.[51]

Rossotrudnichestvo's opaque statements make it difficult to understand why an institution that, given its objectives, should have seen its funding increase as Russia's policy becomes more aggressive has not received the previously promised funding. The following factors may be at play:

---

49 Russia's GDP was RUR 106.6tn in 2020. Kommersant. "Rosstat: VVP Rossii v 2020 godu snizilsia na 3.1%" [Rosstat: Russia's GDP decreased by 3.1% in 2020]. February 1, 2021. https://www.kommersant.ru/doc/4671959.

50 RIA Novosti. 2016. "V GD obespokoiieny sokrashcheniiem finansirovaniia programm Rossotrudnichestva" [State Duma concerned about funding cuts for Rossotrudnichestvo programmes]. October 7, 2016. https://ria.ru/20161007/1478733956.html.

51 Primakov (@evgenyprimakov). 2023. "Novaia Russkaia Kultura" [New Russian Culture]. Forwarded from @akimapachev. Telegram, February 24, 2023. https://t.me/evgenyprimakov/3047.

1. *Russia's foreign policy priorities shift as the regime opts for hard power.* Russia's neighbouring states were expected to become the primary focus areas in 2013–2015, and Rossotrudnichestvo planned to open 9 out of its 11 new offices in those countries. Ukraine was likely a top priority: in March 2014, Konstantin Kosachev, then Head of Rossotrudnichestvo, complained that USAID's budget in Ukraine doubled Rossotrudnichestvo's total for all countries. He insisted that Russian universities significantly increase the quota for Ukrainian students (Khimshiashvili 2014). However, the subsequent annexation of Crimea and the military invasion of the Donbas demonstrated that Russia prioritised hard power over soft power in Ukraine.
2. *Russia's stagnant economy and foreign policy challenges cripple the agency's activities.* Early in the 2010s, Russia's economic growth began decelerating, and its GDP fell by 2 per cent in 2015.[52] This left Russia with fewer resources for foreign policy. In 2015, this was reflected in the shrinking budgets of RT and MIA Rossiya Segodnya, the principal Russian propaganda outlets.[53] Rossotrudnichestvo was not exempt from budget cuts.
3. *Bureaucratic warfare between various governmental entities as well as organisational inefficiency, torpedoed Rossotrudnichestvo's activities.* In 2015, Russia's Accounts Chamber reported that Rossotrudnichestvo was not spending efficiently, and the desired pace of opening new offices abroad did not match the available resources: it opened only three out of the eleven planned for 2013-2015.[54] Numerous violations were found in other categories of spending. This may

---

52 The World Bank. "GDP growth (annual %) — Russian Federation." n. d. https://data.worldbank.org/indicator/NY.GDP.MKTP.KD.ZG?locations=RU.
53 RT na russkom [RT in Russian]. "Biudzhet telekanala RT sokrashchen na 10%" [The RT budget is cut 10%]. January 16, 2015. https://russian.rt.com/article/69298.
54 Regnum. "Rossotrudnichestvo neeffektivno ispolzovalo biudzhetnyiie sredstva — SP RF" [Rossotrudnichestvo used budget funding inefficiently — Accounts Chamber of the Russian Federation]. June 9, 2016. https://regnum.ru/news/2142931.html.

have necessitated revaluating the initial plans to increase funding for Rossotrudnichestvo.

2.3 World League of Russian Houses: Rossotrudnichestvo's foreign representations

As of 2021, the infrastructure of offices inherited by Rossotrudnichestvo from its predecessors has evolved into a network of Russian Centres of Science and Culture and Russian Houses. Additionally, it inherited established relationships and contacts with foreign and Russian organisations worldwide. As a result, Rossotrudnichestvo is now an organisational behemoth with a maximum of 251 full-time employees at its central office and 548 employees abroad at its offices and representations in other countries.[55]

According to Rossotrudnichestvo's Statute, its apparatus abroad comprises the so-called Russian centres of science and culture, Russian information and culture centres, Russian houses of science and culture abroad, and Russian cultural centres abroad. Still, the term used in the organisation's annual reports and public communication is the Russian Centre of Science and Culture/RCSC. In places where Rossotrudnichestvo does not have full-fledged offices, there are individual representatives at Russia's diplomatic missions who are not part of the diplomatic personnel. According to Rossotrudnichestvo's website, the Agency's offices operate in 80 countries.[56]

Rossotrudnichestvo's offices and representatives are subordinate to the Russian state and are managed centrally from Moscow. Russia's president decides on any alterations to the structure and functions of these offices.[57] According to the Statute of Rossotrudnichestvo offices, their work is regulated by the laws of the Russian

---

[55] Russian Federation. President. Ukaz [Decree] #1315 "O nekotorykh voprosakh gosudarstvennogo upravleniia v oblasti mezhdunarodnogo sotrudnichestva" [On Some Aspects of Governance in the Field of International Cooperation]. Adopted 6 September 2008. http://www.kremlin.ru/acts/bank/28020.

[56] Rossotrudnichestvo. "O Rossotrudnichestve" [About Rossotrudnichestvo]. n. d. https://rs.gov.ru/about-foiv/.

[57] Russian Federation. President. Ukaz [Decree] #1315 "O nekotorykh voprosakh gosudarstvennogo upravleniia v oblasti mezhdunarodnogo sotrudnichestva"

Federation, as well as by the decrees, resolutions, and orders of the president, government, ministries, and Rossotrudnichestvo central apparatus, Russia's international agreements, and the laws of the host countries.[58] The central apparatus is responsible for the offices' property management, while the ambassador of Russia to the host country exercises general management and oversight, this limiting the independence of each representation. The analysis of administration at Rossotrudnichestvo abroad representations demonstrates that representational offices work is generally defined and tightly controlled by the central office in Moscow.[59]

With the appointment of Yevgeny Primakov Jr. as head of Rossotrudnichestvo, the organisation began a rebranding effort to modernise and consolidate its image. As the word "Rossotrudnichestvo" is allegedly difficult for foreign audiences to pronounce, a suggestion was put forward in late 2020 to change its name to something more colloquial. In March 2021, Russian science and culture centres were renamed Russian Houses, and Rossotrudnichestvo ended up with the Russian House ("Russkiy Dom") as its second unofficial name.[60] Its new logo, based on the new name, was publicly introduced in September 2021.[61]

It appears that the rebranding was done in preparation for implementing the strategy to create a network of non-state Russian Houses, which was announced in September 2021.[62] The declared goals of these changes include expanding the geographic presence

---

    [On Some Aspects of Governance in the Field of International Cooperation]. Adopted 6 September 2008. http://www.kremlin.ru/acts/bank/28020.
58 Ibid.
59 Rossotrudnichestvo. "Russkiie doma za rubezhom" [Russian Houses abroad]. n. d. https://rs.gov.ru/predstavitelstva-za-rubezhom/.
60 Russkii dom [Russian House]. "Welcome to Russian House!" Facebook, March 2, 2021. https://www.facebook.com/rsgov/photos/a.420750617960319/3717949421573739/.
61 Rossiia s mirom [Russia with peace]. "O novom logotipe Russkikh domov" [About the new logo of Russian Houses]. September 10, 2021. http://web.archive.org/web/20220129005549/https://rwp.agency/press-sluzhba/zayavleniya/?ELEMENT_ID=295.
62 Rossiia s mirom [Russia with peace]. "Rossotrudnichestvo predstavilo novyi firmennyi stil Russkikh domov za rubezhom" [Rossotrudnichestvo presents a new brand style for Russian Houses abroad]. September 3, 2021. http://web.archive.org/web/20210916191444/https://rwp.agency/news/282/.

of Rossotrudnichestvo, primarily going beyond the capitals of the host countries where its offices are currently concentrated and thus engaging a larger foreign audience. Under the new guidelines, a Russian House abroad can be opened by foreign and Russian partner organisations, private Russian schools and local higher education institutions, non-profit or "compatriots" organisations, and graduates of Russian universities. According to Nadana Fridrikhson, press-secretary for Rossotrudnichestvo, the Russian House is transforming into a "franchise" of sorts.[63] The information that the Agency's officials were broadcasting remained confusing. In his Telegram in April 2022, Polikanov, when reporting about signing an agreement about opening such an office in Egypt, claimed that only three non-state centres had been opened, namely, in China, Sudan, and in the so-called "DPR" (occupied by Russia).[64] However, in his large programmatic interview in April 2023, he stated that in 2022, these new "franchise" offices were established in Sudan, Algeria, Mali, and Egypt, with countries in Africa, the Middle East, and Latin America expected to follow suit (Polikanov 2023). Still, in its 2022 annual report, the Agency admitted that only two such offices were to be opened in 2022, with another two, in Sierra Leone and Uganda, being negotiated (Rossotrudnichestvo 2023, 3).

Establishing Rossotrudnichestvo agencies with a non-government status could accelerate and simplify the emergence of new offices and increase their number, thereby promoting the Kremlin's agenda faster and more effectively. The office opened in Sudan in early 2022 provides one example in support of this assumption: its director was already spreading the Kremlin's false narratives about the causes and context of Russia's war against Ukraine in the first

---

63   Russkii dom [Russia with peace]. "Brifing press-sekretaria Rossotrudnichestva Nadany Fridrikhson" [Briefing by Rossotrudnichestvo press-secretary Nadana Fridrikhson]. YouTube video, 13:40, December 21, 2021. https://youtu.be/s89EA9KtcUY.
64   Polikanov govorit (@polikanovgovorit). "Podpisali soglashenie segodnia ob otkrytii negosudarstvennogo Russkogo doma v Khurgade" [Today, we have signed an agreement on the opening of a non-state Russian House in Hurghada]. Telegram, April 20, 2022. https://t.me/polikanovgovorit/99.

month after it began *(see the subsection on Rossotrudnichestvo after the beginning of Russia's full-scale invasion of Ukraine below for more details).*

According to Rossotrudnichestvo's 2022 annual report, the Agency is established across 80 countries via 87 foreign representations. Despite the announced rebranding, Rossotrudnichestvo continues to refer to its offices as either the Russian Centre of Science and Culture or the Russian House. For example, the office in Moldova uses different names for its website[65] and Facebook page.[66]

---

65 Predstavitelstvo Rossotrudnichestva v Respublike Moldova [Rossotrudnichestvo representation in the Republic of Moldova]. "Kontaktnaiia informatsiia" [Contact information]. n. d. http://www.rcnk.md/kontaktnaya-informaciya/.
66 "Russkiy dom v Kishineve / Casa Rusă din Chișinău" [Russian House in Chișinău]. Facebook, n. d. https://www.facebook.com/MoldovaRCNK.

Table 2. Host countries for foreign offices of Rossotrudnichestvo[67]

Region	Number	Countries[68]
CIS, occupied parts of Georgia: Abkhazia and South Ossetia	16	Azerbaijan, Armenia (2),[69] Belarus (3), Kazakhstan (2), Kyrgyzstan (2), Moldova, Tajikistan (2), Uzbekistan, occupied territory of Georgia: Abkhazia and South Ossetia
The Middle East and North Africa	9	Egypt (2), Israel, Jordan, Lebanon, Morocco, Palestine, Syria, Tunisia
Asia	21	Afghanistan, Bangladesh, Vietnam, India (5), Indonesia, Iran, Cambodia, China, Laos, Malaysia, Mongolia, Nepal, Pakistan, South Korea, Singapore, Sri Lanka, Japan

---

67 It is important to note that the total number of offices and representatives listed in the Russian Houses (https://rs.gov.ru/predstavitelstva-za-rubezhom/) section on the website and in the chart below, respectively, (considering that six of them have been shut down) is smaller than the number specified in the Programmes (http://web.archive.org/web/20220218091030/https://rwp.agency/programmy/) section and seems to be incomplete (85 versus 87 representations; information provided as of spring 2023). For example, the Russian House in Donetsk is mentioned in other sections of the website but is not on the list in the Russian Houses section. One must still keep in mind that the number of offices might still decrease due to the sanctions and respective decisions by the authorities.

68 Rossotrudnichestvo uses the vocabulary and categorization for countries and territories that are typical for the Russian regime. For example, the occupied territories of Georgia, Abkhazia, and South Ossetia, recognised unilaterally as independent by Russia, are placed in the same cohort as independent countries. Also, it uses such vocabulary for the countries that used to be part of the Soviet Union. For example, it uses Belorussiya, Kyrgyzia, and Moldavia instead of their current official names: Belarus, Kyrgyzstan, and Moldova. This is just one illustration of the way Rossotrudnichestvo approaches naming other countries. Other documents and communications by Rossotrudnichestvo persistently use old Soviet or Russian imperial names for the countries that used to be part of the Soviet Union, not their official names. Examples include *Pribaltica* for the Baltic States or *na Ukraine* instead of *v Ukraine* for the phrase "in Ukraine." This practice points to the preservation of Russia's imperialist perspective on the countries in the post-Soviet space and attempts to legitimise quasi-entities established with Russia's support but unrecognised by most countries across the world. See Rossotrudnichestvo. "Russkiie doma za rubezhom" [Russian Houses abroad]. n. d. https://rs.gov.ru/predstavitelstva-za-rubezhom/.

69 The number in the brackets hereinafter marks the number of offices in the country. If there is no number in brackets next to a country's name, this means that it hosts just one office of Rossotrudnichestvo.

Europe	22	Austria, Albania, Belgium, Bulgaria, Hungary, Germany, Greece, Denmark, Spain, Italy, Cyprus, Luxembourg, Malta, Poland (2), Portugal, Serbia, Turkey, Finland, France, Czechia, Switzerland *Closed after 2022*: Croatia, Montenegro, North Macedonia, Romania, Slovakia, Slovenia, United Kingdom (had a representative at the Russian Embassy and not a proper office)[70]
America	12	Argentina, Brazil (2), Venezuela, Canada, Cuba, Mexico, Peru, USA (2), Chile Nicaragua *(representative at the Russian Embassy, not a full-fledged office)*
Africa	5	Zambia, Congo, Tanzania, Ethiopia South Africa *(representative at the Russian Embassy, not a full-fledged office)*
Total	**85**	

---

[70] The countries listed according to Rossotrudnichestvo's 2022 annual report. One more, Romania, was closed down by the Romania authorities already in 2023. Not surprisingly, all seven of them happened to be in Europe (Rossotrudnichestvo 2023, 3). See also: RIA Novosti. 2023. "Rumyniia priostanovit deiatelnost Rossiiskogo tsentra kultury i nauki" [Romania will suspend the activities of the Russian Centre of Science and Culture]. February 21, 2023. https://ria.ru/20230221/kultura-1853462534.html.

Figure 2. Rossotrudnichestvo's offices abroad (as of April 2023)

In numerous public documents, the countries covered by Rossotrudnichestvo are typically categorised into the "CIS countries," which include a number of post-Soviet states as well as the Baltic States and Georgia, and the "far abroad," which refers to the remainder of the world. This outlines two major operational areas. One is the territory of the former Soviet Union, which may confirm Russia's strategic aspiration to maintain control over all post-Soviet countries in one way or another. The other is the rest of the world, which, according to Rossotrudnichestvo's publicly available documents, including the annual statement (Rossotrudnichestvo 2021), plan of activities,[71] public declaration of goals and objectives[72] and others, appears rather vaguely defined as these documents offer no nuanced strategies for various regions of the world, (or at least they are not publicly articulated).

On the contrary, in public documents and on the official website, CIS countries, a traditional focus of Russia's cultural diplomacy, are identified as the geographic coverage priority.[73] In a briefing on Rossotrudnichestvo's performance in 2021 and its plans for 2022,[74] press-secretary Nadana Fridrikhson also highlighted the organisation's projects in CIS countries. She cited the Agency's activities in Ukraine, which were implemented despite sanctions imposed against the organisation by the Ukrainian National Security

---

71 Rossiia s mirom [Russia with peace]. "Plany" [Plans]. n. d. http://web.archive.org/web/20220625041323/https://rwp.agency/agency/open-a/index-detail/plany/.
72 Rossotrudnichestvo. "Publichnaia deklaratsiia tselei i zadach Rossotrudnichestva na 2022 gg." [Public declaration of Rossotrudnichestvo goals and objectives for 2022]. n. d. https://rs.gov.ru/app/uploads/2023/04/fin_publichnaya-deklaracziya-czelej-i-zadach-na-2022-god.pdf.
73 Rossiia s mirom [Russia with peace]. "Programmy Agentstva" [Agency's Programmes]. n. d. https://web.archive.org/web/20220218091030/https://rwp.agency/programmy/.
74 Russkii dom [Russian House]. "Brifing press-sekretaria Rossotrudnichestva Nadany Fridrikhson" [Briefing by Rossotrudnichestvo press-secretary Nadana Fridrikhson]. YouTube video, 13:40, December 21, 2021. https://youtu.be/s89EA9KtcUY.

and Defence Council in 2021.[75] This indicates that Rossotrudnichestvo prioritised Ukraine despite the Ukrainian government's ban on its operations. Even more illustrative of this point is that the Russian House in Kyiv (https://www.facebook.com/ukrrsgov/) maintains its Facebook account and continues to post content until this day.

Another evidence of the political use of Rossotrudnichestvo's representations abroad are the alleged plans of the Kremlin to open new Centres of Science and Culture in Mogilev, Grodno, and Vitebsk in Belarus within its programme of political and economic subjugation of Belarus, as outlaid in the "Strategic Objectives of the Russian Federation in the Belarusian Direction" published by the Dossier Center (Dosie 2023).

Finally, Rossotrudnichestvo branches are apparently pursuing a destabilising agenda in countries outside of Russia's direct sphere of interest, as, for instance, in Germany. A recent journalistic investigation by Reuters implies that there might be connections between the Russian House in Germany, a Rossotrudnichestvo branch in that country, and pro-Russian nationalist activists standing behind a social movement pleading for the halt of German support of Ukraine in the current Russian-Ukrainian war (Nikolskaya et al. 2023).

2.4 A focus on gathering "compatriots": Offices in Ukraine[76]

As soon as Rossotrudnichestvo was reformed in 2008 to prioritise former Soviet Union countries, Ukraine became a focal point of its activities. In 2008, the Russian Centre of Science and Culture was opened in Kyiv, and the one in Simferopol in 2012 (the latter was closed in 2014). Another representative office was at the General

---

75 Ukraine. President. Ukaz [Decree] #140/2021 "Pro rishennia Rady natdionalnoi bezpeky i oborony Ukrainy vid 2 kvitnia 2021 roku 'Pro zastosuvannia personalnykh spetsialnykh ekonomichnykh ta inshykh obmezhuvalnykh zakhodiv (sanktsii)'" [On the resolution of the National Security and Defense Council of Ukraine from April 2, 2021 "On the application of personal special economic and other restrictive measures (sanctions)"]. Adopted 3 April 2021. https://www.president.gov.ua/documents/1402021-38381.
76 We express gratitude to the Centre of Defence Strategies for the materials provided for this section.

Consulate of Russia in Odesa. All in all, Ukraine was considered a battleground for an uncompromising fight against American or, more generally, Western soft power, and thus a significant number of resources were invested there. As Konstantin Kosachev, the Head of Rossotrudnichestvo (2012–2014), claimed in 2014:

> "Our competitors and adversaries have been expanding their influence on the minds of Ukrainians all these years using soft power tools. Here is a serious difference in our approaches: while we traditionally assumed that the factors of cultural, linguistic, and historical proximity, economic ties, and a large Russian diaspora would act on their own without constant external impetus from our side, the competitors have invested massively in the local NGOs and, through them, they have consistently peddled onto the population the "European" idea as their goal for Ukrainian civil society, not only in the West but also in the East of Ukraine." (Cited in Khimshiashvili 2014)

These offices operated activities customary for Rossotrudnichestvo, although the substance of their work in Ukraine has caused increasing concern, especially after 2014 (Hrupa z analizu hibrydnykh zahroz 2020). Despite Russia's military aggression against Ukraine, the Kyiv office of Rossotrudnichestvo kept operating after 2014. According to some data, it held nearly 700 cultural events across the country in 2017 alone, despite the Russian occupation of a part of Ukraine's territory. Most of the criticism of Rossotrudnichestvo was aimed at its attempts to reconstruct a common identity in the post-Soviet space through organising events that promoted (outdated) Russian historical narratives, fostering contacts and support for militarised youth groups, persistently promoting the learning of the Russian language, culture, and literature among children and youth in some regions, proactively encouraging local students to study at Russian universities, and implementing other projects to engage educational, cultural, and academic professionals. Furthermore, its offices were suspected of spying on and incorporating agents of influence among central and local authorities.

For example, the work of Rossotrudnichestvo's "local partners" in Ukraine, such as the International Pedagogical Club in Kharkiv, the Kyiv Society of Russian Compatriots Homeland, the Kharkiv Society of East Slavs, and the International Association of

Slavic Unity, was frequently unambiguously pro-Russian. Rossotrudnichestvo's activities in Ukraine often sparked scandals. For example, its office in Ukraine brought 70 Ukrainian school students to Moscow and Saint Petersburg as part of the *Hello, Russia!* Programme;[77] activists from Ukrainian nationalist organisations broke into its office in Kyiv;[78] its operations were blocked,[79] and the Security Service of Ukraine, SBU[80] and parliamentarians[81] made multiple attempts to ban Rossotrudnichestvo in Ukraine to protect Ukraine's national interests.

Multiple instances of Rossotrudnichestvo representatives acting against Ukraine's national interests were uncovered. For example, in 2018, SBU counterintelligence revealed and terminated Rossotrudnichestvo employees' anti-Ukrainian activities at the Russian Consulate General in Odesa.[82] It was discovered that these representatives engaged Ukrainian citizens who were members of pro-Russian civic associations and movements in anti-Ukrainian activities under the guise of so-called Humanitarian and Social Programmes of the Russian Federation. One Consulate employee was

---

77 Ukrainska Pravda. "Rosiiany khvaliatsia, shcho vidpravyly do RF velyku hrupu ukrainskykh shkoliariv" [Russians boast about sending a big group of Ukrainian school students to Russia]. August 16, 2017. https://www.pravda.com.ua/news/2017/08/16/7152369/.
78 Ukrainska Pravda. "Natsionalisty uvirvalysia do budivli 'Rosspivrobitnytstva' v Kyievi" [Nationalists break into the office of Rossotrudnichestvo in Kyiv]. February 17, 2018. https://www.pravda.com.ua/news/2018/02/17/7171957/.
79 Ukrainska Pravda. "U Kyievi aktyvisty, iaki 'zamurovuiut' rosbanky, zablokuvaly 'Totalnyi dyktant'" [The activists who "wall up" Russian banks block the Total Dictation in Kyiv]. April 8, 2017. https://www.pravda.com.ua/news/2017/04/8/7140655/.
80 Ukrainska Pravda. "V SBU rozpovily, iak borolys' z rossiiskym tsentrom, shcho vozyt ditei do RF" [SBU tells how it targeted the Russian centre that brings children to Russia]. September 19, 2017. https://www.pravda.com.ua/news/2017/09/19/7155628/.
81 Ukrainska Pravda. "Rada rozhliane zakon pro zaboronu rossiiskoho kulturnoho tsentru" [Verkhovna Rada considers a law to ban Russian cultural centre]. September 19, 2017. https://www.pravda.com.ua/news/2017/09/19/7155664/.
82 Tsenzor.net [Censor.net]. "Kontrrozvidka SBU rozkryla antyukrainsku diialnist 'Rosspivrobitnytstva' i dyplomata RF v Odesi. FOTO" [SBU counterintelligence discovers anti-Ukrainian operations of Rossotrudnichestvo and a Russian diplomat in Odesa. PHOTOS]. May 21, 2018. https://censor.net/ua/n3069021.

suspected of working for Russian security services. His illegal activities on the territory of Ukraine were proven, and he was declared *persona non-grata*.

The road towards a legislative ban of Rossotrudnichestvo operations in Ukraine was arduous,[83] partly because the Agreement Between the Cabinet of Ministers of Ukraine and the Government of the Russian Federation on the Establishment and Operations of Information and Culture Centres had to be repealed.[84] Finally, with decree No140/2021 in April 2021, the President of Ukraine enacted the decision of Ukraine's National Security and Defence Council, "On Personal Special Economic and Other Restrictive Measures (Sanctions)." Among other things, this decision applied various unilateral restrictions on Rossotrudnichestvo for three years, disabling and de facto terminating its operations in Ukraine (Yermolov 2021). The request to the National Security and Defence Council that resulted in sanctions against Rossotrudnichestvo was made after the Russian Centre of Science and Culture held an event in Kyiv on March 9, 2021, titled "Summarizing the International Creative Competition of Modern Poets On the Commemoration Day for the Russian-Ukrainian Poet Taras Shevchenko" (emphasis added). This attempt at cultural appropriation of Shevchenko, considered to be the most important national poet, was met with resentment and

---

83 Stukanov, Serhii. "Rosiiskyi kulturnyi tsentr u Kyievi — tse mistse promyvannia mizkiv, — Podoliak" [Podoliak: Russian cultural centre in Kyiv is a brainwashing spot]. *Hromadske Radio*. September 22, 2017. https://hromadske.radio/podcasts/kyiv-donbas/rosiyskyy-kulturnyy-centr-u-kyyevi-ce-misce-promyvannya-mizkiv-podolyak.

84 Ukraine. Verkhovna Rada. "Uhoda mizh Kabinetom Ministriv Ukrainy i Uriadom Rosiiskoi Federatsii pro zasnuvannia ta umovy diialnosti informatsiino-kulturnykh tsentriv" [Agreement Between the Cabinet of Ministers of Ukraine and the Government of the Russian Federation "On the Establishment and Conditions for Information and Culture Centres"]. Ratified 8 April 1999 by the law #583-XIV. https://zakon.rada.gov.ua/laws/show/643_090#Text.

condemnation from Ukraine's MFA and civil society.[85] On November 30, 2021, a Russian House was opened in Donetsk that Russia temporarily occupies.[86]

Importantly, Rossotrudnichestvo leaders have long served as mouthpieces for Russian propaganda on Ukraine, echoing identical talking points to Russia's state media and MFA top officials in the media and their social network accounts. In March 2014, Konstantin Kosachev, then head of Rossotrudnichestvo, spoke about "the US and EU investing giant resources in ideology in Ukraine, which resulted in EuroMaidan."[87] Eleonora Mitrofanova echoed this point in 2018 when she spoke about the $ 1.5 billion the US allegedly spent on NGOs in Ukraine to "undermine the regime."[88]

3. A Three-Headed Dragon: Key Areas of Work

Rossotrudnichestvo operates in three broad areas: (1) supporting and expanding Russian cultural and humanitarian presence abroad by endorsing Russian culture and accomplishments of Russian science, promoting Russian education abroad, and strengthening the presence of the Russian language in the world; (2) supporting "compatriots," and (3) assisting international development (Rossotrudnichestvo 2021).

---

85 Radio Svoboda. "Zaperechuiemo bud'-iaki rosiiski naratyvy stosovno Tarasa Shevchenka—MZS" [MFA: We object to any Russian narratives on Taras Shevchenko]. March 29, 2021. https://www.radiosvoboda.org/a/news-mzs-shevchenko-ros-tsentr/31174651.html.
86 Rossiia s mirom [Russia with peace]. "Russkiy dom otkrylsia v Donetske" [A Russian House opens in Donetsk]. November 30, 2021. http://web.arc hive.org/web/20220423154234/https://rwp.agency/news/770/.
87 Vzgliad. 2014. "Kosachev: ES i SShA vlozhyli v ideologiiu na Ukraine gigantskiie resursy" [Kosachev: EU and US have invested giant resources in ideology in Ukraine]. March 13, 2014. https://vz.ru/news/2014/3/13/676829.html.
88 RBK. "Glava Rossotrudnichestva obiasnila proval 'miagkoi sily' Rossii na Ukraine" [Head of Rossotrudnichestvo explains the failure of soft power in Ukraine]. May 26, 2018. https://www.rbc.ru/politics/26/05/2018/5b0931c49a7947552a58086d.

3.1 Culture, language, youth: expansion of Russian presence in the world

Russia's expanding cultural and humanitarian presence abroad can be roughly categorised into the following subgroups: cultural diplomacy projects, projects to engage the youth, and projects to promote the Russian language abroad.

A)   Cultural diplomacy projects

Russian culture and the achievements of Russian science are promoted with the conventional means of exhibitions: cinema screenings and film days, thematic festivals, tours of Russian music or theatre groups, lectures, roundtables and thematic workshops, and through cooperation with educational facilities abroad.[89] Since 2010, Rossotrudnichestvo has supported and maintained burial sites of "historical and memorial significance for Russia." Before 2019, the financial sources for this had been drawn from the money earned by the Rossotrudnichestvo offices. In 2020–2022, state budget funding was also utilised for this purpose (Kuzmin 2019). In 2022, Rossotrudnichestvo planned to launch a system of microgrants from $ 300 to $ 1,000 to implement projects that are thematically related to Russia in science, environment protection, and preservation of historical memory.[90] These microgrants will be issued to non-commercial organisations or citizens.

Under this category, Rossotrudnichestvo proactively advances Russian narratives. For example, Russian Houses abroad extensively and comprehensively cover the topics of wars of the past and Russian military prowess. For instance, in 2020, a series of documentaries was subtitled in eight foreign languages for the 100th

---

89   Russkii dom [Russian House]. "Brifing press-sekretaria Rossotrudnichestva Nadany Fridrikhson" [Briefing by Rossotrudnichestvo press-secretary Nadana Fridrikhson]. YouTube video, 13:40, December 21, 2021. https://youtu.be/s89EA9KtcUY.

90   Belgiiskaia Federatsiia Russkoiazychnykh Organizatsii [Belgian Federation of Russian-Speaking Organizations]. "Rossotrudnichestvo budet vydavat mikrogranty na kulturnyie meropriiatiia" [Rossotrudnichestvo will allocate microgrants for cultural events]. July 22, 2021. https://www.bfro.be/ru/rossotrudnichestvo-budet-vydavat-mikrogranty-na-kul-turnye-meroprijatija.html?cmp_id=80&news_id=33463.

anniversary of the imperial Black Sea fleet departing from Crimea (Rossotrudnichestvo 2021, 6); the Russian House in Belgrade prepared an exhibition project on the Serbian-Ottoman Wars;[91] a conference on the war in Yugoslavia and NATO bombing was organised.[92] At least seven different events commemorating the 250th anniversary of Czar Peter I were held in Russia, Belgium, France, Montenegro, and Germany in 2022.

Nevertheless, the biggest effort is invested in spreading Russian myths and interpretations of World War II, or the "Great Patriotic War," in contemporary Russian parlance. The Russian President's Decree No. 211, dated May 9, 2018, "On Preparations and Celebration of the 75th Anniversary of the Victory in the 1941-1945 Great Patriotic War," outlined the activities to celebrate the 75th anniversary of the end of World War II across the world in 2020. The content for some events was distributed from headquarters to all offices worldwide and subsequently translated into seven languages. Monitoring the titles and topics of events proves that Rossotrudnichestvo focused on strengthening the narrative of the "great victory of the Soviet people" and its role in the global context. The events included the St. George Ribbon initiative;[93] eight documentary chronicle films with subtitles screened via 26 online platforms of Rossotrudnichestvo offices; ten feature films of the

---

91 Ruski Dom u Beogradu [Russian House in Belgrade]. 2022. "O prvim ruskim dobrovoltsima u Srbii" [About the first Russian volunteers in Serbia]. Facebook, March 17, 2022. https://www.facebook.com/watch/?v=391796205632766&ref=sharing.
92 Evgeniy Pavlov. "K 22 godovshchine nachala aggressii NATO na SRIu" [For the 22nd anniversary of NATO aggression against SFR Yugoslavia]. Ruski dom [Russian House]. March 3, 2021. https://ruskidom.rs/2021/03/23/k-22-j-go dovshhine-nachala-agressii-nato-na-srju/.
93 A two-colour ribbon with three black and two orange stripes, used in Russian state decorations and awards. It is mostly known as a symbol of the Soviet Union's fight and victory over Nazism through the medal "For Victory Over Germany in the Great Patriotic War of 1941-1945." The ribbon is known to have been used since the 18th century, when the Russian empress Catherine the Great founded the Order of Saint George, a military award of the Russian Empire (hence its name). Among other things, Russian propaganda is exploiting it today as a symbol of Russia's aggression against Ukraine since 2014. The use of these symbols has been banned in Ukraine since 2017. A number of other countries, including Estonia, Latvia, Lithuania, and Moldova, have restricted its use as well.

20th century; and the premiere of the *Immortal Regiment: A Global Movement* in seventy offices of Rossotrudnichestvo.[94] Rossotrudnichestvo does not need anniversary dates to substantiate its intense exploitation of the topic of World War II. Forty-five out of 105 publications on the website of its Ukrainian office between May 1 and July 16, 2020, were at least somehow related to World War II (Hrupa z analizu hibrydnykh zahroz 2020).

Another important aspect of the Russian Houses' work in the CIS countries is nostalgia management, which aims to preserve and fuel positive interpretations of the Soviet experience. In 2022, a hashtag #вкладСРСР (#USSRcontribution) was used to mark Rossotrudnichestvo's social media posts on how former Soviet republics in general and Uzbekistan, Turkmenistan, and Kyrgyzstan in particular, have benefited greatly from their membership in the USSR. But this nostalgia management is in no way limited to the CIS. For instance, when the Russian House opened a centre for the Russian language at a school in Ulaanbaatar, the school was renamed in honour of Semen Budennyi. The Facebook post about the event described him as *"Marshal of the Soviet Union, holder of three Hero of the Soviet Union titles... first head of the Society of Soviet-Mongolian Friendship, founded in 1958."*[95]

At the same time, Rossotrudnichestvo does not shun providing open ideological support for the Kremlin's aggressive policy in the international arena. In 2022, it held a series of events for the eighth anniversary of the "reunification of Crimea with Russia" that pushed false messages in direct violation of international law

---

94 The Immortal Regiment started in 2017 as a civic initiative to commemorate those who perished in WWII, or the Great Patriotic War, as it is called in Russia. In recent years, Russian federal authorities have supported this march with photographs of family members who fought in the war. Along with the St. George ribbon, now a symbol of "Russkiy Mir" supporters, the function of the Immortal Regiment march is to glorify the military experience of the Soviet Union and to shape a militarist, imperialist and anti-West Russian-Soviet identity.

95 Russkii dom v Ulan-Batore [Russian House in Ulaanbaatar]. 2023. "Dvum shkolam v Ulan-Batore prisvoili imena geroiev Rossii i otkryli dva novykh Tsentra russkogo iazyka" [Two schools in Ulaanbaatar have been named after heroes of Russia, and two new Centres of Russian language have been opened]. Facebook, March 27, 2023. https://www.facebook.com/RussianhouseMongolia/posts/4928199357265022.

and well-aligned with Russian propaganda narratives. Examples include a photo exhibition about Crimea at the Russian House in New Delhi,[96] the screening of the "Militant Girl" («Ополченочка») film at the Russian House in Chisinau[97] focused on presenting Russian narratives on Russia's military aggression in the Donbas, or a photograph exhibit in Beirut, Lebanon, under the title "Why the special military operation in Ukraine started. Donbas 2014–2015," which referred to Ukraine's defence against the Russian army in the Donbas as a "punitive operation."[98] As a high point of Rossotrudnichestvo's warmongering effort, it also composed, translated into thirteen languages, and published online a brochure, "The Civil War in Ukraine: 2014–2022," which strove to create the impression of the total economic and political decline of Ukraine during the thirty years of independence, postulated the ubiquity of nefarious nationalism in Ukraine under Poroshenko and Zelensky, continued the Russian official line that a coup d'état occurred in Ukraine in 2014, and interpreted the current invasion as ensuring peace by the Russian army.[99]

Among the events that help Rossotrudnichestvo promote the Russian official propaganda discourses are also those that would suit more, in the genre, the activities of the Gorchakov Fund (*see*

---

96 Russkii dom [Russian House]. 2022. "V Russkom dome v Niu-Deli otkrylas fotovystavka o Kryme" [A photograph exhibition about Crimea has been launched in the Russian House in New Delhi]. Facebook, March 18, 2022. https://www.facebook.com/rsgov/posts/pfbid0no8GHwoMJSt66DU2kSoe kcvS4zmvPBwbjiN5dDMgzcmLGjoU2n8z4bQRWTX5F3XPl.
97 Russkii dom v Kisheneve / Casa Rusă din Chișinău [Russian House in Chișinău]. 2021. "V Russkikh domakh proidet nekommercheskii pokaz filma 'Opolchenochka'" [A non-commercial screening of the film "Opolchenochka" will be held in Russian Houses]. Facebook, May 17, 2021. https://www.face book.com/MoldovaRCNK/posts/pfbid02BDvjSgoqGc3QXy3R2UQnpRc4N bJNpraTLe1Bp6nhjjp6rARE8s8dPKmXr57rEKCW1.
98 Russkii dom (@rossotrudnichestvo). 2022. "V Russkom dome v Bierute otkrylas fotovystavka 'Pochemy nachalas spetsialnaiia operatsiia na Ukraine. Donbass 2014–2015'" [A photograph exhibit "Why the special military operation in Ukraine started. Donbass 2014–2015" opened in the Russian House in Beirut]. Telegram, April 29, 2022. https://t.me/rossotrudnichestvo/5732.
99 Rossotrudnichestvo. n. d. "Civil War in Ukraine: 2014–2022." http://warcri mesofkiev.com/.

Chapter 3), namely, those promoting the Russian foreign policy vision directly, without the veil of cultural diplomacy. Those would, for instance, include a public discussion on "The West's Marches to the East in the Light of the Ukrainian Crisis," held in the Russian House in Belgrade, which featured Serbian academics who strove to essentialize "the relation of a Western person to the Russian civilization."[100] In 2022, in cooperation with Diplomatic Academy of Russia, it launched the "Laboratory of Analytics at the Institute of Contemporary International Studies," a two-month course in foreign policy analysis for Russians and citizens of CIS countries[101]. Another example would be a series of public discussions featuring influential Russian international relations experts in Armenia, organised by Rossotrudnichestvo's representation in this country.[102]

Regarding the topics it covers, Rossotrudnichestvo primarily targets events from the past and offers far less coverage of modern culture and art. For instance, its many art events, especially the ones marking memorable dates, traditionally represent classic Russian culture, including literature, poetry, music, art, ballet, and cinema, and the best-known representatives from each category, such as Fyodor Dostoevsky, Leo Tolstoy, Dmitri Shostakovich, Sergei Rachmaninoff, Ivan Aivazovsky, and Sergei Diaghilev.[103] Particularly numerous are the references to Alexander Pushkin: in 2022,

---

100 Russkii dom (@rossotrudnichestvo). 2022. "Zapad i Vostok—budushchee otnoshenii" [The West and the East—the future of relations]. Telegram, April 18, 2022. https://t.me/rossotrudnichestvo/5583.
101 Russkii dom (@rossotrudnichestvo). 2022. "Otkrylas' Laboratoriya analitiki Instituta aktual'nyh mezhdunarodnyh problem" [The opening of the Laboratory of Analytics at the Institute of Contemporary International Studies]. Telegram, April 30, 2022. https://t.me/rossotrudnichestvo/5742.
102 Russkii dom (@rossotrudnichestvo). 2022. "Predstavitelstvo Rossotrudnichestva v Armenii #RusskiiDomYerevan nachinaiet seriiu publichnykh vystuplenii v Yerevane i drugikh gorodakh strany vedushchikh rossiiskikh ekspertov v oblasti vneshnei politiki" [Rossotrudnichestvo's representation in Armenia is launching a series of public appearances of the leading Russian experts in international relations in Yerevan and in other cities of the country]. Reposted from @RSGOVArmenia. Telegram, April 2, 2022. https://t.me/rossotrudnichestvo/5370.
103 See, for instance, the publication about the opening of a picture of Fyodor Dostoyevsky on a building of an educational institution in Naples, Italy: Russkii dom (@rossotrudnichestvo). 2022. "V Neapole poiavilsia portret Dostoievskogo v znak borby s rusofobiei" [In Naples, a portrait of Dostoyevsky appeared as a

there was an online competition "Lets read Puskin" in New-Delhi, a "Pushkin-fest" in Cyprus, a Paris exhibition about the first Pushkin museum, a Tel-Aviv exhibition on Pushkin's life and work, a podcast "What would Pushkin say?" in Tajikistan, a flash-mob "Pushkins are walking around Kazakhstan," etc.

This backward perspective stems from Russian propaganda concerning the greatness of the country's past accomplishments and Russia's overreliance on well-known, classical representations of its culture. Although this "traditionalism" as a feature of Russian cultural diplomacy is constantly criticised, both internally and externally, it remains in place. The attempts to modernise the activities of Rossotrudnichestvo may concern shifting attention to other topics, like promoting Russian science or education, or even directions, like humanitarian assistance, but they still avoid contemporary, experimental, non-traditional art. Therefore, Konstantin Kosachev, former head of Rossotrudnichestvo, emphasised the importance of using the Russian language and the country's artistic heritage after discussing the failure to promote "Russian brands" in the world:

> "All this is without exaggeration the world's treasury, and all this is our unique heritage. We do not need to invent new brands artificially. We just need to preserve what we have, love it as much as we can, and know how to make it serve our national interests." (Fediakina 2014)

Further underscoring such a conservative framework, Rossotrudnichestvo consistently refers to religious motifs. Rossotrudnichestvo's Statute lists cooperation with religious organisations as one of its functions.[104] Plans to open an Orthodox church in collab-

---

sign of fight against Russophobia]. Telegram, March 18, 2022. https://t.me/rossotrudnichestvo/5182. Another example: Russkiy dom (@rossotrudnichestvo). 2022. "Izvestnyi khudozhnik-monumentalist Milan Milosavlevich Deroks narisoval vtoroi mural s Dostoievskim na stene shkoly v serbskom gorode Štrpce" [A famous muralist painted the second mural with Dostoyevsky on a wall of a school in the Serbian town of Štrpce]. Telegram, March 24, 2022. https://t.me/rossotrudnichestvo/5237.

104 Russian Federation. President. Ukaz [Decree] #1315 "O nekotorykh voprosakh gosudarstvennogo upravleniia v oblasti mezhdunarodnogo sotrudnichestva"

oration with the office of Rossotrudnichestvo (the 2020 report mentions this initiative in Singapore) are a recent example (Rossotrudnichestvo 2021, 12–13). Finally, constant referring to the folk symbols of Russian culture, like *matryoshka* doll, *samovar* tea parties, *Ded Moroz* New Year mythical figure, bears and birch-trees related imagery, are common for many events organised by Rossotrudnichestvo and its foreign representations.

B)   *Youth-oriented projects*
Former Rossotrudnichestvo head Eleonora Mitrofanova identified a focus on working with the youth as the top priority for reorganising the organisation's work in 2018 (Khimshiashvili 2018). Rossotrudnichestvo proactively cooperates with students and young professionals from foreign countries as part of this effort. This includes primarily events and programmes engaging this audience in studies, internships, or work in Russia. This is intended to immerse them in the country's culture and, most importantly, facilitate forming and maintaining an extensive network of personal connections between foreigners and their peers in Russia.

Given the organisation's extensive network of partner institutions in host countries, the Concept of promoting Russian education abroad via Rossotrudnichestvo representations was approved in 2014.[105] Rossotrudnichestvo appeals to dozens of thousands of foreigners and engages them in visiting Russia and studying there. According to its 2020 report, it held "awareness-raising events" in sixteen countries to present and promote education in Russia. Over 16,500 people in total attended those events. Russia's Ministry of Foreign Affairs and Ministry of Education and Science participated in the 2020/2021 campaign to recruit students for Russian universities together with Rossotrudnichestvo. The quota for international

---

[On Some Aspects of Governance in the Field of International Cooperation]. Adopted 6 September 2008. http://www.kremlin.ru/acts/bank/28020.
105 Russian Federation. Ministry of Foreign Affairs. "Kontseptsiia prodvizheniia rossiiskogo obrazovaniia na baze predstavitelstv Rossotrudnichestva za rubezhom" [The Concept of Promoting Russian Education Through Rossotrudnichestvo Offices Abroad]. Approved by the Minister 27 March 2014. https://rulaws.ru/acts/Kontseptsiya-prodvizheniya-rossiyskogo-obrazovani ya-na-baze-predstavitelstv-Rossotrudnichestva-za-rubezhom/.

students from 171 countries was 15,000 (Rossotrudnichestvo 2021, 8), but it was increased to 23,000 places for the 2022/2023 academic year and is expected to reach 30,000 in the following academic year.[106] The countries that benefited most from these quotas were, as listed in Rossotrudnichestvo's annual report, Belarus, Vietnam, China, Syria, Tajikistan, Uzbekistan, Ukraine (apparently, people from the occupied territories), Mongolia, Kazakhstan, and Kyrgyzstan (Rossotridnichestvo 2023, 4). The purposeful intensification of this policy demonstrates Russia's increasing reorientation towards its Soviet-era Global South practices of generous provision of education opportunities in Russian higher education institutions to ensure loyal, educated strata in the home countries. Among the primary targets of such activities, former Soviet republics occupy a significant place.

Rossotrudnichestvo places particular emphasis on IT and international relations, among other areas. Its 2020 performance report highlighted the engagement of "talented foreign students" to study computer technologies and participate in the DIGITAL PEOPLE competition to develop international cooperation with Russia regarding the digital economy (Rossotrudnichestvo 2021, 7). The InteRussia programme of research internships offers another example that seeks to establish international contacts, establish close cooperation throughout the programme and develop regular professional relations among its alumni beyond the programme.[107] Implemented jointly with the Moscow State Institute of International Affairs and the Gorchakov Fund since 2021, it targets young foreign professionals aged 25-35 who specialise in international relations and political studies. It offers visits to Russian government institutions, universities, think tanks, and non-governmental organisations and collaboration with Russian experts. These are efforts to

---

106 Russkii dom (@rossotrudnichestvo). 2023. "V sleduiushchem uchebnom godu Rossiia vydelit 30 tysiach mest dlia zarubezhnykh studentov v rossiiskikh vuzakh" [In the next academic year, Russia will allocate 30,000 places in Russian universities for foreign students]. Telegram, January 5, 2023. https://t.me/rossotrudnichestvo/9742.

107 MGIMO University. "Internship programme InteRussia: call for applications is open." January 31, 2022. https://english.mgimo.ru/announce/interussia-03-22.

indoctrinate foreigners with Russian (geo)political and cultural narratives. In 2022-2023 InteRussia programme has also widely targeted international journalists, in particular from African countries, as well as specialists in Russian language.

The New Generation long-term programme has been in place since 2011 and is currently the key Rossotrudnichestvo programme for bringing foreign youth into the country. Through that programme, young professionals between the ages of 25 and 35 from the political, social, academic, and business communities travel to Russia short-term to establish professional contacts and long-term partnerships with Russian state and non-state entities, as well as youth and social organisations, in various spheres. This programme made three hundred sixty-nine foreigners from 54 countries visit Russia in 2021,[108] and representatives of 49 countries were reported to participate in 2022, taking part in events devoted to topics as diverse as library management, international relations (the InteRussia programme), youth parliaments, journalism and propaganda (the SPUTNIK.pro workshops), as well as culinary diplomacy. Some of these visits take place in the occupied Crimea, for instance in October 2022, a special program "Ambassadors of the Russian Kitchen"[109] was organized for young chefs in Yalta and covered in detail on the Agency's social media for several months in a row.

Generally, Rossotrudnichestvo pays much attention and invests generously in working with young people in an effort to increase the number of people who have a favourable perception of Russia, share its worldview, and develop a certain degree of loyalty to it as they become adult professionals. In addition to this long-term objective, Rossotrudnichestvo pursues more attainable and immediate goals. Among other things, it collaborates with the state

---

108 Russkii dom [Russian House]. 2022. "Programma 'Novoie pokolenie' v 2021 godu" [Programme "New Generation" in 2021]. Facebook, March 18, 2022. https://www.facebook.com/photo?fbid=286916526924426&set=a.2360607720 10002.

109 Russkii dom (@rossotrudnichestvo). 2022. "Molodye povara priedut v Krym po programme 'Novoe pokolenie'" [Young chefs will arrive to Crimea in the framework of 'Novoe Pokolenie' programme]. Telegram, October 1, 2022. https://t.me/rossotrudnichestvo/8008.

corporation Rosatom on humanitarian projects in countries where nuclear power plant construction is planned. Quotas for students from these countries to study in Russian universities and eventually obtain employment at Rosatom are the key instrument here.[110]

C) *Projects to promote the Russian language abroad*

Promoting the Russian language abroad is an integral part of Rossotrudnichestvo's operations. It encompasses a vast array of events of various scales and vectors, such as Russian language courses at Russian Houses; assistance with the opening of affiliate organisations, preparatory sections, and departments of Russian educational facilities in foreign universities; professional development courses for teachers at Russian schools and of Russian as a foreign language, organising different festivals and competitions for Russian language students worldwide, as well as summer camps for children and youth studying Russian.

In 2022, 70 Russian houses offered Russian language courses to students in 60 countries (notably, a few years ago, the courses in the US suspended operations "for political reasons"). As of 2020, the number of students amounted to 18,000; nearly 3,000 events were held to promote the Russian language worldwide and approximately 900,000 people attended them (Rossotrudnichestvo 2021, 10).

This operation field is supported by the content platforms of the System of Support for Russian Schools, an electronic resource for educational institutions abroad, and My Russian, an e-library for a wide range of users that has already had over 150,000 "book borrowings" over 2020 (Rossotrudnichestvo 2021, 11). Rossotrudnichestvo even used the 2018 FIFA World Cup hosted by Russia to promote the Russian language. In the lead-up to the championship,

---

[110] REIN Rosatom. "Pri uchastii Rosatoma v RUDN proshel II Molodezhnyi forum 'Rossiia—Afrika: iadernoie obrazovaniie dlia ustoichivogo razvitiia'" [The 2nd Youth Forum "Russia—Africa: Nuclear Education for Sustainable Development" was held at RUDN with the participation of Rosatom]. November 25, 2021. https://rusatom-energy.ru/media/rosatom-news/pri-uchastii-rosatoma-v-rudn-proshel-ii-molodezhnyy-forum-rossiya-afrika-yadernoe-obrazovanie-dlya-u/.

it opened "fan houses" in 35 countries and held Russian language classes in 11.[111]

In this context, the work to promote the Russian language and Russian-language literature in certain post-Soviet countries and Russian-occupied territories is particularly important. The 2020 report mentions "spreading the model of expanding the presence of the Russian language in preschool education using Russian preschool education techniques in teaching Russian in Abkhazia, Moldova, Tajikistan, Uzbekistan, and South Ossetia"; providing Rossotrudnichestvo employees with all types of textbooks and methodology guidance for teaching Russian; fiction and non-fiction literature in Russian that is to be "subsequently gifted to Russian schools/classes." Notably, over 100,000 copies of books were provided to Abkhazia and South Ossetia, the occupied territories of Georgia, in 2020, and slightly over 60,000 to the "far-abroad" countries (Rossotrudnichestvo 2021, 11). A similar trend persisted in 2021: Rossotrudnichestvo provided over 169,000 copies of books to foreign countries. More than 94,000 of these were handed over to the CIS countries and the occupied territories of Georgia, Abkhazia, and South Ossetia.[112] This points to the priority of preserving and strengthening the status of the Russian language in the region. The activities directed of promotion of Russian language learning have also remained a key priority of the Agency in 2022 and 2023, encompassing opening new centres for Russian language learning, organising readings of classical literature, poetic battles, and dictations, proposing workshops, conferences, and camps for Russian language instructors from foreign countries, supporting organiza-

---

111 RBK. 2018. "Rossotrudnichestvo otkrylo 35 'domov bolelshchikov' dlia prodvizheniia ChM-2018" [Rossotrudnichestvo opens 35 "fan houses" to promote 2018 World Cup]. May 22, 2018. https://www.rbc.ru/rbcfreenews/5b03dfdf9a79475aad4e002d.
112 Russkii dom [Russian House]. 2022. "Postavka knig v 2021 godu" [The Delivery of Books in 2021]. Facebook, March 10, 2022. https://www.facebook.com/rsgov/posts/pfbid0VU8BpUtTDVdvUxNa8dhrVn6uBd1vjvbayfv2EQUcicgvGqqdWUyTh4ytVXMet3qxl.

tionally and financially Russian citizens working abroad as teachers of Russian language, providing books and manuals, mobile applications for learning Russian, etc.

In addition to promoting and supporting studying the Russian language, Rossotrudnichestvo is visibly engaged in the media campaign against any measure that could curb the use of Russian internationally. The News section on its website features numerous articles about Russian officials' statements on what they refer to as "discrimination" against the Russian language in other countries.[113] These statements are not necessarily related to the work of Rossotrudnichestvo. One example is Sergei Lavrov's statement on the discrimination against the Russian language in Ukraine. According to him, Ukraine has "declared an open war on the Russian language and Russian-language education," which is "a violation of its Constitution." He spoke about "guarantees for the Russian, Russian-speaking and national minorities."[114] Other similar news stories, based on statements made at the informal Arria formula meeting of the UN Security Council and posted on the website in late December 2021, peddle the narrative about linguistic oppression. The titles speak for themselves: "The problems of national minorities and heroizing Nazism in the Baltic States and the Black Sea region were discussed at the UN Security Council online meeting;"[115] "An appeal of the 13-year-old Faina Savenkova from Luhansk to the UN Security Council."[116]

---

113 Rossotrudnichestvo. "Novosti" [News]. n. d. https://rs.gov.ru/novosti/.
114 Rossiia s mirom [Russia with peace]. "Sergei Lavrov o diskriminatsii russkogo iazyka na Ukraine" [Sergei Lavrov about the discrimination against the Russian language in Ukraine]. September 6, 2021. https://web.archive.org/web/20220125044553/https://rwp.agency/news/285/.
115 Rossiia s mirom [Russia with peace]. "Problemy natsionalnykh menshinstv i geroizatsii natsizma v stranakh Baltii i Chernomorskom regione obsudili na onlain vstreche SB OON" [Problems of national minorities and the heroization of Nazism in the Baltic countries and in the Black Sea region have been discussed at the online meeting of the UN Security Council]. December 23, 2021. https://web.archive.org/web/20220117061622/https://rwp.agency/news/883/.
116 Rossiia s mirom [Russia with peace]. "Obrashcheniie 13-letnei Fainy Savenkovoi iz Luganska k Sovetu Bezopasnosti OON" [Address by thirteen-year-old

Despite Rossotrudnichestvo's efforts to promote the Russian language, the number of Russian language learners in the world has been steadily declining since the collapse of the Soviet Union. From 2004 to 2018, it shrank from 13 to 8.3 million (Gubernatorov 2019). Therefore, it is no surprise that Rossotrudnichestvo and the "Russkiy Mir" Foundation work so hard to promote the Russian language. Interest in learning Russian is decreasing in most regions of the world. The only exceptions are Sub-Saharan Africa and North America, where the number of learners has increased from 19,000 to 30,000 over the past fifteen years. While Russia's aggressive policy toward its neighbours explains the steep decline of the Russian language in post-Soviet countries, the fact that the number of Russian language learners in Asia has fallen from 570,000 to 185,000 raises questions about the effectiveness of Russian soft power institutions in this region.

3.2 Gathering them all: Support for "compatriots"

Work with "compatriots" focuses on two primary objectives: encouraging Russian-speaking citizens of other countries and Russians abroad to move to Russia and spreading its influence on other countries via organisations of "compatriots" Rossotrudnichestvo cooperates with. As an investigation by *The Insider* implies, there are reasons to believe that the effective activation of attempts by the Russian government to instrumentalise "compatriot" organisations for political purposes took place only after the occupation of Crimea by Russia in 2014. Since then, these organisations have been closely keeping in touch with Russian embassies and Rossotrudnichestvo representations abroad, receiving both resources and directions from them (Fishman 2022). After Russia's full-scale invasion of Ukraine on February 24, 2022, these organisations have been exploited even more extensively *(see the section Doves of Peace, Hawks of War: Rossotrudnichestvo after the Full-Scale Invasion for more details)*.

Faina Savenkova from Luhansk towards the UN Security Council]. December 23, 2021. https://web.archive.org/web/20220117071028/https://rwp.agency/news/885/.

Regarding its target audience, the term "compatriots" appears frequently in Rossotrudnichestvo's external communication and the description of its projects and long-term programmes. It has been used more regularly since the beginning of the full-scale Russian invasion of Ukraine on February 24, 2022; for instance, 157 times between January and June 2022 and as many as five times on some days. In its social media posts, Rossotrudnichestvo refers to participants in various events in support of Russia abroad as "compatriots."

Figure 3. Frequency of mentions of the word "compatriot" on Russkiy Dom Telegram channel within a week, 2021-2022.

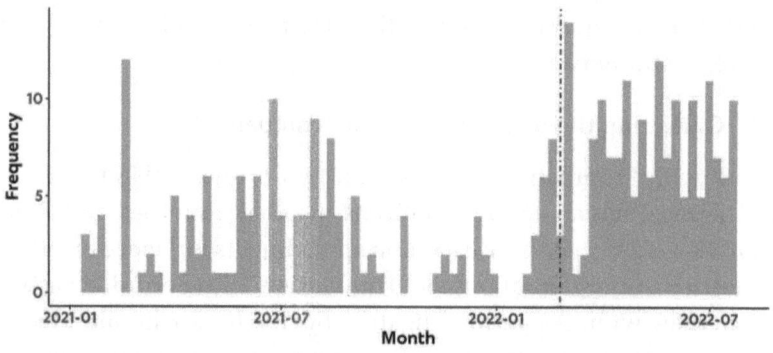

Source: calculations based on posts at *Russkiy Dom* Telegram channel.

At the same time, the term "compatriot" is not well defined, which benefits Russian propaganda and foreign policy because it can be filled with whatever suits any situation. The term encompasses a wide range of people, including those whose ties with contemporary Russia are questionable. According to articles 1 and 3 of Federal Law No99-ФЗ "On the State Policy of the Russian Federation on Compatriots Abroad," the term "compatriots" is much broader and goes far beyond individuals with Russian citizenship.

In addition to the audience that meets this criterion, Russia considers compatriots people and their descendants who permanently reside outside the Russian Federation and are part of the peoples that "... historically reside on the territory of the Russian

Federation..." as well as "... people who have freely chosen spiritual, cultural, and legal ties with the Russian Federation, whose direct ascending line family members resided on the territory of the Russian Federation in the past...". These include those who reside in the countries formerly a part of the Soviet Union and hold their citizenship or have no citizenship, as well as those who emigrated from these countries and obtained citizenship from other countries or have become persons without citizenship.[117]

On March 28, 2022, Konstantin Zatulin, a member of the State Duma and director of the Institute of CIS Countries who works on citizenship, migration policy, and "compatriots," filed a bill to amend the law on Russia's state policy regarding "compatriots." Among other things, he proposed to include knowledge of the Russian language as a criterion for the term "compatriot" and to more clearly outline the concept of "peoples that historically reside on the territory of the Russian Federation" by adding a list of these peoples. This list would include Belarusians and Ukrainians, among others, because he thinks they are connected to the Russians, considered state-founding people, "through the commonality of historical fate and culture."[118] Essentially, he proposed to codify Russia's political and cultural expansion over the populations of Ukraine and Belarus. While Zatulin is an ardent supporter of the concept of "compatriots" and their repatriation to Russia, he appears to have been unsuccessful in gaining the Kremlin's support for his effort to maintain consistency between the concept of the "Russian World" and the term "compatriot." His bill was still pending review in early August 2023 and ended up with negative feedback from the Russian government after two and a half months of waiting.[119] This

---

[117] Russian Federation. Federalnyi zakon [Federal Law] #99-FZ "O gosudarstvennoi politike Rossiiskoi Federatsii v otnoshenii sootechestvennikov za rubezhom" [On the State Policy of the Russian Federation on Compatriots Abroad]. Adopted by the State Duma 5 March 1999, approved by the Federation Council 17 March 1999. http://webcache.googleusercontent.com/search?q=cache:https://docs.cntd.ru/document/9003489.

[118] Sistema obezpecheniia zakonodatelnoi deiiatelnosti [Support System for Legislative Activity]. "Zakonoproekt No 95462-8" [Draft Law No 95462-8]. Introduced on March 28, 2022. https://sozd.duma.gov.ru/bill/95462-8.

[119] Ibid.

decision was probably delayed but will likely resurface amidst possible attempts to assimilate forced Ukrainian deportees from Russian-occupied territory.

Rossotrudnichestvo's top official, Yevgeny Primakov Jr., voiced similar ideas in 2021, long before this legislative proposal:

> "There are descendants of white émigrés; dissidents of the Soviet era; economic immigrants of the late 1980s and early 1990s; global Russians of the modern time who live where they are most comfortable and travel the globe. However, there are millions upon millions of people who did not choose to become compatriots because new borders were imposed upon them when one country fell apart, and they found themselves in the new republics outside of Russia. When it comes to how their lives are, they vary greatly, but assimilation is an issue everywhere."[120]

This Russian policy of preventing the assimilation of the groups that meet the Russian definition of "compatriots" in other countries appears to seek their assimilation into the Russian cultural space in the future, whether it is to influence the policy of any given target country or to encourage "compatriots" to resettle to Russia.

Other statements by Rossotrudnichestvo top officials suggest that speaking Russian is the primary criterion for identifying a person as a "compatriot," as opposed to having relatives who had lived in the territory of the Russian Federation in the past (even several generations ago) or belonging to an ethnic group that makes up the population of modern Russia. According to Yevgeny Primakov Jr.,

> "...there are four million compatriots in Ukraine, for example, according to this data. And we are well aware that there are significantly more Russian speakers there. Five million in Kazakhstan. And the number in Belarus is ridiculous, slightly over 700,000 people! But we understand that in Belarus, roughly speaking, all are compatriots." (Steshin 2021)

This variety of definitions and the "Russian language" factor provides ample room for foreign policy manoeuvres in the context of work with "compatriots," including repatriation programmes,

---

[120] @evgenyprimakov. 2021. "#poradomoi" [#timetogohome]. Telegra.ph, November 30, 2021. https://telegra.ph/poradomoj-11-30.

pressure on the countries with the Russian diaspora for alleged violations against the Russian-speaking population, and armed aggression under that very same pretext.

Rossotrudnichestvo's focus on "compatriots" is hardly surprising given the global network of their associations. The President of Russia issued a decree in 2011 to establish a Fund to Support and Protect the Rights of Compatriots Residing Abroad in over 30 countries. As of summer 2022, it had 49 "human rights entities" in over 30 countries, such as legal support centres and consultation desks.[121] In addition, the World Coordinating Council of Russian Compatriots Living Abroad (WCCRC) was established in Russia, bringing together national coordination councils in 99 countries.[122] They provide a convenient platform for Rossotrudnichestvo's events abroad. Only eight countries that host a Rossotrudnichestvo office do not have a "compatriots" organisation.

---

121 Sovet Federatsii Federalnogo sobraniia Rossiskoi Federatsii [The Federation Council of the Federal Assembly of the Russian Federation]. 2021. "Programma zasedaniia Soveta po mezhnatsionalnym otnosheniiam i vzaimodeistviiu s religioznymi obiedineniiami pri Sovete Federatsii Federalnogo Sobraniia Rossiiskoi Federatsii" [Program of the meeting of the Council for International Relations and Interaction with Religious Societies at the Federation council of the Federal Assembly of the Russian Federation on the topic]. December 3, 2021. http://council.gov.ru/media/files/VTdeqAIudImWu0jMEbj1oxSxsTUzQyZk.pdf.
122 Vsemirnyi koordinatsionnyi sovet rossiiskikh sootechestvennikov, prozhivaiiushchikh za rubezhom [World Coordinating Council of Russian Compatriots Living Abroad]. n. d. "Koordnatsionnyie sovety" [Coordination councils]. https://vksrs.com/koordinatsionnye-sovety/map/?TYPE=REGION.

Figure 4. Countries with organisations of Russian compatriots and Rossotrudnichestvo offices (as of April 2023)

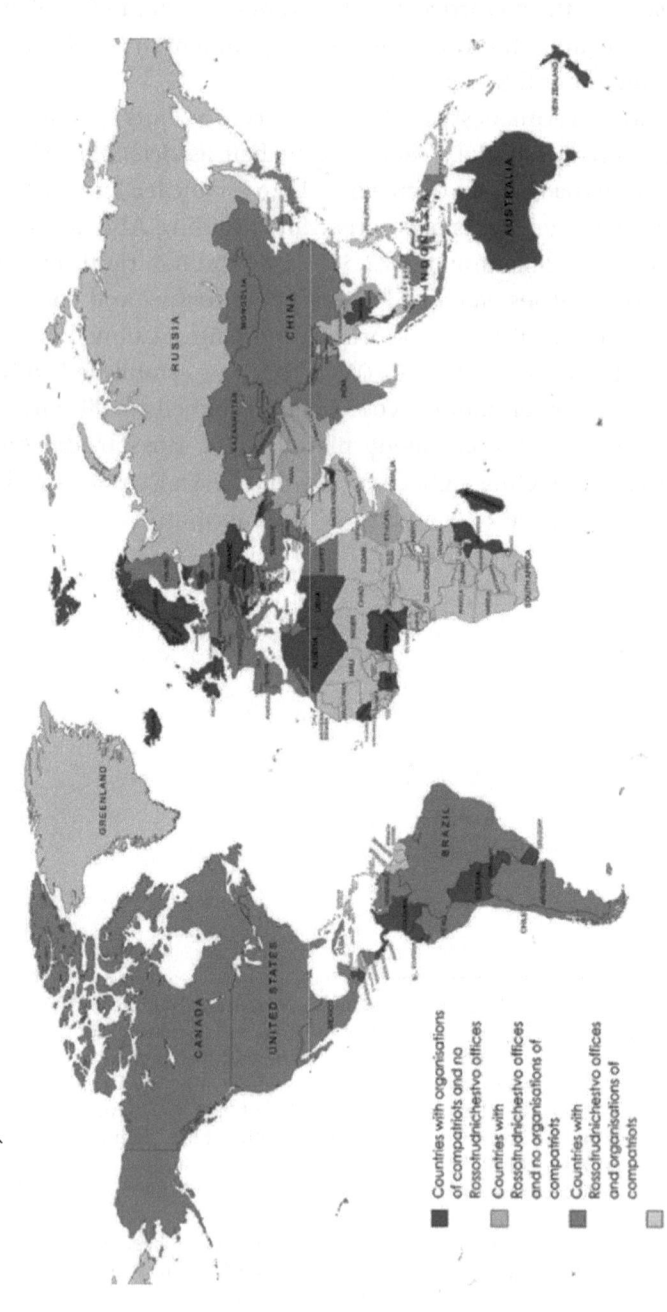

Source: Rossotrudnichestvo and World Coordinating Council of Russian Compatriots Living Abroad websites

There are several ways that Rossotrudnichestvo collaborates with "compatriots":

- *Financial support for organisations of compatriots in other countries.* In 2020, Rossotrudnichestvo supported over 300 "compatriot" non-governmental organisations initiatives in 60 countries (Rossotrudnichestvo 2021, 18).
- *Hello, Russia!* Since 2014, this programme has offered cultural and educational trips to Russia for 14- to 19-year-old Russians living abroad. The objective is to acquaint them with contemporary life and culture in Russia, assist them in improving their Russian through practice, and encourage them to establish new contacts. Participants include the winners of creative contests and contests on Russian history, culture, and language held at Russian Houses abroad. Each year, over 700 people visit Russia through this programme.[123]
- *Resettlement of compatriots.* Running since 2006, this programme focuses on the voluntary resettlement to Russia of people who ended up outside of Russia following the collapse of the Soviet Union and who wish to return to their "historical homeland" for permanent residency in a territory of strategic importance to Russia.[124] It is co-implemented with the Ministry of Internal Affairs of the Russian Federation. The Russian government lists the Republic of Buryatia, the Republic of Sakha (Yakutia), Zabaykalsky Krai, Kamchatsky Krai, Primorsky Krai, Khabarovsk Krai, Amur Oblast, Magadan Oblast, Sakhalin Oblast, Jewish Autonomous Republic, and Chukotka Autonomous Okrug as "the territories of strategic importance to Russia" that are also "the territories for priority settlement." All these are

---

123 Rossiia s mirom [Russian with peace]. "Zdravstvui, Rossiia!" [Hello, Russia!]. September 1, 2021. https://web.archive.org/web/20220129035439/https://rwp.agency/programmy/news.php?ELEMENT_ID=53.
124 Rossia s mirom [Russia with peace]. "Pereseleniie sootechestvennikov" [Resettlement of compatriots]. September 1, 2021. https://web.archive.org/web/20220218203332/https://rwp.agency/programmy/news.php?ELEMENT_ID=607.

the remote regions of the Russian Far East, which are significantly less populated than the oblasts of Central Russia.[125] Virtually all priority regions are non-Russian ethnically, and nearly all are experiencing a demographic crisis. Therefore, the resettlement policy for "compatriots" may also have an economic and security rationale. According to the Russian Ministry of Internal Affairs, 826,000 people moved to Russia under this programme between 2006 and 2018. Most came from former Soviet Union countries, including Kazakhstan, Ukraine, Tajikistan, Armenia, and Moldova.[126]

Given the flexible definition of "compatriots" and their actual number, this concept applies to many former Soviet Union countries. Given the nature of Russia's migration policy, this threatens their national interests. Russia's approach to using elements of the "compatriot" resettlement policy to the occupied Ukrainian territory's population before and after its full-scale invasion should serve as an additional warning to other countries. Similar to its predecessors, the Soviet Union and the Russian Empire, Russia seeks to resolve its demographic, economic, and security issues through the use of force and a policy of relocating large populations across its territory.

3.3. "Russia with peace/world?" International development aid

This area was added to Rossotrudnichestvo's portfolio in 2014 when Russia adopted the Concept of State Policy for International Development Aid. The rationale for the Concept was that, in the past, Russia assisted with multilateral projects led by international organisations. As a result, according to Rossotrudnichestvo's top

---

125 Posolstvo Rossiiskoi Federatsii v Respublike Kazakhstan [Embassy of the Russian Federation in the Republic of Kazakhstan]. "Gosprogramma pereseleniia" [State program for resettlement]. n. d. http://www.consular.rfembassy.ru/lm/konsulskie_voprosy/sootechestvenniki/.
126 Izvestiia. 2019. "Nazvano chislo vernuvshikhsia v Rossiiu po programme pereseleniia sootechestvennikov" [The number of compatriots who returned to Russia under the resettlement program reported]. March 29, 2019. https://iz.ru/861860/2019-03-29/nazvano-chislo-vernuvshikhsia-v-rossiiu-po-programme-pereseleniia-sootechestvennikov.

officials, the recipients were unaware of the aid's origins and did not associate it with Russia. The Russian leadership decided to copy the approach of the US and provide bilateral assistance through an international development aid agency comparable to USAID. This role was bestowed on Rossotrudnichestvo. All of Russia's international assistance would now be channelled through it, not through the Ministry of Finance as it had before 2014.

In the briefing on Rossotrudnichestvo's performance in 2021 and plans for 2022, this area was still mentioned as a priority for 2022 as "an important mechanism for promoting Russian humanitarian policy in the world."[127] The speakers highlighted that these projects would contribute to the socio-economic development of the countries in which they are implemented in science, education, and healthcare. The stated objectives are to improve the quality of life for the population, shape a favourable image of modern Russia, and reduce "Russophobic" sentiments in certain countries.

> "We need to reject the old interpretation of "humanitarian" in the political and social sphere—in foreign and domestic (!) policy… for us, the international terms "humanitarian policy" and "humanitarian cooperation" are broader, more comprehensive, more interesting and more promising. In practice, this will mean a greater emphasis on international development, human rights, and a major focus on charity—but by no means at the expense of "promoting" the Russian language and art."
> —Yevgeny Primakov Jr.

As listed on its website, the partners that co-implement these projects with Rossotrudnichestvo include the Russian Humanitarian Mission, the Association of Volunteer Centers, and the Humanitarian Map.

- *The Russian Humanitarian Mission (RHM)* is portrayed as a non-state commercial organisation that focuses on international humanitarian activities in Russia and abroad, including Palestine, Uzbekistan, Lebanon, Syria, Nagorno-Karabakh, Kyrgyzstan, Bosnia and Herzegovina, Serbia,

---

127 Russkii dom [Russian House]. "Brifing press-sekretaria Rossotrudnichestva Nadany Fridrikhson" [Briefing by Rossotrudnichestvo press-secretary Nadana Fridrikhson]. YouTube video, 13:40, December 21, 2021. https://youtu.be/s89EA9KtcUY.

Tajikistan, and Georgia. Its stated mission is to "help people and communities in crisis as a result of conflicts, natural disasters, catastrophes, and poverty."[128] In essence, RHM often acts not as a partner for Rossotrudnichestvo but rather its humanitarian assistance tool. Not incidentally, Yevgeny Primakov Jr., one of RHM's founders, is the current Head of Rossotrudnichestvo.[129] Rossotrudnichestvo's social media accounts frequently share RHM content, and RHM employees often appear at events that are exclusively about the activities of Rossotrudnichestvo, such as the opening of the Russian House in Donetsk.[130] In 2017, RHM and Rossotrudnichestvo signed an agreement on state subsidies from Rossotrudnichestvo. In 2018, these subsidies amounted to 37.7 million roubles (around $600,000) and thus accounted for 50.5% of the total RHM's budget (Burlinova et al. 2020, 18).

- *The Association of Volunteer Centers* has been declared one of Russia's largest non-profit organisations. It encompasses a vast network of volunteer organisations throughout Russia.[131] Its "federal programmes" include Dobro.Universitet, an education programme; #МЫВМЕСТЕ (We Are Together), an award presented by the President of Russia; ДОБРО.РФ (Kindness.RF) platform; and more. It interacts

---

128 Russkaiia gumanitarnaiia missiia [Russian Humanitarian Mission]. n. d. https://rhm.agency/.
129 Russkaiia gumanitarnaiia missiia [Russian Humanitarian Mission]. "Ye. Primakov. Istoriia sozdaniia ANO RGM; gumanitarnyie proekty za rubezhom i v Rossii; vostrebovannost podderzhki rossiiskikh NKO v krizisnykh regionakh; polozheniie del v rossiiskoi nekommercheskoi sfere. Chasti 1–3" [Yevgeny Primakov. History of the establishment of ANO RHM; humanitarian projects abroad and in Russia; demand for support of Russian non-profit organisations in the regions in crisis; state of affairs within the Russian non-profit sector. Parts 1 to 3]. March 2, 2020. https://rhm.agency/radio/e-primakov-istoriya-sozdaniya-ano-rgm-gumanitarnye-proekty-za-rubezhom-i-v-rossii-vostrebovannost-podderzhki-rossijskih-nko-v-krizisnyh-regionah-polozhenie-del-v-rossijskoj-nekommercheskoj-sfere/.
130 Regnum. 2021. "V Donetske sostoialos otkrytie Russkogo doma" [A Russian House opens in Donetsk]. November 30, 2021. https://regnum.ru/news/3437052.html.
131 Assotsiatsiia volonterskikh tsentrov [Association of Volunteer Centres]. n. d. https://www.авц.рф/.

closely with several federal entities and initiatives. Among its numerous listed partners are the Russian government and a number of ministries, the Presidential Grant Foundation, ROSATOM, RIA Novosti, and others.

- *The Humanitarian Map* is a digital portal developed as part of the Humanitarian Monitor project. Its mission is to "increase the awareness of Russian and foreign audiences about various aspects of international humanitarian cooperation and Russia's contribution to international development aid."[132] The project's website aims to demonstrate "how Russia helps foreign partners in emergencies and peaceful times, for instance, by supporting their socio-economic development."

Rossotrudnichestvo defines *Missiya Dobro (Mission Kindness)* as its flagship project implemented in the international development aid area. Launched in 2021, it is run jointly by Rossotrudnichestvo, the Association of Volunteer Centers, and the Russian Humanitarian Mission. Its objective is to promote international volunteering in Russia and humanitarian cooperation with other countries in environmental protection, education, and culture. Currently, it is available to Russians who are interested in international volunteering. Kazakhstan and Uzbekistan were partner countries in 2021. A mirror project for foreigners in Russia is planned.[133]

This shortlist of international development aid partners reflects the status of this component in Rossotrudnichestvo's portfolio in general. Despite its designation as a provider of international assistance, Rossotrudnichestvo can hardly be put in a row with similar institutions from other countries due to the limited resources allocated to this portfolio component. As mentioned in Section II, Rossotrudnichestvo assumed responsibility for international development in 2014 and aimed to expand it significantly by 2020. However, funding was reduced in 2015 for various reasons, and the

---

132 Gumanitarnyi monitor [Humanitarian monitor]. "Gumanitarnaia karta" [Humanitarian map]. n. d. https://russianassistance.ru/about/.
133 Rossiia s mirom [Russia with peace]. "Missiia Dobro" [Mission Kindness]. n. d. https://web.archive.org/web/20210904024453/https://rwp.agency/programmy/news.php?ELEMENT_ID=60.

most recent report on its international development aid work is from that year. While Rossotrudnichestvo's leaders have spoken about the need to expand international humanitarian cooperation, the organisation's efforts on this front were primarily motivated by inertia, at least until the full-scale invasion of Ukraine in February 2022. Since then, Russian Humanitarian Mission became the main instrument on providing "humanitarian aid" in the occupied territories of Ukraine, each and every of its actions have been covered and promoted in the Rossotrudnichestvo social networks (see in more detail below).

4. Doves of Peace, Hawks of War: Rossotrudnichestvo After the Full-Scale Invasion

When Russia launched its full-scale invasion of Ukraine in 2022, Rossotrudnichestvo participated directly in state propaganda and provided support for the war effort through events at its headquarters and offices abroad, as well as through website and social media content.[134] In practice, this entailed two significant components: facilitating and promoting "humanitarian assistance" to the conquered and occupied regions of Ukraine and conducting pro-war information campaigns, including efforts to demonstrate support for Russia and its war in other countries. Local organisations of compatriots in different countries and the Coordinating Council of Russian Compatriots Living Abroad frequently co-organised such events.[135]

---

134 As mentioned at the beginning of this chapter, the Rossotrudnichestvo's Head Evgeny Primakov Jr. is a passionate and radical supporter of the Russia's war against Ukraine. See, for instance, one of the posts on his personal Telegram channel from as late as March 2, 2023. The text goes as follows: "As a private person, I would like to see a *ground zero* in the centre of Kyiv, while avoiding casualties among civilians if possible. I do not think that the civil authorities of Ukraine, let alone the military personnel and commanders, can be considered peaceful civilian population."

135 One example is the car rally in Cyprus in support of Russia. Russkii dom [Russian House]. 2022. "Na Kipre proshel avtoprobeg v podderzhku Rossii" [In Cyprus, a motor rally in support of Russia was held]. Facebook, April 9, 2022. https://www.facebook.com/watch/?v=556996232279652. Another example is the 15th conference of organisations of Russian compatriots in Buenos Aires.

Since the early days of the full-scale invasion in late February, the official Facebook account of Rossotrudnichestvo (https://www.facebook.com/rsgov), with 41 thousand followers, its Telegram channel (https://t.me/rossotrudnichestvo) with 12 thousand subscribers (both titled Russkiy Dom), and the Facebook accounts of its offices have been the primary platforms for Rossotrudnichestvo to share the official position of Russia.[136] Increased activity of its social media accounts since February 2022 highlights the importance of the social media assault by Rossotrudnichestvo: the number of its posts increased from 25-35 per week in February-March 2021 to 50-70 in the same period of 2022.

Figure 5. Frequency of publications at Russkiy Dom Telegram channel, 2021–2022

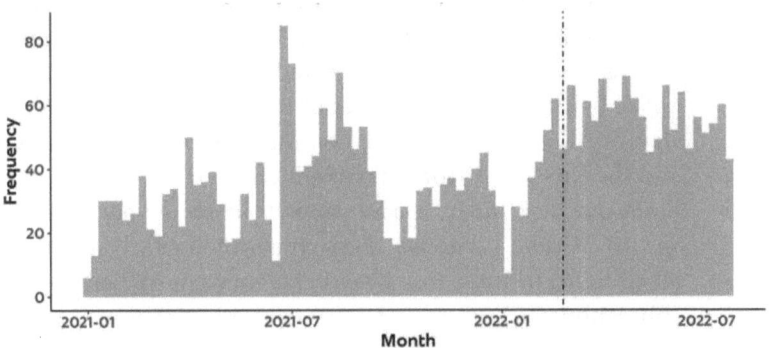

Source: calculations based on the posts at *Russkiy Dom* Telegram channel.

The posts on both channels have identical content. Some posts are duplicated in English, but most content is written in Russian, primarily aimed at Russians and Russian-speaking compatriots. The analysis of Rossotrudnichestvo's central office's social media

---

Russkii dom [Russian House]. 2022. "26 marta v Buenos Airese proshla XV Stranovaia konferentsiia organizatsii rossiiskikh sootechestvennikov, prozhivaiushchikh v Argentine" [On March 26, the 15th conference of organisations of Russian compatriots residing in Argentina was held in Buenos Aires]. Facebook, March 27, 2022. https://www.facebook.com/watch/?v=1006802196604276.

136 Rossotrudnichestvo's social media performance was as follows, according to its 2020 performance report: 700,000 total account subscribers; total post reach – 51 million accounts.

content between February 24, 2022, and June 20, 2022, reveals that all posts from this time can be classified into several clusters. Similar trends emerged in the accounts of its foreign offices, with minor variations.

- *Publications on programmed activities of Rossotrudnichestvo*: announcement, fact or result of events with hashtags #Россотрудничество (Rossotrudnichestvo) and #Русский Дом (Russian House) comprised between one-third and one-half of all weekly posts. Some of these posts and events were related to the previous, hybrid phase of the Russia-Ukraine war (2014-2022) and were promoting relevant Russian narratives."[137]
- *General information posts* included memorable dates, brief stories about the geographical diversity or peoples of Russia, notable figures, and announcements of partner organisations' events. These constituted roughly a third of all posts. Before May 9, posts about the "Great Patriotic War" stood out as a meta-theme central to Rossotrudnichestvo and the Russian historical narrative.
- *Posts that were direct media support for the all-out invasion against Ukraine*. Likewise, these constituted nearly a third of all content. In turn, this broad category comprises several subsections:
  - Posts on international development aid (#CMP for "содействие международному развитию" in Russian), "humanitarian assistance" to some areas in Ukraine or "refugees", often forcibly deported individuals from the Donbas to the territory of Russia.
  - Propaganda posts on the Russia-Ukraine war, news on Rossotrudnichestvo's events or third-party events in support of Russian war effort, dissemination of

---

137 Russkii dom [Russian House]. 2022. "31 marta v Russkom Dome v Ulan-Batore proshla vystavka 'Tragediia Donbassa'" [An exhibition 'The Tragedy of the Donbas' was held at the Russian House in Ulaanbaatar on March 31]. Facebook, April 4, 2022. https://www.facebook.com/rsgov/posts/pfbid07KkiZRHqt UqcFW6UJLBKXrnsrn3WbkFohDhcd64cAd5m7EczyYos36TWEqtH6QLJl.

Kremlin narratives about it, portraits of the Russian "heroes" of the "special operation," etc.
- o Posts tagged with #Русофобия (Russophobia) / #StopHatingRussians/#StopCancellingRussia: posts devoted to denouncing attempts to limit Russian influence or counter Russian narratives in foreign countries, especially related to cultural field.

4.1. Wolf in sheep's clothing: Imitating humanitarian assistance

On February 22, 2022, the day after Russia recognised the "independence" of the quasi-entities in parts of Donetsk and Luhansk oblasts, the so-called "LPR" and "DPR," Rossotrudnichestvo published a statement on its official website "On the recognition of DPR and LPR." It states that Rossotrudnichestvo intends to "continue supporting humanitarian projects in the Donbas" to "improve people's lives."[138] In the following days, the first articles appeared in the News section (24.02.2022[139] and 01.03.2022[140]) regarding humanitarian support and Russia's assistance to the refugees from the Donbas in Rostov oblast. Between the beginning of the full-scale Russian invasion of Ukraine and June 20, 2022, Rossotrudnichestvo almost daily posted on its social media accounts about humanitarian aid provided by itself, its partners, and other Russian organisations as part of what it refers to as "international development aid." This assistance was offered to people in the parts of the Donetsk, Luhansk, Kherson, Mykolayiv, Kharkiv, Chernihiv and even Kyiv

---

138 The web page containing this address was removed from Rossotrudnichestvo's website but it is still possible to read its first paragraph from the archived version of this website's home page as of February 23, 2022. Rossiia s mirom [Russia with peace]. n. d. "Novosti" [News]. http://web.archive.org/web/20220223083950/https://rwp.agency/.

139 Rossiia s mirom [Russia with peace]. 2022. "Moskvichi peredali bolee 2 tonn produktov bezhentsam DNR i LNR" [Muscovites have handed over more than 2 tons of foodstuffs to the refugees from DPR and LPR]. February 24, 2022. https://web.archive.org/web/20220428040923/https://rwp.agency/news/1135/.

140 Rossiia s mirom [Russia with peace]. 2022. "V Izraile obiavlen sbor sredstv dlia detei-sirot i detei-invalidov iz DNR i LNR" [A fundraising for orphan children and children with disabilities from DPR and LPR has been launched in Israel]. March 1, 2022. https://web.archive.org/web/20220501083234/https://www.rwp.agency/news/1151/.

oblasts that are or were temporarily occupied by Russia, even for the shortest amount of time. A case of the distribution of "humanitarian aid" to the residents of Dymer, a small town in Kyiv oblast, which was occupied until early April 2022, at the end of March 2022, is a good example.[141]

Occasionally, these regions were mentioned without any reference to Ukraine, and some posts referred to them as "demilitarised" or "liberated." These posts manipulated the topics pertaining to war victims, such as the children of the Donbas or Mariupol residents.[142] They constructed a narrative, excluding Russian responsibility for attack, destruction, death and injuries, humanitarian crisis, and claimed instead that these groups suffered from the military aggression of the Armed Forces of Ukraine. In this narrative, Russia was allegedly providing humanitarian assistance, and 'evacuating" civilians, including children, from the frontline territory to protect them.

Publications about the "humanitarian assistance" work of the Russian Humanitarian Mission in the cities and villages under occupationare a dominant thread in this narration. As previously mentioned, it has become the primary organization for this type of activity and each instance of its operations was reported on the social networks run by Rossotrudnichestvo. On the official Rossotrudnichestvo Telegram account, there were about 190 posts about various aspects of Russian "humanitarian assistance," mostly from RHM, but also from Rossotrudnichestvo itself, the Russian Ministries of Defence, Emergency Situations, Construction, and other organisations. In autumn 2022, the narration of humanitarian assistance to affected populations gave way to the narration of re-

---

141 Russian House in Bethlehem. 2022. "Zhiteli Kievskoi oblasti poluchili 20 tonn gumanitarnoi pomoshchi ot Rossii" [Residents of the Kiev region received 20 tons of humanitarian aid from Russia]. Facebook, March 31, 2022. https://www.facebook.com/Russian.House.Bethlehem/videos/515696510175508/.
142 Russkii dom [Russian House]. 2022. "Pri podderzhke Rossotrudnichestva v Minsk byla privezena delegatsiia detei s Donbassa" [With support from Rossotrudnichestvo, a delegation of children has been brought to Minsk]. Facebook, April 1, 2022. https://www.facebook.com/watch/?v=939448043420242&ref=sharing.

construction and "return to normal life" of cities ruined as a consequence of the Russian attack, starting with the destroyed city of Mariupol. An important part of this story was highlighting an all-Russian effort to provide this humanitarian assistance, with some regions of Russia proper taking responsibility for providing aid and financing the reconstruction of given occupied cities or regions. Closer to the end of the year, the occupied territories were routinely described as the (new) Russian regions or cities.

4.2 Empire's mouthpieces: Spreading military propaganda

A second way of Rossotrudnichestvo's supporting Russia's war effort was by facilitating and covering local audience-oriented events on the so-called "special operation" in Ukraine, either held by Russian Houses abroad or created and promoted from inside Russia. It directly focuses on disseminating propaganda and engaging in targeted efforts to rally public support for Russia's war against Ukraine abroad.

Since early spring 2022, the official accounts of Rossotrudnichestvo on social media have started sharing announcements of rallies in Israel, Armenia, Tunisia, Serbia, Turkey, Cyprus, and other countries, with direct or disguised appeals to support Russia in the war it launched against Ukraine on February 24, 2022, echoing the Kremlin's narratives about the causes of this war. These rallies were presented as initiatives of some organisations or individuals, presumably without the involvement of Rossotrudnichestvo. Still, they were diligently covered on its social media, and striking similarities in their conduct and key messages at least hint at a centralised organisation. The car rally in Limassol with the slogan "Let us stop neonazism together with Russia. No to NATO in Ukraine and Cyprus. Russia speaks the truth!" is an illustration. The SMM team of Rossotrudnichestvo created this announcement's teaser, which featured the letter Z, a symbol that propagates Russia's aggression against Ukraine.[143] Another example comes from Lebanon, where

---

143 Russkii dom (@rossotrudnichestvo). 2022. "Aktsii na Kipre v podderzhku Rossii" [Demonstrations in Cyprus in support of Russia]. Telegram, March 30, 2022. https://t.me/rossotrudnichestvo/5320.

people formed the phrases *Za Россию* and *Za Победу* ("For Russia" and "For Victory") using candles. During the rally on April 17 in Nicosia, the message alleging the fake nature of the Bucha Massacre was pushed.[144] Additionally, media coverage of events abroad in support of Russia was sometimes accompanied by the condemnation of the collective West's sanctions against Russia due to Russia's invasion of Ukraine. Russia's sanctions, not its military aggression, are portrayed in this case as the cause of the global food price increase.[145]

As to the events organised by the central office, they concentrated on producing alternative narration and translating it into as many languages as possible to broadcast Russian views on the war, its causes, Ukrainians and their history, etc. For example, Rossotrudnichestvo's organised and live-streamed the press conference titled "War crimes of the Kyiv regime: Testimony of eyewitnesses" on May 25, 2022, with Rossotrudnichestvo's Head Yevgeny Primakov Jr., representatives of the Russian government and other state organisations, propagandists Armen Gasparian and Kirill Vyshinsky. A special website was designed, and relevant disinformation leaflets were prepared and translated into thirteen languages. These contained Kremlin propaganda clichés about Ukraine and its army, presenting them as "irrefutable facts of manifestation and encouragement of the Nazi regime in Ukraine on the state level." The presentation's key points were then published on Rossotrudnichestvo's social media platforms, citing an open ambition to become a regime propaganda hub:

> "We had an idea — to collect in one place a cheat sheet, FAQ, for the average person, which will give him basic knowledge about the civil war in Donbass

---

[144] Russkii dom (@rossotrudnichestvo). 2022. "17 aprelia v Nikossii u zdaniia Posolstva Rossii v Respublike Kipr proshla chetvertaiia v strane massovaia aktsiia v podderzhku Rossii" [On April 17, a mass demonstration in support of Russia, the fourth in the country, has been held near the building of the Russian Embassy in the Republic of Cyprus]. Telegram, April 17, 2022. https://t.me/rossotrudnichestvo/5568.

[145] Russkii dom [Russian House]. 2022. "V tsentre peruanskoi stolitsy proshel miting v podderzhku Rossii" [A meeting in support of Russia has been held in the center of Peru's capital]. Telegram, April 19, 2022. https://t.me/rossotrudnichestvo/5591.

and the special military operation. The next idea was to make it as user friendly as possible. We will distribute it free of charge in printed form and post it in pdf format in different languages so that people in any country of the world know what is happening in the Donbass and Ukraine. Our network of Russian Houses will be the anchor point for this brochure to be distributed worldwide."

Evgeny Primakov Jr.[146]

A similar example of propaganda appears in "Besogon," an author's programme by pro-regime filmmaker Nikita Mikhalkov, where he created an alternative scenario of what happened during the EuroMaidan protests in 2013-2014, based on the memories of so-called "eyewitnesses" that Western media outlets allegedly do not dare to discuss.[147] This Mikhalkov show episode is available in Ukrainian, Spanish, Portuguese, Japanese, Italian, Hindi, German, French, and English. It is distributed through the online resources of Russian Houses across the world.

Rossotrudnichestvo exploited the theme of World War II to promote the narrative of "the crimes of the Ukrainian Nazi regime." It posted its own and shared content from the Russian Ministry of Defence page, drawing parallels between World War II and the current Russia-Ukraine war and portraying Ukrainians as those who continue the cause of Nazism, a message typical of Russian propaganda. On April 22, Rossotrudnichestvo's Telegram account shared the Russian Ministry of Defence's post about the project "Mariupol. Liberation," with reference to the 1943 Donbas operation and a phrase about the "bloody legacy between Nazis of that time and Ukrainian radicals today." It follows this approach in other publications on similar topics. In addition, biographies of at least a dozen

---

146 International multimedia press-centre 'Russia Today'. 2022. Press-conference "Voennye prestupleniya kievskogo rezhima: pokazaniya ochevidcev". [War Crimes of the Kyiv Regime: Testimony of the Eyewitnesses]. Moscow, May 25, 2022. https://pressria.ru/20220525/953669980.html.
147 Russkii dom [Russian House]. 2022. "Spetsvypusk avtorskoi peredachi 'Besogon' Nikity Mikhalkova posviashchen istokam natsionalizma na Ukraine, a takzhe prichinam i posledstviiam Maidana" [A special episode of Nikita Mikhalkov's programme 'Besogon,' dedicated to sources of nationalism in Ukraine, as well as the reasons and consequences of Maidan]. Facebook, March 8, 2022. https://www.facebook.com/watch/?v=740775000243243.

"heroes of the special operation" were featured on the Rossotrudnichestvo Telegram channel in 2022.

Finally, Rossotrudnichestvo continues with either supporting or promoting propaganda-heavy exhibitions and films. A number of exhibitions devoted to Russian narrative of events in the Donetsk region before and after the all-out invasion were demonstrated in Ulaanbaatar (Mongolia), Limassol (Cyprus), Beirut (Lebanon), and Ankara (three different exhibitions in one year), and "Crimean Spring: Together Forever," on the anniversary of Annexation, in Armenia. The films as of 2022 were created by Russia Today, main propaganda TV channel, and included a "documentary," "Russophobia," shot with the support of the Russian House in Tel Aviv, and two films on Mariupol, "I am alive" (with a localization in English) and "Mariupol is a Russian City" (demonstrated in the Russian Centre in Beijing). Quite a limited geography of offline events can be explained by the effect of the sanctions on Rossotrudnichestvo.

On the contrary, in Western countries, the Agency was compelled to downscale its operations and restrict overt propaganda. Instead, it came out with the idea of a neutral series of events "From Russia with warmth,"[148] anticipating that a reduction in Russian gas supplies would cause cold in European households. As a result, Rossotrudnichestvo offices could become locations where Europeans could get warm and watch some Russian/Soviet animated or feature films. In autumn-winter 2022-2023, such screenings were held in Paris, Brussels, Bucharest, Warsaw, Gdansk, Copenhagen, and Helsinki.

4.3 Russian cultural diplomacy's collateral damage: Fighting "Russophobia"

Since the beginning of Russia's full-scale invasion of Ukraine, Rossotrudnichestvo's communication strategy has incorporated criticism of the allegedly pervasive "Russophobia" in Europe and the

---

[148] Russkii dom (@rossotrudnichestvo). 2022. "Russkie doma otkryvayut punkty obogreva dlya evropejcev" [Russian Houses open warming stations for Europeans]. Telegram, October 21, 2022. https://t.me/rossotrudnichestvo/8368.

wider West and the fight against calls to "cancel" Russian culture. This refers to the war-induced refusal to collaborate with Russian cultural actors and institutions and attempts to reflect on imperialistic or colonial Russian artistic objects critically. In the meantime, Rossotrudnichestvo employees seek to appeal to the discourse of human rights, the need for dialogue and understanding, and the apolitical nature of culture, which some Western audiences find relatable and frequently acceptable.

On February 28, 2022, on the fifth day of Russia's full-scale war against Ukraine, Rossotrudnichestvo published a confusing and abstract statement by then-deputy head Natalia Poklonskaya[149] on its website. She spoke of new cases of what she termed "violation of the rights of compatriots and discrimination for citizenship and national affiliation abroad" "as a result of the current situation" and announced the launch of a hotline in Telegram "to protect compatriots" where they could seek assistance and called for peace. One of Rossotrudnichestvo's posts on its Facebook account is more specific about the hotline, stating that it focuses on providing psychological support. The statement's tone and content correspond to the narratives about the inadmissibility of "Russophobia" and its negative impact on "ordinary" Russian civilians. Since the Russia-Ukraine war began and Russia's military aggression against Ukraine was condemned by various countries, the Russian state media and some opinion leaders have promoted these narratives. The official Facebook account bolsters the argument against "Russophobia". Examples include the announcement of the Motorcade against "Russophobia" and racism with slogans like "For Peace! For Russia! For Greece!"[150] in Athens; a post about a rally against Russophobia held in Brussels;[151] a petition of Italian cultural actors to

---

149 Verber, Nikol'. "Nataliia Poklonskaia soobshchila o zapuske goriachei linii v Telegram dlia podderzhki rossiian" [Natalia Poklonskaya's statement on the launch of a Telegram hotline for the protection of compatriots abroad]. Life.ru. February 28, 2022. https://life.ru/p/1475095.
150 Russkii dom [Russian House]. 2022. "V Gretsii proidet aktsiia v podderzhku Rossii" [A demonstration in support of Russia will be held in Greece]. Facebook, March 31, 2022. https://www.facebook.com/rsgov/posts/pfbid033c LiG2xGtfTx711ry72JfD46JAP5z2m5HcKuLErrAXhzLrsvcu8mUeR7nHq3Mxg Vl.
151 Russkii dom [Russian House]. 2022. "V Briussele proshla aktsiia protiv rusofobii" [A protest against Russophobia took place in Brussels]. Facebook,

protect Russian culture; a rally supporting Russian culture in the centre of Rome;[152] and more. The photographs of these events reveal few attendees.

Individual appeals of people from various countries calling to stop "Russophobia" without identifying themselves or their names have become the characteristic content on Rossotrudnichestvo's accounts in the context of combating "Russophobia."[153] This content is typically accompanied by manipulative titles, such as "Country X joins the #StopHatingRussians flash mob." This campaign is intended to give the impression that ordinary people worldwide support Russia. Shared from the account of RT, the video appeal of an athlete, Jeff Monson, with a number of hostile and misleading Kremlin narratives on Ukraine, justifying the war on Ukraine, offers another example of imitating support for Russian policies from foreign audiences. These posts were quite active between February and August-2022 (42 posts hash tagged #StopHatingRussians in total) and then disappeared completely.

To create the impression of general grassroot support, the Agency's posts on rallies "against Russophobia" use impersonal language. This suggests that the local populace supports the activities on the ground. For instance, the post on the fight against "Russophobia" in Mexico has the title "Posters against Russophobia appear on the streets of Mexico City," and the text refers to unspecified "activists."[154] The post on the rally in Rome prior to Cosmonautics Day mentions the representatives of the local communist

---

March 28, 2022. https://www.facebook.com/rsgov/posts/pfbid02LDuJDPsyL65uJ5gHfCarbmc6Zi1eHmik8KHcVSVrKvyZ8cCfYPK3fqACHz6o7eq6l.

152 Russkii dom (@rossotrudnichestvo). 2022. "12 maia v Italii v tsentre Rima na ploshchadi Sviatogo Apostola proshel miting v podderzhku russkoi kultury" [A rally in support of Russia took place at Piazza Santi Apostoli in Rome, Italy, on May 12]. Telegram, May 13, 2022. https://t.me/rossotrudnichestvo/5954.

153 See, for instance, one example: Russkii dom (@rossotrudnichestvo). 2022. "Vse bolshe liudei po vsemu miru prizyvaiut prekratit rusofobiiu" [More and more people around the globe call for an end to Russophobia]. Telegram, April 14, 2022. https://t.me/rossotrudnichestvo/.

154 Russkii dom [Russian House]. 2022. "Na ulitsakh Mekhiko poiavilis plakaty protiv rusofobii" [Posters against Russophobia appear on the streets of Mexico City]. Facebook, April 6, 2022. https://www.facebook.com/rsgov/posts/pfbid02J42rJzsWJjSrxbVcthJFQtnHbgLunarc3u6cFPDJ59bwBUBrrgbcgsRfwxQjPAoZl.

youth organisations who put up posters depicting Yuri Gagarin in Rome. However, it provides no information regarding the public's reaction to this.

The few public art events that Rossotrudnichestvo manages to organise in Western countries also come with messages on preventing the "cancellation" of Russia. For example, a local art critic reported an exhibition's opening by the Russian artist Andrey Yesionov in Rome, saying, "If an artist is Russian, we should not judge him based on his nationality."[155]

The "cancelling" context, too, has incorporated the meta-narrative of the victory in World War II. Rossotrudnichestvo's social media accounts published sporadic articles about "vandalism" against Soviet-era Russian institutions or artefacts in March and April. The Russian embassy in Germany urged "citizens who care" to report vandalism "to prevent xenophobia and racism" after someone painted over the Treptower Park memorial to Soviet soldiers. The news that someone painted the monument to Soviet soldiers in Otepää, Estonia, in the colours of the Ukrainian flag was also accompanied by the hashtag #Russophobia.[156] Notably, that mass grave turned out to be fake when the city tried to transfer it to the cemetery. It was discovered to contain no actual remains of soldiers.[157] On May 23, Rossotrudnichestvo's social media accounts launched a media campaign with similar videos for several countries. In these videos, the statement about the significant assistance of the Soviet Union before or after World War II, for which the

---

155 Russkii dom (@rossotrudnichestvo). 2022. "V Rime okrylas vystavka russkogo khudozhnika Andreiia Esionova 'Puti Very Iskusstvo Andreiia Esionova v semi tserkviakh Rima'" [An exhibition "Paths of Faith. The Art of Andrei Esionov in seven churches of Rome" of a Russian painter Andrei Esionov opened in Rome]. Telegram, May 24, 2022. https://t.me/rossotrudnichestvo/6099.
156 Russkii dom (@rossotrudnichestvo). 2022. "V estonskom gorode Otepia oskvernili pamiatnik sovetskim voinam" [A monument to Soviet soldiers was desecrated in the Estonian town of Otepää]. Telegram, April 12, 2022. https://t.me/rossotrudnichestvo/5507.
157 Fokus. 2022. "Bratska mohyla v estonskomu misti vyiavylasia radianskym feikom" [Mass grave in an Estonian city turns out to be a Soviet fake (photo)]. June 17, 2022. https://focus.ua/uk/world/519379-bratskaya-mogila-v-estonskom-gorode-okazalas-sovetskim-feykom-foto.

country in question should allegedly be grateful, is followed by accusations of "Russophobia" or sanctions against Russia with the hashtag #МЫПОМНИМ (We Remember). In total, twelve such videos have been produced.

All of these and other communication cases, such as statements by Rossotrudnichestvo leaders, news, social media posts to allegedly cover humanitarian and other areas of its work, and the work of its partner organisations, are designed to spread and bolster propaganda narratives among Russian and foreign audiences. Several of these narratives are hostile toward Ukraine. The narrative of the "people of the Donbas suffering from Ukraine's aggressive actions and seeking refuge and assistance in Russia" and the narrative of "nationalism and Nazism in Ukraine" are examples. Once again, this demonstrates the political bias of Rossotrudnichestvo and its role as a mouthpiece for Russian propaganda through its extensive network of offices abroad and media platforms.

Conclusions

Reinvented by the Russian government in the 2000s out of the Soviet-era organisations of "friendship and cooperation" with other countries, Rossotrudnichestvo was designed to dramatically strengthen the soft power and attractiveness of the Russian Federation in the world, especially among its neighbouring countries that were becoming increasingly interested in Western development models. Rossotrudnichestvo preserved and reworked the approaches and traditions of its predecessors, such as solid integration into the state structure and administration close to the top tiers of the Russian government; centralised governance and political bias; non-transparent funding and concealed motives and tools of work, up to spying and subversions. Having established Rossotrudnichestvo at the same time as waging its war on Georgia in 2008, Russia began to back up its hard power from day one. The objective was to relativise or justify armed or hybrid aggression against other states in the international arena.

In the network of Russia's cultural and public diplomacy institutions, Rossotrudnichestvo appears to be the most powerful, thanks to the resources at its disposal. These include generous state funding, the extensive network of offices it inherited from the past, which is likely to grow exponentially after the recent innovation in authorising "non-state" foreign offices and friendly organisations in the world; an extensive partner network with federal institutions; media outlets banned in the EU; programmes and projects, including those supported by the president. All this translates into hundreds of thousands of personal contacts and millions of media users' exposure. Still, these resources are partially offset by the excessively ambitious goals and the weakness of Russia's economy, which has been investing much more into militarisation, i.e., hard power, leaving soft power tools on the sidelines.

However, Rossotrudnichestvo does have massive objectives and ambitions. It deals with cultural diplomacy, as well as international development aid, and the support of "compatriots" abroad. Notable is the emphasis on promoting the glorious past of Russian culture over modern, future-oriented art, as well as the intense ideological exploitation of history and identity myths for political purposes. Self-presentation as an international donor of humanitarian aid intended to strengthen Russia's role as a global powerhouse. In fact, this has become a tool of media support for the military aggression that covers up the massive destruction caused by the indiscriminate attacks. Finally, support for the loosely defined "compatriots" helps Russia solve its political challenges in the target countries through its work with the Russian-speaking minorities and the demographic challenges of Russia through the passportisation policy and resettlement in Russia's remote regions.

Russia's war against Ukraine has revealed all the potential of Rossotrudnichestvo's threatening impact. It openly acts as a mouthpiece for propaganda and a tool of war through institutional ties, networks of representatives, and media platforms. Given Rossotrudnichestvo's active support of the Russo-Ukrainian war, the Agency will not only have to undergo a rebranding (which it must be accustomed to) but also a revaluation of its values to again pose itself as a neutral organisation specialising in cultural and humanitarian cooperation and "soft power" agent. As of now, its history and the history of related organisations and the characteristics of Russia's political regime do not support any forecasts for such a development.

"The Russian flag will be flown wherever Russian is spoken"
The "Russkiy Mir" Foundation

Yulia Masiyenko, Kateryna Zahryvenko, Nadiia Koval, Denys Tereshchenko

1. Assembling the "Russian World": From Concept to Political Strategy

> The trouble is not that the USSR broke up—that was inevitable. The real trouble, and a tangle for a long time to come, is that the breakup occurred mechanically along false Leninist borders, usurping from us entire Russian provinces. In several days we lost 25 million ethnic Russians—18 per cent of our entire nation—and the government could not scrape up the courage even to take note of this dreadful event, a colossal historical defeat of Russia, and to declare its political disagreement with it—at least in order to preserve the right to some negotiations in the future. No... In the heat of the August (1991) 'victory', all this was allowed to slip away.
> — Aleksandr Solzhenitsyn, *"The Russian Question" at the End of the Twentieth Century*

The 2007 Russian President's Decree establishing the "Russkiy Mir"[158] Foundation was the first attempt to institutionally re-evaluate the importance of public and cultural diplomacy to Russia's foreign policy. This was precipitated by the failure of Russian foreign policy in neighbouring states, as witnessed by the Rose Revolution of 2003 in Georgia and the Orange Revolution of 2004–2005 in

---

158 The literal translation of the Russian "русский мир" into English as "Russian world" does not fully convey the meaning of this concept, as it misses a number of connotations present in the Russian language (such as those related to the multiple meanings of the Russian word "мир," which can mean "world," "peace," and "community"). In the absence of a suitable alternative, we adhere to the official English name of the foundation, "Russkiy Mir" Foundation, by transliterating the Russian expression. Whenever "русский мир" refers to the ideology espoused by this Foundation and wider circles of Russian elites, we translate it as "Russian World," bearing in mind all the limitations and attempting to explain the plethora of meanings later in this chapter.

Ukraine. These two events demonstrated the weakness and impotence of Russia's soft power and its lack of attractiveness even in the former Soviet republics and sparked an in-depth debate within Russia about the need to rethink Russian policy in the post-Soviet space.

As early as 2005, in a speech to the Russian Federal Assembly, Putin described the collapse of the Soviet Union as the greatest geopolitical catastrophe of the 20th century, citing the enormous number of Russians who remained outside the country. Therefore, the new institution, the "Russkiy Mir" Foundation, was tasked with promoting the Russian language and culture among Russian diasporas/minorities abroad, particularly in the former Soviet republics. For this purpose, the concept of the "Russian world" as one of the tools aimed at correcting the consequences of Putin's alleged "catastrophe" came in handy.

The Foundation's avowed mission is to "promote the Russian language, which is Russia's national heritage and an essential component of Russian and world culture, and to support Russian language research programmes abroad." In addition to promoting Russian language and teaching methods, providing access to Russian educational materials, and assisting Russian language teachers, the Foundation's list of tasks also includes more comprehensive ones:

- Promotion of "objective" information about contemporary Russia and "compatriots" to build a favourable public perception of Russia worldwide.
- Support for the activities of Russian diasporas abroad, protection of their identity, and preservation of the Russian language as a medium of interethnic communication.
- Support for the Russian-language media primarily focused on achieving the Foundation's objectives.
- Collaboration with the Russian Orthodox Church and other denominations to promote the Russian language and culture.

Executives and supporters of the Foundation have said on multiple occasions that "Russkiy Mir" was founded as a Russian counterpart to renowned Western institutions such as the British Council, Alliance Française, and Goethe-Institut (Viperson 2007). Particularly noteworthy is the case of the Alliance Française, which seems to have served as a model to emulate. Founded a few years after the defeat of France in the Franco-Prussian War of 1870-1871, it was tasked with restoring French foreign policy prestige by promoting and supporting the French language and culture. At first glance, "Russkiy Mir" followed a comparable objective for the Russian language and culture. However, in order to realize the expansionist ambitions of "assembling the Russian world," "Russkiy Mir" has politicized language and culture well beyond any precedent.

The "Russkiy Mir" Foundation has the main structural characteristics of institutions engaged in cultural diplomacy, i.e., the statute, goals, objectives, long-term programmes, grants, and conferences, the declaration of aspirations for cooperation with leading academic and cultural institutions around the world, etc. At the same time, the Foundation does not appear to share the values and spirit of its Western counterparts, nor does it adhere to the ideas of openness and cultural interchange. Moreover, its ideology aims for geopolitical expansion and is marked by aggressive attitudes towards other cultures (Popovic, Jenne, and Medzihorsky 2020). The precise political objectives of the Foundation are also indicated by its name, which directly refers to the eponymous revanchist ideology, and by the peculiarities of its organisation (see the following chapter) as well as by the content of analytical and ideological documents published on the Foundation's website (Nikonov 2010).

The vast majority of these ideological works have not been translated into other languages, which is remarkable. The foreign-language editions of the website mostly give general information about the Foundation, as well as some broad statements regarding the preservation of cultural heritage and the promotion of cultural identity. However, the Foundation's imperial-civilizational and revanchist principles, goals, and values are not translated. Consideration of the structure and activities of the "Russkiy Mir" Foundation should therefore begin with an examination of the ideology and values of this concept: what exactly is the "Russian world" ideology, and how is its meaning conveyed in the public communication of the Foundation's staff, key Russian politicians, and Foundation documents.

1.1 The Russian world as a revitalization instrument for Russia

The history of the "Russian world" concept has already been examined in-depth; therefore, for the sake of this study, we will merely cover the essential points (Laruelle 2015; Suslov 2018). Various literary and philosophical aspects of the "Russian world" can be traced back at least several centuries. The political argument for the "Russian world" as a civilizational framework for development and a means of (re)interpreting Russian-speaking communities in other countries was first advanced in the history of post-Soviet Russia at the end of the 1990s by political technologists Pyotr Shchedrovitsky and Yefim Ostrovsky.[159] As they assert, it was a method for creating a concept of Russian policy toward the Commonwealth of Independent States (CIS):

> I can tell you precisely when the word emerged. It appeared around New Year's Eve of 1998 when we were preparing a concept of Russia's policy in the CIS at the request of one of the government officials. In the text of this concept, the existence of a particular socio-cultural reality was suggested as the basic formula, the fundamental myth that set the principles of policy in the CIS (it was being transformed at the time). The critical point of understanding was that the same number of Russian ("russkie") people lived in Russia as abroad. (Russkiy Arkhipelag 2001)

Nevertheless, numerous conservative intellectual and journalistic groups contributed to the conception and development of this idea. For instance, in 2023, Konstantin Zatulin, a member of the Russian parliament and a prominent promoter of the "compatriots" policy, publicly claimed, in a frank revelation, that Russians, after having lost their "greater Russia" in the form of the USSR, "found comfort" in the "Russian world" as an idea of assembling Russians

---

159 In an interview with the online publication "Russkiy Arkhipelag" (Russian Archipelago), Shchedrovitsky himself made this claim. See more on this in: Russkiy Arkhipelag 2001; Laruelle 2015; Sorokina 2021; Nikonov 2010, 4–14.

and sympathisers around the globe in order "not to lose the influence upon the minds."[160] However, the deliberate avoidance of unambiguous distinctions and definitions, i.e., providing straightforward answers to the questions of what the "Russian world" is and who or what belongs to it, is a remarkable aspect of the discussion around the concept of the "Russian world." Foundation's ideologists and leaders actively employ an extensive array of abstract concepts to describe the "Russian world." For instance, it may be regarded as a language, a culture, a universe, an empire, a world power, a supraethnic formation, a community, or peace. Apparently, this ambiguity never changed even up to 2022, as testified by the conference panel on the concept and policy of the Russian world co-organised by Rossotrudnichestvo and the "Russkiy Mir" Foundation. The term's polysemantic character makes its accurate translation impossible (Kozdra 2018, 61). Its immensity and abstractness make it impossible to operationalize, but they are meant to represent a deeper meaning that implies competition with other "great worlds" (Anglo-Saxon, Arabic, etc.).

The fundamental contradiction between the broadest possible definition of "Russian world" necessitated by geopolitical claims and the highly restrictive, conservative, and archaic definition of cultural Russianness upon which the very term is built is, in our opinion, the source of this vagueness. In addition, according to Foundation documents, improving global attitudes toward Russia or the "Russian world" is a secondary objective of the "Russian world's" development. It is asserted, for instance, that Russia needs a "positive image" to "strengthen the positions of our civilization in global competition" or that it is crucial to "appeal not only to Russian citizens but also to compatriots living abroad, to citizens of the former Soviet Union, and, ideally, to a wider audience of those

---

160 Vserossiiskaiia nauchno-prakticheskaiia konferentsiia "Rossiia: edinstvo i mnogoobraziie" [All-Russian Scientific and Applied Conference "Russia: Unity and Diversity]. "Sektsiia 7. Russkiy mir kak garant obespecheniia mezhnatsionalnogo mira i soglasiia" [Section 7. Russian world as a guarantor of ensuring interethnic peace and harmony"]. n. d. https://единство-и-многообразие.рф/program/sekcija-7-russkij-mir-kak-garant-obespechenija-mezhnacionalnogo-mira-i-soglasija/.

who are potentially not indifferent to Russia" (Nikonov 2010, 108–109).

Nonetheless, in 2010, during a discussion over the Foundation's aims, its then-executive director, Vyacheslav Nikonov, made an unsubstantiated claim about the size of the Russian diaspora while jumping to an expansionist conclusion:[161]

> "Today, the Russians are the largest diaspora nation in the world. According to the "Russkiy Mir" Foundation, the Russian-speaking diaspora (which includes, for example, Germans from Kazakhstan) has already surpassed the Chinese. In addition, the number of people who speak Russian worldwide is comparable to the population of the Russian Federation. In fact, this is a second Russia outside of Russia. But it is sand. It is a scattered, atomised civilization that our Foundation, like many others, is trying to unite. But sand is also used to build cement and concrete, which can be fused into glass or something very tough when subjected to severe external forces." (Nikonov 2010, 39)

It is this idea that as many Russians ("russkie," in the cultural and civilizational sense, not necessarily ethnic Russians) live outside Russia as in Russia itself, which is a possible source of the rebirth of power and hope for Russia, that is the semantic core of the "Russian world" concept.

1.2 Indicators of affiliation with the "Russian world"

The concept of the "Russian world" raises the problematic questions of what principle should be used to determine a person's or community's belonging to the "Russian world" and what policy should be implemented in response. In fact, to answer these questions, in the first years of the Foundation's existence, its founders and activists relentlessly engaged in organisational introspection, holding numerous round tables. The ensuing texts, entitled "Meanings and Values of the Russian World" (Nikonov 2010), posted only on the Russian-language version of the Foundation's website, can

---

[161] In fact, the Russian diaspora is at least the fourth largest in the world, judging by its size, after Indian, Mexican, and Chinese. See Papadopoulos, Anna. "Countries with the largest diaspora population in the world, 2019." *CEOWorld Magazine*. September 18, 2019. https://ceoworld.biz/2019/09/18/countries-with-the-largest-diaspora-population-in-the-world-2019/.

be considered the Foundation's programmatic document. The publication of the results was put together as a raw synopsis of round tables that were attended by the Foundation's leaders and staff, political technologists and philosophers, philologists-activists from the regions, heads of key research institutions, propaganda journalists, and the Russian Orthodox Church Patriarch Kirill, on the one hand, demonstrates the inability of these groups to reach a compromise, and on the other, suggests a plethora of meanings that have yet to be analysed and summarised.

The primary criterion of the "Russian world" is still a linguistic marker. The round tables' reports explicitly state that the Russian language is the "binder" of the Russian world since it contains its historical codes and meanings (see Gromyko's contribution in Nikonov (ed.) 2010, 22). In the Foundation's printed materials about the current status of the Russian language, a sense of threat and dissatisfaction with the status of the Russian language in the world predominate. The topic of (losing) the worldwide stature of the Russian language takes on an aggressive, even bellicose tone for the Foundation's leaders and activists. Typical statements that refer to this issue comprise the following:

- Following the collapse of the Soviet Union, the Russian language suffered from a "rapid loss of positions," which was allegedly a "catastrophe in Eastern Europe:" "Russian is the only major language that has not only lost its position in the world over the past two decades but also lost it rapidly." (Nikonov 2010, 7, 9)
- The Russian language is "punished" in the countries of the former Soviet Union for "actual or perceived sins of tsarism and the USSR," while the civilising role of the Russian language in the former Russian Empire or the Soviet Union is ignored. (Nikonov 2010, 7)
- The Russian language's adversaries will be defeated. According to Vladimir Kochin, the Foundation's executive director, "The Russian language is a political matter. Its promotion worldwide is a very significant political task about which our President has frequently spoken. Of course, our

case is righteous. The enemy will be defeated, and the victory will be ours." (Kochin 2016, 26)
- A classic example of the enemy of the Russian language and Russia is Ukraine, where, after the collapse of the Soviet Union, a generation of "young people hostile to Russia who have been educated in the West" has grown up. (Kochin 2016, 23)
- "The Russian flag will be flown wherever Russian is spoken," In an interview with the newspaper "Izvestiya" ("The News") in 2015, Vladimir Kochin joked about a plan by the Russian Ministry of Education and Science to spend 3.75 billion roubles on promoting the Russian language abroad. "Promoting the Russian language is a multifaceted endeavour; we will not receive this funding. If we had such resources, the Russian flag would already be everywhere" (Kornatskii 2015).

However, the language criterion cannot be sufficient, given the Foundation's repeatedly articulated desire to also attract to the "Russian world" the descendants of the previous waves of emigration who have lost their language but still identify as Russians or people who are simply interested in the Russian language and culture.

The second essential criterion is religious affiliation, specifically with the Russian Orthodox Church. The inclusion of Patriarch Kirill's speech at the Third Assembly of the Russian World in the programmatic documents of the "Russkiy Mir" Foundation is thus no coincidence. Kirill's definition of the "Russian world" based on this religious criterion includes not only Russia within its contemporary borders but also Ukraine, Belarus, and even Moldova.

> "It seems that if we consider the Russian Federation within its modern borders the only centre of it (of the "Russian world" — Authors), we will be sinning against the historical truth and will artificially alienate many millions of people who are aware of their responsibility for the fate of the Russian world and who consider its establishment their life's work. The core of the Russian world today is Russia, Ukraine, and Belarus, and St. Rev. Laurentius of Chernihiv expressed this idea in a famous phrase: "Russia, Ukraine, and Belarus are Holy Rus." This understanding of the Russian world is enshrined in the modern self-designation of our Church. It is called Russian

not on ethnic grounds; rather, this name indicates that the Russian Orthodox Church carries out a pastoral mission among peoples who accept the Russian spiritual and cultural tradition as the basis of their national identity or as an essential component." (Patriarch Kirill in Nikonov 2010, 29)

However, this criterion is also insufficient due to the diversity of religious traditions in Russia, including a large number of Muslims residing in it, and the wish to engage with representatives of other Christian denominations related to the Russian language and culture within the project.

The cultural dimension of the "Russian world" is typically not discussed in terms of ancient or modern phenomena, trends, or representatives of Russian culture but rather in terms of the "values" and "meanings" that the "Russian world" carries. In this effort to define values, the ambivalence between the Foundation's broad goals and its limited resources, which was previously mentioned, is well observed. On the one hand, it is stated that the "Russian world" presupposes harmony and mutual respect, as well as peaceful coexistence with other states: "It would be desirable if this civilization (the "Russian world") brought to the world the ideals of freedom, dignity, justice, sovereignty, and mutual respect for states, faith, and traditions" (Nikonov 2010, 14). On the other hand, it is emphasised that the defining characteristic of the values of the "Russian world" is their unmistakable Russocentrism in the broadest sense, i.e., that they must be "produced within the country" (Nikonov 2010, 14).

The 2022 panel discussion "The Russian World as a Guarantor of Interethnic Peace and Harmony," mentioned above, did not present any radically new ideas about the essence of the Russian world concept and its application. It featured predominantly the same key speakers, including Konstantin Kosachev, Anatoliy Torkunov, Sergey Stepashin, Fyodor Lukyanov, Vyacheslav Nikonov, and Konstantin Zatulin, among others. Torkunov, for instance, claimed that the Russian world, in stark contrast to the "ethnonationalist approaches of other countries" (apparently implying Ukraine or maybe Poland), aimed to build "Russian civil unity," a utopian picture of Russian society that would account for numerous ethnic and religious differences but would still be dominated by the Russian component. Throughout the conference, criticism of Russian nationalism was a recurrent point, and several speakers, including Zatulin, referred to suggestions to build a purely Russian national republic in a negative light (they never mentioned who put those suggestions forward, however). This criticism perfectly makes sense given that Russian imperial and national narratives have long been conflicting since the latter would imply that nationally non-Russian territories would have or would be able to secede, which means a huge loss for the imperial project. Generally, the importance of the Russian world for a harmonious "national" policy featured prominently in those discussions. Fyodor Lukyanov, for instance, using Fukuyama's critique of the "identity politics" of the West, suggested that Russia should construe its minority policy in a consolidating, not divisive, way. However, even the ardent supporters of the Russian world had to admit that their project had lost significantly within the previous thirty years, and the Russian world's postulates are not as easy to universalise and sell abroad as the Soviet ones used to be.[162]

On the Foundation's website, the understanding of the ideology of the "Russkiy mir" is presented in a rather diverse way:[163]

- "'Mir' as a community," a term associated with "communality," "conciliarity," and "collectivism." It is noted that the key problem of contemporary Russia is individualism and the rupture of social ties; therefore, the restoration and strengthening of the *community* are precisely the basis of the concept of the "Russian world."
- "Russian world" is also about loyalty to Russia because everyone's vocation is to help the motherland and to care

---

162 Vserossiiskaiia nauchno-prakticheskaiia konferentsiia "Rossiia: edinstvo i mnogoobraziie" [All-Russian Scientific and Applied Conference "Russia: Unity and Diversity]. "Sektsiia 7. Russkiy mir kak garant obespecheniia mezhnatsionalnogo mira i soglasiia" [Section 7. Russian world as a guarantor of ensuring interethnic peace and harmony"]. n. d. https://единство-и-многообразие.рф/program/sekcija-7-russkij-mir-kak-garant-obespechenija-mezhnacional nogo-mira-i-soglasija/.
163 Fond "Russkiy Mir." n. d. Informatsionnyi portal Fonda "Russkiy Mir" [Information Portal of the "Russkiy Mir" Foundation]. https://russkiymir.ru/fund/.

for one's neighbour ("what each of us can do for the Motherland").
- "Russian peace" is the absence of enmity, notably in the Russian sense ("Russian reconciliation, rapport, Russian order, overcoming the ruptures of the 20th century"), examples of which are the unity of the Churches under the auspices of the Russian Orthodox Church and the reburial of significant émigrés.

In his article "Russian World: Concepts, Principles, Values, and Structure," Alexey Gromyko (head of the Foundation's European programmes at the time) described and even categorised the values of the "Russian world" in a more structured manner.[164] This attempt once again reveals the fundamental internal contradiction of the concept. On the one hand, multiculturalism and multiethnicity are declared to be the functional values of the "Russian world." Still, at the same time, they are only possible under "Russian dominance" (see Gromyko in Nikonov 2010, 21). And the majority of the listed values (see the table below) are extremely conservative (their exact content is not disclosed or elaborated upon). They are presented as a categorized, flimsily substantiated list of concepts immanently opposed to Western values, notably conservative, authoritarian, and even archaic. Thus, "functional values" conceal imperialism, "political values" conceal an authoritarian leaning, "spiritual values" imply Orthodox irrationalism, and "worldview values" indicate passivity and patience (humility).

---

164 Alexey Gromyko (born in 1969) is the Director of the Foundation's European programmes and the Chairman of its Institute of Linguistic-Civilizationist and Migration Processes' Expert Council. He is also the grandson of Andrey Gromyko, Foreign Minister of the USSR from 1957 to 1985 and Chairman of the Presidium of the Supreme Soviet from 1985 to 1988. A. Gromyko is a migration historian, a doctor of political science, the Director of the Institute of Europe at the Russian Academy of Sciences. His work for the Foundation focuses primarily on academic and analytical writing.

Table 3. Core values of the "Russian world" according to A. Gromyko

Functional values	Multinationality and polyethnicity with Russian dominance Multilingualism with Russian dominance Multi-religiousness with the dominance of Eastern Orthodoxy Multiculturalism
Political values	The sacredness of power Paternalism Sovereignty
Spiritual values	Spirituality as the dominance of the spiritual over the material Messianism (Moscow is the Third Rome) Idealism Humility Martyrdom
Worldview values	Contemplation Justice Providentialism (up to fatalism) Sacrifice
Behavioural values	Benevolence Sociability Openness Lenience/tolerance Generosity Hospitality

Twelve years later, the list of values identified by Gromyko, in a much more succinct form, was officially adopted by the Russian president in a special decree establishing the "principles of state policy for saving and enhancing traditional Russian spiritual and moral values." The decree itself (no. 809 from November 9, 2022), defined as a "document of strategic planning in the field of ensuring the national security of the Russian Federation," lists the following traditional values to be supported and promoted:

- Life
- Dignity
- Human rights and freedoms
- Patriotism
- Civic consciousness («гражданственность»)

- Service to the Fatherland and the responsibility for its fate
- High moral ideals
- Strong family
- Creative labour
- Priority of the spiritual over the material
- Humanism
- Mercy
- Justice
- Collectivism
- Mutual help and mutual respect
- Historical memory and the continuity of generations
- Unity of the peoples of Russia.

These "traditional values" are picked and espoused as a counterweight to what is perceived to be liberal "Western" values. This geopolitical dimension is evident in the document wherever it refers to the USA and its alleged attempts to destroy Russian society from within with the help of promoting its "destructive ideology," which includes "the cultivation of egoism, permissiveness, immorality, the negation of the ideals of patriotism and the serving to the Fatherland, of the natural continuation of life, the value of strong family, marriage, having many children («многодетность»), creative labour, the positive contribution of Russia to the world history and culture, the destruction of traditional family with the help of propaganda of non-traditional sexual relations."[165]

In the decree, the diversity of religions is recognised as "part and parcel of Russian historical and spiritual heritage," but Orthodoxy is given "a special role in establishing and enhancing traditional values."[166] Although the Russkiy Mir ideology is never directly referred to in this document, its entry is largely consistent

---

[165] Russian Federation. President. Ukaz [Decree] #809 "Ob utverzhdenii Osnov gosudarstvennoi politiki po sokhraneniiu i ukrepleniiu traditsionnykh rossiiskikh dukhovno-nravstvennykh tsennostei" [On the Adoption of the Principles of State Policy for the Preservation and Enhancement of Traditional Russian Spiritual and Moral Values]. Adopted 9 November 2022. http://www.kremlin.ru/acts/bank/48502.

[166] Ibid.

with the writings and doctrine of the Fund. It signifies the latter's rise into the ranks of Russia's official ideology.

Given the profound duality and ambiguity of the concept, Vyacheslav Nikonov, the unalterable leader of the Foundation, turns to the least tangible criterion of "Russian world" membership, *self-identification*, in his most often cited definition:

> "Russian world is multiethnic, multireligious, and polysemantic. This is a global phenomenon that any single concept cannot unambiguously describe. We consider the Russian world to be Russia plus the Russians abroad ('zarubiezhie'). And mentally [it is] everyone conscious of their involvement in the Russian world. In this sense, belonging is defined through self-identification." (Nikonov 2010, 5–6)

Unsurprisingly, the ideologues tend to conceptualise the "Russian world" as a series of concentric circles based on the imagined proximity of countries or communities to the "core values" of language, religion, or others. Thus, according to the former head of Rossotrudnichestvo, Konstantin Kosachev:

> "Our dream is to initiate a union, a consolidated "Russian world" centred on the Russians, then, moving outward from the centre, it will include those who studied in Russia, married Russians, started families, have business interests in Russia, or are otherwise professionally or personally connected (to Russia). Then another group of individuals is simply interested in Russia, its literature, ballet, and space." (quoted after Popovic, Jenne, and Medzihorsky 2020, 1459)

Similar concentric circles can be seen in the geographical definition of the Russian world, which can be found in the previously mentioned article by Alexey Gromyko.

- Core: Russia and the post-Soviet Slavic countries, namely Ukraine and Belarus.
- Inner sphere: other post-Soviet countries and regions.
- Outer sphere:
    - Countries with substantial Russian-speaking minorities (Germany, Israel, USA, UK).
    - Countries with an Orthodox Christian majority (Serbia, Cyprus, Romania, Montenegro, Bulgaria).

- Countries without Russian-speaking minorities and the Orthodox Church but with a historical interest in Russian culture and trade with Russia (e.g., Italy or Finland).

The unconditional appropriation of Ukraine and Belarus by the "Russian world" echoes the approach of Patriarch Kirill cited previously, and the application of the religious criterion is notable. Moreover, such spatial structuring reveals Russia's strategic interests: the revival of the "fraternal peoples" concept and the restoration of control over the countries of the former Soviet Union, followed by the countries with Russian-speaking minorities that are religiously or economically close to Russia.

The passage of the "Russian world" concept from political operators to Kremlin cabinets is highly symbolic. If Shchedrovitsky complained in 2000 that the idea of the "Russian world" (as opposed to the mere statement about a large number of Russians abroad) did not resonate with customers in the late 1990s (Russkiy arkhipelag 2001), it was picked up in Kremlin-connected circles in the early 2000s (Sorokina 2021). The phrase "Russian world" first appeared in Putin's speeches in 2001, became fully politicized after Ukraine's Orange Revolution, and was finally institutionalised in 2007 with the establishment of the "Russkiy Mir" Foundation.

Mikhail Suslov splits the evolution of the concept of the "Russian world" in Russian intellectual and political discourse into three stages, beginning with an idealistic image of Russian diasporas as a "Russian archipelago" that had to enrich Russia in the 1990s and progressing to the concept's adaptation to the concept of "sovereign democracy" and restoration of the spheres of influence in Putin's policies in the 2000s. During this second period, the concept of the "Russian world" began to serve the needs of Russia's "soft power," appearing in primary foreign policy documents such as the concept of Russian foreign policy (from 2008 onwards to 2023) and its appendix that defined the priorities of cultural and humanitarian cooperation (2010), as perhaps the most important tool of Russian cultural diplomacy. Finally, in the third stage, the "Russian world" has begun to form the foundation of an irredentist isolationist project that fits the logic of presenting Russia as a non-Western power model. Efforts to consolidate the ostensible "core" of the "Russian world" through gradual subordination of Belarus and armed aggression against Ukraine occurred during this period. Finally, in his 2014 "Crimean speech," Putin exacerbated the politicization of the "Russian world" notion by expressing hope that "German citizens will also support the aspirations of the 'Russian world' historical Russia, to restore unity" (Prezident Rossii 2014).

2. "Russkiy Mir" As a Vocation: The Foundation's Organisational Structure

"Russkiy Mir" was established as a non-governmental organisation, namely a foundation, by a decree issued by Russian President Vladimir Putin in 2007. Its existence has recently been extended until 2025. Its founders are the Russian Federation's Ministry of Foreign Affairs and the Russian Federation's Ministry of Education, and the relevant ministers serve on the Foundation's Board of Trustees.[167]

The Foundation's management structure, as of April 2023, is comprised of three bodies, namely the Board of Trustees, the Supervisory Board, and the Management Board:

- The Board of Trustees is the main supervisory body for the Foundation's activities and the deployment of its funds, and it is chaired by the deputy head of the Presidential Administration, Dmitry Kozak. Sergey Lavrov (Minister of Foreign Affairs), Sergey Kravtsov (Minister of Education), Olga Lyubimova (Minister of Culture), and Valery Falkov (Minister of Higher Education and Science) serve on the Board.
- The Supervisory Board, chaired by an Adviser to Russian President Vladimir Tolstoy, is the highest collegiate body determining the Foundation's main directions. The Supervisory Board includes representatives of the Presidential

---

[167] Fond "Russkiy Mir." Informatsionnyi portal Fonda "Russkiy Mir" [Information Portal of the "Russkiy Mir" Foundation]. n. d. https://russkiymir.ru/fund/.

Administration, rectors of Russia's leading universities (Moscow State University, Moscow State Institute of International Relations, Literature Institute, St. Petersburg State University, etc.), representatives of the Ministry of Foreign Affairs, the Director of Hermitage museum, as well as Metropolitan Antony (Head of the External Relations department of the Moscow Patriarchate), Margarita Simonyan (Editor-in-Chief of the international propaganda channel Russia Today), and Yevgeny Primakov (Head of Rossotrudnichestvo).

- The Management Board is a collegiate executive body that oversees the Foundation's operations directly. The Chairman of the Board is Vyacheslav Nikonov, the permanent (de-facto, not by design) Head of the Foundation (see Box below), who is now the First Deputy Chairman of the State Duma Committee on International Affairs. In addition, the Management Board includes representatives from the Ministry of Foreign Affairs, key academic institutions, and Rossotrudnichestvo. Vladimir Kochin is the Foundation's executive director.

The manner in which members of the Foundation's governing bodies are appointed and their prominent figures' personalities highlight the Foundation's apparent involvement in the Russian regime's executive hierarchy of governance and the leading institutions tasked with influencing overseas audiences. Furthermore, the Foundation has recently become even more closely aligned with the presidential governance hierarchy. The management and each member of the Foundation's three governing bodies are appointed personally by the President of the Russian Federation, according to the Decree of the President of the Russian Federation No. 215 of April 12th, 2021.[168] For example, from 2007 to 2019, the Foundation's Board of Trustees was chaired by Lyudmila Verbitskaya, rec-

---

168 Russian Federation. President. Ukaz [Decree] #215 "O nekotorykh voprosakh fonda 'Russkiy mir'" [On certain questions of the "Russkir Mir" Foundation]. Adopted 12 April 2021. http://publication.pravo.gov.ru/Document/View/0001202104120042?rangeSize=1.

tor of St. Petersburg University and chairperson of the Russian Union and the International Association of Experts in Russian Language and Literature. Following her death, one of Putin's closest associates, Vyacheslav Nikonov, assumed her position.

Vyacheslav Nikonov is a textbook example of a hereditary party boss ('nomenklaturshchik' in Russian, i.e., a member of the Soviet party elites): his grandfather was Vyacheslav Molotov, a long-time People's Commissar (and later Minister) for Foreign Affairs of the USSR. Molotov and his German counterpart signed the infamous Molotov-Ribbentrop Pact in 1939, which divided the spheres of influence in Eastern Europe between the USSR and Nazi Germany. Nikonov joined the Communist Party during the Soviet era. Still, after the Soviet Union's demise, he continued his political career within other parties, eventually ending up in the parliamentary faction of the "United Russia" that has ruled Russia for decades.

Nikonov is a notable actor in Russia's political system: he has been elected repeatedly to the State Duma, where he led the Education Committee for eight years, and he has served as Deputy Chairman of the Duma's Foreign Affairs Committee since October 2021. Nikonov's combination of positions in the government and nongovernmental organisations is typical of Russian elites: he is a member of the Russian parliament's lower house, Chairman of the Management Board of the "Russkiy Mir" Foundation, member of the Foreign and Defense Policy Council's praesidium, President of the "Politika" ("Polity") Foundation,[169] and Dean of the Department of Public Administration at the Lomonosov Moscow State University. Having obtained a degree in history, like his parents, Nikonov authored many works full of propagandist and pseudo-scientific statements, in which he stands as a sentimental advocate of his grandfather's policies during Stalin's times, promotes the concept of the "decline" of the West and the need for the establishment of a new multipolar world, as well as ideas of Russia's unique civilizational role. Nikonov appears to use the Foundation not only to carry out the Russian state's policy of expanding the "Russian world" but

---

169 Fond Politika ["Polity" Foundation]. "President." n. d. http://www.polity.ru/president.html.

also to carry out personal propaganda projects, such as the website "Twenty-Eight Moments of the Spring of 1945,"[170] which narrates the author's perspective on the events of April 1945 that led to the Allies' victory over Nazi Germany. Much emphasis is placed on the USSR's unique role in these events, as well as Joseph Stalin and Vyacheslav Molotov.

Nikonov served as the Foundation's executive director for the first four years before being promoted to Chairman of the Management Board in 2011. Nikonov's statements were published every few days by the Foundation's information portal before and after the full-scale Russo-Ukrainian war on February 24th, 2022. These statements mostly repeat the Russian regime's anti-Ukrainian and anti-Western rhetoric with great precision and regularity. Its leitmotif is the idea of an unprecedented confrontation between Russia and the entire Western world, combined with the pressing need to expand the "Russian world" in any way possible. Nikonov's speech to the State Duma plenary session a month after the start of the full-scale war is an example:

> "Now is the time to call everything by its name. The clash of two worlds over the future of the planet continues. For Russia, it is a matter of survival — a life-and-death struggle. We have accepted the challenge of contenders for world dominance — the United States and its allies, who consider themselves to belong to a higher race and wish to impose their will on all humanity. Today there is a battle between the forces of freedom and the forces of dictatorship ... The clash between the world of Light and the world of Darkness continues. And the world of Light turned out to be larger than expected. One billion people on the planet belong to the West. Seven billion are with us: Asia, Africa, and much of Latin America. The clash of the world of truth, in which the fight is against fascism, against the world of lies, in which fascism is either not noticed or openly supported, continues. And there is no room for compromise here. There is a clash between the culturally open world, in which Goethe and Beethoven are not banned, and the world of bans on Dostoevsky, Tolstoy, Tchaikovsky, and Gergiev. They did not understand us. We cannot be bought! We will win. Because our cause is righteous, and victory will be ours."[171]

---

170 Fond "Russkiy Mir." "Dvadtsat vosem mgnovenii vesny 1945-go. Proekt Vyacheslava Nikonova" [Twenty-Eight Moments of the Spring of 1945. Project by Vyacheslav Nikonov]. n. d. https://28.russkiymir.ru/.
171 Fond "Russkiy Mir." "Vyacheslav Nikonov: Idet stolknovenie dvukh mirov za bushchee planety" [Vyacheslav Nikonov: There Is a Clash of Two Worlds for

Nikonov's hegemony over the Foundation's activities is evident not only in the news feed, which is replete with his statements and comments. Nikonov's creativity has also overrun the "Books" section of the Foundation's information portal, which featured sixteen of his works as of May 2023.[172]

The Foundation's headquarters are in Moscow, and there are two branches, one in St. Petersburg and one in the Far East (Vladivostok), established to support academic and pedagogical research and other activities to spread the Russian language throughout the country. There is no information on the official number of employees or the internal structure of the Foundation, but previous research suggests that the staff may number around 80 people.[173]

The main partners of the Foundation listed on its website as of 2023 are:

- Rossotrudnichestvo (Federal Agency for the Commonwealth of Independent States Affairs, Compatriots Living Abroad, and International Humanitarian Cooperation), with which the Foundation has close ties not only through mutual participation of the heads in each other's governing bodies but also through the wide range of activities that both institutions undertake jointly. The Foundation explains the division of labour between the two institutions: Rossotrudnichestvo promotes the state's political messages, whereas "Russkiy Mir" focuses solely on cultural and humanitarian cooperation (Kornatskii 2015).
- Associations of Russianists reflect the linguistic focus of the Foundation's activities. (International Association of Teachers of Russian Language and Literature (MAPRYAL), Rus-

---

the Future of the Planet]. April 5, 2022. https://russkiymir.ru/news/299605/?sphrase_id=1230901.

172 Fond "Russkiy Mir." "Knigi" [Books]. n. d. https://russkiymir.ru/the-modern-world-and-its-origins/index.php.

173 Data as of 2014, see Lutsevych (2016, 14). In 2022, job boards, where the foundation's vacancies occasionally appear, contained information on 20 to 50 employees, and as of March 2022, LinkedIn contained profiles for 23 employees.

sian Society of Teachers of Russian Language and Literature (ROPRYAL), American Council of Teachers of Russian Language and Literature (ACTR))
- Non-governmental and pseudo-non-governmental organisations and foundations, for many of which, according to Marlène Laruelle's study, the "Russkiy Mir" Foundation serves as an umbrella platform (Laruelle 2015, 14). These organisations may apply for Russian government funding via grants, but they can also receive funds from other sources; they reproduce and disseminate Russian official narratives, and there are no single independent NGOs among them. (Institute of CIS Countries, Russian Foundation of Culture, Foundation named after Likhachov, Foundation of Historical Perspectives, Civic Chamber of the Russian Federation, The Alexander Gorchakov Public Diplomacy Fund, International Foundation for Slavic Literature and Culture, Public Diplomacy Corps. Foundation (Kingdom of the Netherlands), Russian-Iranian Public Relations Council, "Eurasia Heritage" Foundation, International Research Agency "Eurasian Monitor")
- Institutions established to coordinate Russian "compatriots" abroad, such as information portals, comprise the largest pool of partners, reflecting the Foundation's priority target audience. (International Council of Russian Compatriots, Interstate Union of Hero Cities, Association for Relations with Compatriots "Rodina" ("Motherland"), International Association of Youth Organisations of Russian Compatriots, International Coordination Council of Educational Institutions Alumni (INCORVUZ-XXI), Moscow House of Compatriots, EU Russian-Speakers' Alliance, russkie.org, Information portal "Russkiy vek" ("Russian Era"), Official Thematic Resource of the Committee on Foreign Relations of St. Petersburg, Portal of the Coordinating Council of Russian Compatriots of Germany "Russkoe pole" ("Russian Field"), Dialogue with Russian-speaking Scientists Working Abroad, TV project "Russkoe vremya novostey" ("Russian News Time")

- Educational and research institutions, given that from a legal point of view, the Foundation's main activity is "scholarly research and developments in the field of social sciences and humanities." (Lomonosov Moscow State University, St. Petersburg State University, Sochi State University, Herzen Russian State Pedagogical University, Pushkin State Russian Language Institute, Russian Academy of Sciences, Vinogradov Russian Language Institute of the Russian Academy of Sciences, Institute of Religion and Policy, Pushkin House (Russian Literature Institute of the Russian Academy of Sciences), Centre for Ukrainian and Belarusian Studies of Lomonosov Moscow State University, Library-Foundation "Russian Abroad", Maxim Moshkov Library, All-Russian Children's Centre "Okean" ("Ocean"))
- Prominent cultural institutions (Russian Publishers Association, State Russian Museum, Boris Yeltsin Presidential Library, State Literary-Memorial and Nature Museum-Reserve of A. S. Pushkin "Boldino", State Film Fund of the Russian Federation)
- Mass media and publishing houses (TASS (Telegraph Agency of the Soviet Union), VGTRK (All-Russia State Television and Radio Broadcasting Company), "Zvezda" ("Star"), TV channel "Kultura" ("Culture"), TV "Bolshaya Aziya" ("Greater Asia"), GTRK (State Television and Radio Broadcasting Company) "Kaliningrad", "Istina i zhizn" ("Truth and Life"), magazine "Russkiy reportyor" ("Russian Reporter"), "Moskva" ("Moscow"), "Neva", "Novoe literaturnoe obozrenie" ("New Literary Review"), "Otechestvennye zapiski" ("Patriotic Notes"), "Radio Rossii" ("Radio of Russia"), "Russkiy yazyk za rubezhom" ("Russian Language Abroad"), "Russkiy zhurnal" ("Russian Journal"), "Russkiy ochevidets" ("L'observateure russe"), Publishing House "Forum", "Yunost" ("Youth"), Russia Beyond the Headlines, Historie&Kultur Forum e.V.)
- Organisations or resources personally associated with Vyacheslav Nikonov (Vyacheslav Nikonov's personal website, BRICS National Research Committee, Foundation

"Polity" ("Politics"), Foundation "Yedinstvo vo imia Rossii" ("Unity for Russia"))
- as well as the Charitable Foundation for the Preservation of the Art of Russian Romantic Song "Romansiada" and the All-Russian Non-Governmental Organisation "National Delphic Council of Russia".

Thus, one can observe a pervasive network of related pro-government organisations, state educational and cultural institutions, and international and regional media, which carry out numerous projects in the near and far abroad, first and foremost focusing on the Russian diaspora and Russian "compatriots" in the broadest sense, with the support or cooperation of the "Russkiy Mir" Foundation.

Russkiy Mir's over-reliance on government funding[174]

State funding of Russian foundations is not transparent. At the same time, once the Russian government effectively barred foreign donor funding for NGOs in 2012 via the "foreign agents" law, government control over the NGO sector became paramount, and state support for these NGOs expanded rapidly. In 2015 alone, governmental assistance for NGOs almost doubled to 4.7 billion roubles ($103 million) (Lutsevych 2016, 11). According to Orysia Lutsevych's calculations based on publicly available information, in 2016, the Russian government spent at least $130 million on projects aimed at influencing foreign public opinion, the vast majority of which targeted post-Soviet and Balkan countries (not to mention funds from state-owned enterprises, private companies loyal to the Kremlin, or presidential grants) (Lutsevych 2016, 11).

Like many Russian organisations, "Russkiy Mir" does not publish detailed financial reports. Following its governing statutes,

---

174 The Foundation's financial information on certain provisions for the years after 2013 is available through public sources, in particular on the Russian-language website Checko.ru, which is dedicated to checking counteragents. Checko: Proverka kontragentov [Checko: Counterparty Verification]. "FOND 'RUSSKIY MIR.'" n. d. https://checko.ru/company/fond-russky-mir-1077799019253.

the "Russkiy Mir" Foundation is funded by the budget of the Russian Federation, private contributions, and is permitted to participate in commercial activities. Almost every year, more than 95 per cent of the Foundation's revenue is derived from the federal budget, as evidenced by its publicly available financial data.

The annual volume of private donations is minimal, fluctuating within a few per cent of the entire budget. Only in 2016 and 2018 did the proportion of external funding grow slightly, but this did not alter the general trend. The Foundation's officials have publicly bemoaned the Foundation's desperate need for private donations, which they claim to account for "just 2 to 3 per cent of the total." They regret that "even in projects directly related to their business interests, our businesspeople are unwilling to invest" (Kornatskii 2015).

Unlike other cultural diplomacy organisations worldwide, the Foundation does not rely on its business activities. The "Russkiy Mir" depends more on state support than China's Confucius Institutes. In Russian Centres (of the "Russkiy Mir" Foundation) abroad, for instance, there are no paid services (such as language classes), and almost all initiatives are funded almost exclusively by government allocations and subsidies. In contrast, the current activities of Confucius Institutes are jointly financed by Chinese and foreign parties (Zhao 2020, 4).

Figure 6. Revenues of the "Russkiy Mir" Foundation, 2013–2021

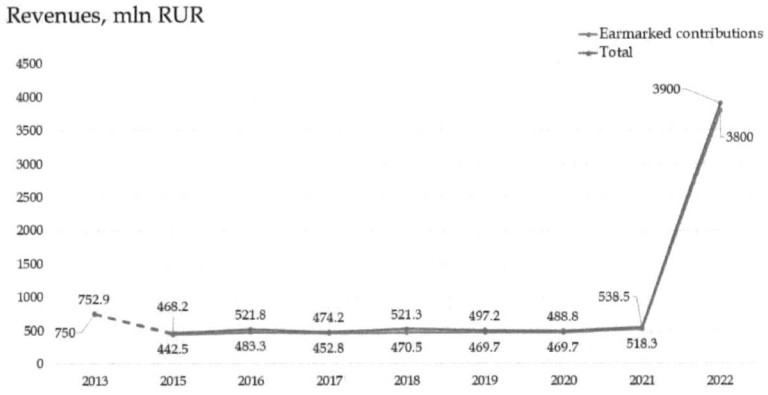

* There is no information for 2014
The line labelled "total" represents the Foundation's annual revenues on the graph. "Target contributions," or budget revenues, individual contributions, and income from the Foundation's commercial activities are included.
Source: revenue information on the "Russkiy Mir" Foundation on the https://checko.ru/.

In 2015, due to fiscal sequestration, the Foundation received over 1.7 times less state funding than in 2013. In the same year, the media stated that this budgeted sum was insufficient for full-scale operations and that administrative expenses would decrease. In 2015, it was reported that the Ministry of Education and Science of the Russian Federation insisted on maintaining funding for the Foundation of 750 million roubles until 2020. Still, the Ministry of Finance opposed and blocked the decision (Khamraiev 2015). In terms of the Foundation's performance, however, neither the overall number of Russian Centres abroad nor the volume of the Foundation's projects decreased much. Only the cancellation of all public projects in Ukraine, which had traditionally been the Foundation's top priority, became a significant change. In addition, the Foundation's non-public activities may have been harmed by the financial reductions. However, "Russkiy Mir" began to rely on state support through other programs, such as Ministry of Education funds for educational projects (Kornatskii 2015).

In 2022, already amidst the full-scale war, the Fund's financial situation dramatically improved. The Fund's revenues reached as high as 4 billion roubles, which was more than seven times more compared to the previous year and the general trends of the last decade. However, since the Fund did not publish a report on its activities in 2022, there is no official information on the reasons for this significant rise in available sources.

As for the Foundation's expenses, unlike the state agency Rossotrudnichestvo, "Russkiy Mir," as an allegedly (or at least legally speaking) non-governmental organisation, reports only to its founders and the President of the Russian Federation (Dmitriieva 2015), so there is virtually no relevant public information. Only the total amounts of expenses are known.

Figure 7.   Expenditures of the "Russkiy Mir" Foundation, 2013–2021

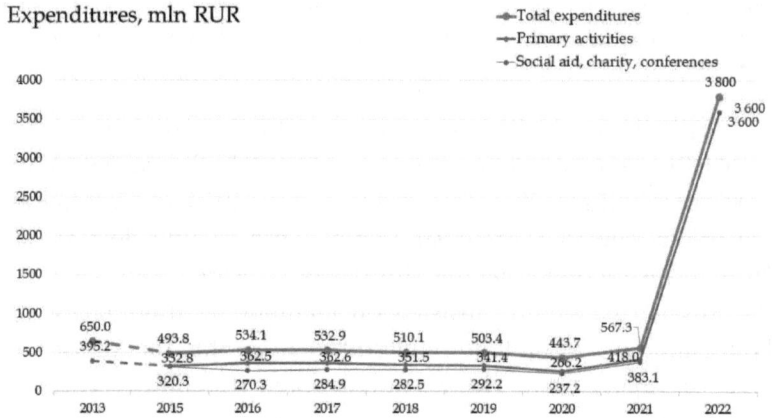

* There is no information for 2014
Source: expenditures information on the "Russkiy Mir" Foundation on the https://checko.ru/

The Foundation's primary activities in previous years accounted for roughly 70 % of its total expenditure structure. The remainder is for administrative expenses. As a result of unused balances from prior periods, total expenditures and revenues may not precisely match. The lion's share of the expenditures on the Foundation's principal activities is comprised of provisions such as "social aid and charity" (obviously the support of Russian Centres and Cabinets of "Russkiy Mir," as well as grants) and "conference organisation"; these two items account for approximately 50-60 per cent of the Foundation's expenditures. In financial statements from 2016 to 2019, there was also a line item for "other" expenses. In conclusion, the Foundation's complete reliance on the presidential hierarchy of governance and federal budget funding reaffirms that it is a tool of centralised state policy designed to spread Russian influence abroad under the guise of cultural diplomacy.

The year 2022 saw an outstanding leap in the Foundation's activities' funding, which corresponded well with the increase in revenues. That year, 3.6 billion roubles were spent to distribute grants and support the Centres and Cabinets of "Russkiy Mir," which meant a nine-fold budget increase vis-à-vis 2021. Since the change in the number of Centres and Cabinets did not match the inflated budget, one might assume that the expenditures were primarily allocated to fund the grants for the popularisation of the Russian language and culture around the world. However, precise information on where this money went is not available.

Information Fronts of "Russkiy Mir"

The media is an integral part of the Foundation's activities. In addition to its extensive cooperation with traditional media and publishing companies (see the section on partners above), the Foundation has established its own media and social networks. Its primary media outlets include the large online portal "Russkiy Mir," the magazine "Russkiy mir.ru," the TV and radio "Russkiy Mir," as well as Russian and international social media profiles.

A.   *Information Portal „Russkiy Mir"*[175]

The Foundation has a relatively active and lively official portal with as many as seven language versions: Russian, English, Chinese,

---

175   Fond "Russkiy Mir." Informatsionnyi portal Fonda "Russkiy Mir" [Information Portal of the "Russkiy Mir" Foundation]. n. d. https://russkiymir.ru/fund/.

German, Spanish, French, and Italian. However, the website's full content is available only in Russian, which appears to hint that the use of the portal is aimed primarily at Russians and those able to speak Russian fluently.

Therefore, only Russian-speaking users can read all the information about the following:

- Foundation activities, its governing bodies, and significant partners
- Publications presenting ideological foundations of the organisation's activities
- Listing of Russian Centres and Cabinets of "Russkiy Mir" with contact information and locations
- Friendly organisations form the Catalogue of the "Russkiy Mir" (not available online as of May 2022)
- Grants, conditions of their allocation, the status of grant applications
- Events, forums, and Assemblies organised by the Foundation
- News of "Russkiy Mir" (the Foundation's own news and information shared from Russian state structures and news agencies)
- Foundation's official annual reports
- Announcements of future events (Foundation-sponsored or those of interest to it)
- Access to the magazine "Russkiy Mir.ru" and TV and radio company "Russkiy Mir."

The English version includes information about the Foundation, its key activities, and its current management structure and news. The websites in other languages are hardly ever updated, contain outdated information, and provide only very general information about the Foundation's ideology, mission, tasks, and activities. According to the report for 2020, a total of 7,500 publications were published online, but only 2,200, or approximately 30%, were translated.

The homepage of the Russian version of the portal includes news, publications, event announcements, and links to video and audio content. All news messages are geographically and thematically catalogued (e. g., relating to diaspora, culture, history, society, and politics). The following categories are used to classify news articles:[176]

- *"In the Russian world"*: Russian and international news about the "Russian world" as defined by the Foundation. This section is the most frequently updated on the portal, with 15–20 new posts published daily. The content is derived primarily from state news agencies, official Ministry of Foreign Affairs announcements, and partner organisations. In the spring of 2022, i.e., during the tensest first weeks of the full-scale Russian invasion of Ukraine, the news reflected the war effort and goals and was primarily concerned with:

A) war with Ukraine and prospects for the development of the "Russian world" in the occupied territories, especially blatant propaganda materials and reports on efforts to rapidly Russify the occupied territories:
  - May 31st, 2022 — Philologists from the liberated territories of Donbas of Ukraine will be retrained in Luhansk
  - May 31st, 2022 — Orphans from Donbas and Ukraine can become Russians under a simplified procedure
  - May 30th, 2022 — In the Zaporizhzhia region, for the first time in eight years, the memory of Russians ("russkie") who perished in the battle of Kalka in 1223 was honoured
  - May 30th, 2022 — More than 200 residents of Donbas want to get a job in Primorye under the resettlement programme for compatriots
  - May 30th, 2022 — Special military operation in Ukraine: the essential for May 30th
  - May 30th, 2022 — Banners about the Russian history of the city appeared on the streets of Kherson

B) "oppression" of Russians and Russian speakers in the world, allegedly anti-Russian measures of other states, "Russophobia:"
  - May 30th, 2022 — A German journalist working in Russia is shocked by the level of Russophobia in Germany
  - May 28th, 2022 — In Kyiv-controlled schools, Russian-speaking children were taught Pushkin's oeuvre in Ukrainian
  - May 28th, 2022 — The Russian Foreign Ministry has accused the IOC of violating the rights of Russian athletes
  - May 27th, 2022 — Latvia is struggling with Russian names on the map

---

176 Fond "Russkiy Mir." "Novosti" [News]. n. d. https://russkiymir.ru/news_a/.

- May 27th, 2022 — Russian Foreign Ministry: The concept of the German centre on World War II distorts the historical truth
- May 31st, 2022 — In Belarus, the intention to demolish the monument of friendship between the Slavic peoples was called barbaric

C) *events related to the popularisation of the Russian language and the achievements of Russian cultural diplomacy around the globe:*
- May 31st, 2022 — Russia has terminated a memorandum of cooperation with the United States in the field of culture
- May 30th, 2022 — Russia and Republika Srpska are increasing educational cooperation
- May 31st, 2022 — The programme for Russian language teachers started in Istanbul
- May 30th, 2022 — The competition for young Russian-speaking elocutionists was held in Strasbourg
- May 30th, 2022 — In Dushanbe, the Day of Slavic Literature and Culture was marked by a competition
- May 30th, 2022 — In Guangzhou, the results of the competition of short videos dedicated to the Day of the Russian language were summed up
- May 30th, 2022 — The "Friendship Marathon" was held in Havana in honour of the anniversary of the Victory

- *"In the "Russkiy Mir" Foundation*: news related to the Foundation's activities, updated irregularly between 1 and 5 times per month.
- *"News of Russian Centres"*: information about the current activities of Russian Centres and Cabinets of "Russkiy Mir"; there are usually 15 news items per week.
- *Grant projects*: about ten messages per month are posted in this section, containing information on activities supported by grants from "Russkiy Mir."

Regarding audience reach, the Foundation projected between 1.5 and 1.6 million unique visitors from approximately 190 countries in 2018–2020.[177] However, the Foundation does not provide information on the quality of the traffic, such as the average length of user visits, the number of pages viewed, etc. According to SimilarWeb, there were 165.1 thousand unique visitors to the "Russkiy Mir" website in February 2022, roughly in line with the Foundation's estimates. These visitors spent an average of only 33 seconds

---

177 Fond "Russkiy Mir." "Godovyie otchety deiiatelnosti Fonda" [Annual Reports on the Foundation's Activities]. n. d. https://russkiymir.ru/fund/reports.php.

on the website, and 74% of users left after viewing only one page.[178] This means that three-quarters of the website's visitors were sporadic, non-loyal visitors who probably only accessed the page through external links.[179] In March 2022, access for users from western countries and Ukraine became significantly more difficult. In April 2022, website traffic decreased threefold compared to February, and the average visit lasted only 33 seconds.

As of March 2023, the website's attendance had significantly improved. The number of visitors had notably risen within the three previous months and reached 232.9 thousand. Provided that the attendance remains the same, the number of visitors might exceed 2.5 million by the end of the year. However, the traffic quality remained relatively the same, with visitors spending on the website on average around one minute and viewing on average 1.5 pages.

Figure 8. "Russkiy Mir" website attendance in February–April 2022

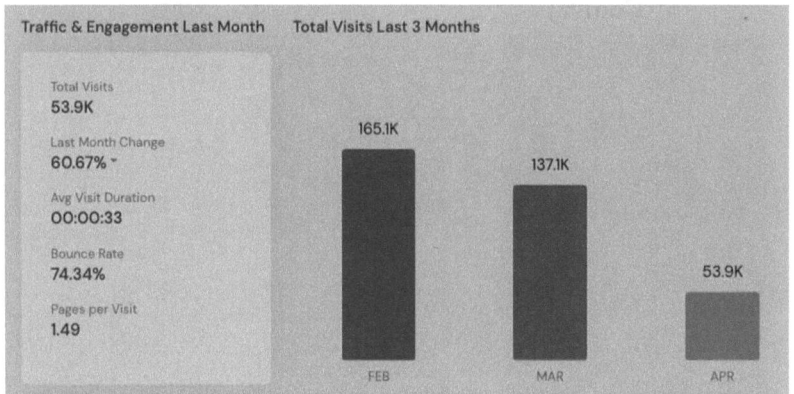

Quantitative and qualitative traffic statistics for the Foundation's website for February–April of 2022. *Data from SimilarWeb website, https://www.similarweb.com*

---

178 Similarweb. "Russkiymir.ru." n. d. https://www.similarweb.com/website/russkiymir.ru/#traffic.
179 Ibid.

Figure 9. "Russkiy Mir" website attendance in February–April 2023

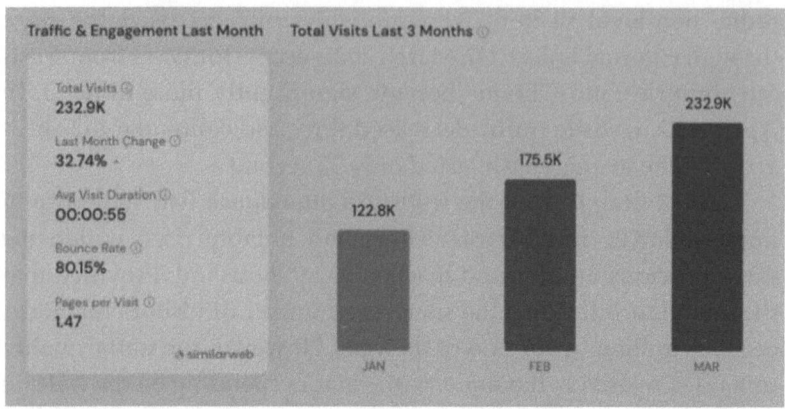

Quantitative and qualitative traffic statistics for the Foundation's website for January–March of 2023. *Data from SimilarWeb website, https://www.similarweb.com*

Figure 10. Distribution of "Russkiy Mir" website visitors by Country

List of countries whose residents ensured the highest traffic volumes on the Foundation's webpage in February, April 2022, and March 2023, respectively. *Data from the SimilarWeb website, https://www.similarweb.com*

According to data, as of February 2022, users from Russia, Ukraine, and the U.S. dominated the website's audience. After the beginning of the war and the imposition of restrictions on access to the website, visitors were primarily from Russia. In 2023, users from Russia still constituted the core of the visiting traffic, the second country being Kazakhstan.

The primary traffic source before the war (as of February 2022) was search queries (almost 77%), and only 17% were direct visits to the webpage. It is also worth noting that social networks and email newsletters do not influence traffic. In 2023, this distribution largely remains the same. The main traffic source was still search queries, while social media provided only a little. However, the number of direct visits to the webpage increased.

Overall, the information portal is abundant with texts and data, but it is still unclear whether it is a systematic source of information about the "Russkiy Mir." Visitors to its website seem to be, in most cases, occasional and to represent somewhat limited geography. The traffic and its qualities appear non-comparable to those of similar western organisations.

Figure 11. Distribution of "Russkiy Mir" website visitors by Source, February 2022

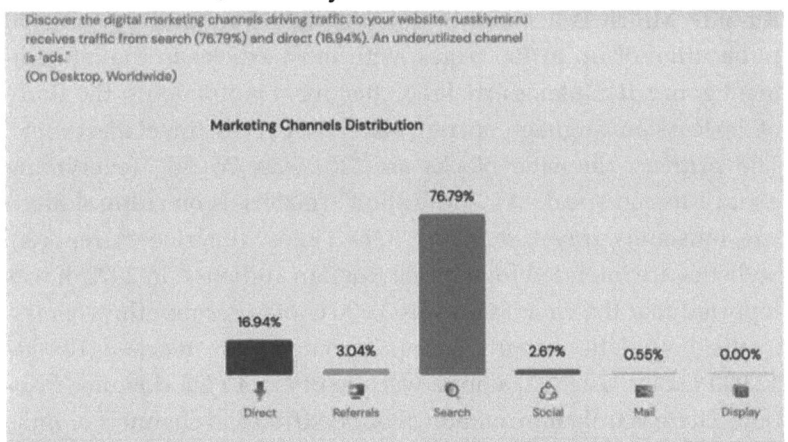

Distribution of website visitors by source (as of February 2022). *Data from SimilarWeb webpage, https://www.similarweb.com*

Figure 12. Distribution of "Russkiy Mir" website visitors by Source, March 2023

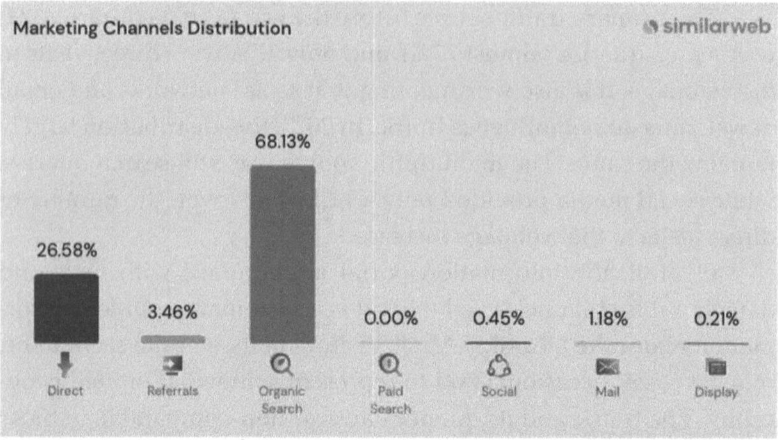
Marketing Channels Distribution
similarweb
26.58%
3.46%
68.13%
0.00%
0.45%
1.18%
0.21%
Direct
Referrals
Organic Search
Paid Search
Social
Mail
Display

Distribution of website visitors by source (as of March 2023). *Data from SimilarWeb webpage, https://www.similarweb.com*

B. Magazine "Russkiy Mir.ru" (https://rusmir.media)

Russkiy Mir.ru is a monthly illustrated cultural and educational publication of up to 100 pages, with most articles in the infotainment genre. It contains articles on historical monuments, the study of the Russian language, current historical events, travel diaries, etc. The primary thematic blocks are "Russian World" (everything about Russian speakers), "Education" (materials on cultural heritage, museums, travel, etc.), and "Our Times" (interviews, reports). Stylistics are intended for a broad Russian audience. In 2022, it was reported that the circulation was 3,000 copies per month, whereas, in the Foundation's early years, the circulation reached 10,000–12,000 copies. The magazine's website offers a PDF download option. There is little information about distribution channels or links to the publication's materials in other media.

The magazine's editor-in-chief is Georgiy Bovt, a Russian journalist, historian, political expert, and politician. He previously worked for "Izvestia" ("The News"), "Kommersant" ("The Businessman"), "Segodnya" ("Today"), "Profil" ("Profile"), and as a host of radio programmes. Although he almost does not speak publicly on behalf of the Foundation, in 2016, he was awarded the Russian government prize in the field of mass media as "the head of information and publishing—editor-in-chief of the "Russkiy Mir.ru" magazine of the "Russkiy Mir" Foundation—for promoting foreign policy on the pages of the "Rossiia v globalnoi politike" magazine" (together with pro-Kremlin expert Sergey Karaganov).[180] It also appears that Nikonov's "Politika" Foundation is the magazine's partner.

C.   *TRK (TV and radio broadcasting company) "Russkiy Mir"*
     (https://tv.russkiymir.ru/)

TRK "Russkiy Mir" produces video and audio content available via the Internet (on its website and Youtube). It does not, however, have its broadcast. TRK targets the Foundation's key Russian-speaking audiences, i.e., Russian "compatriots," emigrants, and anyone interested in the Russian language and culture. Interestingly, TRK asks the audience to provide content and invites them to become correspondents and produce videos on topics related to the "Russian world" in different countries. Main products: cultural news, educational and entertainment programmes, children's programmes, and music.

---

180 Russian Federation. Pravitelstvo Rossiiskoi Federatsii [The Government of the Russian Federation]. Rasporiazheniie [Order] #2584-p „O prisuzhdenii premii Pravitelstva Rossiiskoi Federatsii 2016 goda v oblasti sredstv massovoi informatsii" [On the Awarding of Government Prizes in the Field of Mass Media in 2016]. Adopted 3 December 2016. http://government.ru/media/files/VoQAyfOBN4lXHGFvLjPoP2HnniA1ncAd.pdf.

Table 4. Social networks of the "Russkiy Mir" Foundation

Telegram (https://t.me/russkiymirpressa)	10.7 thousand subscribers (as of April 28, 2023)	The channel's content consists partly of its productions and reposts of materials from other sources, such as RIA Novosti, TASS, the Russian Foreign Ministry, Rossotrudnichestvo, etc. Typically, several dozen subscribers will view each published article.
YouTube (https://www.youtube.com/user/russkiymir)	20.5 thousand subscribers (as of April 28, 2023)	The vast majority of materials are of a cultural or educational nature. Still, some are about current events and phenomena worldwide (for example, the "rampant Russophobia" in the West). The number of views of publications on the channel varies greatly, from several hundred to several tens of thousands.
Vkontakte (https://vk.com/club41275461)	4.2 participants (as of April 28, 2023)	Most of the page's content comes from the informational portal "Russkiy Mir." Each publication receives between 50 and 150 views, and posts receive few likes and shares. The content is updated almost daily, similar to the Foundation's other media platforms.
Twitter (https://twitter.com/fondrusskiymir)	1.5 thousand subscribers (as of April 28, 2023)	Despite the pause in publication in the spring of 2022, the page tweeted regularly a year later. Most posts copy the Foundation's news from its website, but the page does not.

Facebook (https://www.facebook.com/FondRusskiyMir/)	16 thousand subscribers (as of April 28, 2023)	It is regularly updated with shared posts from the Foundation's information portal or other online resources, which receive only a small number of likes (several dozen) and shares (just a few).
Russian Centres community on Facebook (inactive) (https://www.facebook.com/russian.centers.RMF/)	850 subscribers (as of April 28, 2023)	The page was meant to consolidate information regarding the activities of Russian Centres around the world, but the most recent posts are from the spring of 2020. Interestingly, after Russia's ban on Facebook, subscribers did not migrate significantly to permitted social media platforms (e.g., VK).
St. Petersburg branch of the "Russkiy Mir" Foundation on Facebook (https://www.facebook.com/nwbranch)	395 subscribers (as of April 28, 2023)	Posts (mostly reposts from other Foundation media) are updated extremely infrequently, a few times per month, with sometimes lengthy gaps of several months. The publications receive a small number of likes and shares.

All in all, this analysis of the "Russkiy Mir" Foundation's social media reveals that their audience engagement, overall traffic, and general importance in disseminating information about the organisation and its activities is relatively low.

3. Archaic Content in The Classical Form: The Activities of the "Russkiy Mir" Foundation

The "Russkiy Mir" Foundation uses conventional methods of cultural diplomacy in the Western tradition. It organises its offices — Centres and Cabinets — abroad, provides grants to support individual projects, manages its media (magazine, TV channel, and radio), hosts sizable events for the representatives of the "Russian world," and arranges Russian language studies abroad. The overarching idea of the "Russian world" dictates the content of the aforementioned activities.

The organisation is proud of its extensive network of representative offices, which can be found from South Korea to Nicaragua and from the United Kingdom to Jordan. The Foundation also works to expand the number of individuals learning Russian abroad, particularly in the CIS. According to published documentation by the Foundation, these two indicators are crucial for the organisation's self-evaluation of its operations.

3.1 Network of cultural representation: Centres and Cabinets of the "Russkiy Mir"

Establishing a network of Russian Centres and Cabinets of the "Russkiy Mir" Foundation in cities and towns worldwide is the core way of organising the Foundation's activities overseas. The Foundation has the authority to "create non-profit organisations, both in the Russian Federation and overseas," and "establish branches and open representative offices both in the Russian Federation and abroad,"[181] according to the statute of the Foundation,

---

181 Fond "Russkiy Mir." "Ustav Fonda 'Russkiy Mir'" [Statute of the "Russkiy Mir" Foundation]. Approved August 6, 2007, changes from March 29, 2022. http://russkiymir.ru/fund/USTAV_2022.pdf.

dated March 29th, 2022. However, in 2015, the Foundation's leadership publicly stated that "Russkiy Mir," a non-profit organisation, could not have branches abroad due to legal restrictions (Kornatskii 2015). As a result, at least in the past, local educational institutions helped open the "Russkiy Mir" Centres and Cabinets. However, the funding for the Centres and Offices was and is nearly entirely flowing from the Foundation, that is to say, from the federal budget of Russia, in contrast, to the Confucius Institute (Zhao 2020, 4). The fact that the Russian government fully funds the representative offices' operations may indicate their significance and priority. The Cabinets and Centres' stated mission is to supply local institutions with equipment, textbooks, instructional materials, direct access to Russian media, etc.

Russian Centres of the "Russkiy Mir" Foundation are well institutionalised. They are established in university Russian studies or Russian language study departments or chairs. They frequently plan contests for language competence, organise academic conferences, offer certification for language proficiency, and hold other sizable activities. In other words, the centres provide systematic data and methodological services pertaining to teaching Russian and access to the "Russian world's" cultural and historical heritage. The Centres should ideologically represent "all the diversity of the Russian world, unified by the dedication to Russian history and culture,"[182] according to the Foundation's perspective. Since they frequently have the status of a separate department or chair, the Centres of "Russkiy Mir" are typically well incorporated within the university systems. They frequently have access to all the academic benefits, including academic councils and the opportunity to defend PhD theses.

Cabinets of "Russkiy Mir"[183] are smaller organisational units that can be quickly established in libraries and civil society organisations. According to the Foundation's reasoning, installing a Cabinet is the initial step in organising a fully-fledged Centre. Cabinets

---

[182] Fond "Russkiy Mir." "Chto takoie russkiy tsentr?" [What is Russian Centre?]. n. d. https://russkiymir.ru/rucenter/.
[183] Fond "Russkiy Mir." "Kabinety Russkogo mira" [Cabinets of the Russian World]. n. d. https://russkiymir.ru/rucenter/cabinet.php.

are stocked with books according to the requirements of a particular nation. Generally, educational and fictional literature, educational equipment, manuals, and network access are provided. Historically, Cabinets outside the Russian Federation were established by non-profit organisations (educational institutions, libraries, etc.) that requested logistical or financial support from the Foundation. Currently, the Foundation has the legal authority to establish overseas representation offices per its statute.

In its public communications, the Foundation emphasises that the Cabinets and Centres of "Russkiy Mir" are distinct structures that it supports and assists but does not manage. In a 2015 interview, for instance, Vladimir Kochin stated that the organisation could not "supervise" Centres and Cabinets outside the country but could only "persuade" them. According to him, the work was organised as follows:

> "We are concluding an agreement with a local university, for instance. According to it, our partners provide a platform and Internet access, appoint personnel to ensure daily operations, and, in particular, organise Russian language classes for students and anyone else interested. We provide equipment, literature, and access to Russian media and television channels to the centre." (Kornatskii 2015)

In addition, there are examples of centres funded by foreign partners with ties to Russia. It is nearly impossible to trace any formal indications of such funding. According to DutchCulture, the actual sponsor of the Centre of "Russkiy Mir" that opened at the University of Groningen in 2010 was "Gasunie,"[184] a major Dutch partner of "Gazprom" in the "Nord Stream" project.[185]

Friendly organisations of the "Russkiy Mir" Foundation. In addition to the Centres and Cabinets serving as branches, the Foundation is responsible for liaising with Russian and foreign public, re-

---

184 DutchCulture. "Russkiy Mir Foundation." n. d. https://dutchculture.nl/en/location/russkiy-mir-foundation.
185 Gazprom. "Gazprom and Gasunie Sign Agreement on Cooperation Within Nord Stream and BBL Projects." November 6, 2007. https://web.archive.org/web/20080304135405/http://www.gazprom.com/eng/news/2007/11/25932.shtml.

ligious, educational, media, and commercial organisations "engaged in activities aimed at preserving and promoting Russian language and culture in foreign countries, as well as maintaining their 'The Whole Russian World' catalogue."[186] These organisations are also part of the "Russkiy Mir" network, but their relationship with the Foundation is less formal. As of February 2022, the Foundation's catalogue included information on approximately 3,000 such friendly organisations.[187] In May 2022, access to the Foundation's online catalogue was discontinued and is now only possible through WayBack Machine tools.

The catalogue comprises primarily non-profit organisations, associations, cultural and educational structures, local media, and digital platforms that protect the Russian language and accommodate the social and cultural needs of "compatriots" living outside Russia. Based on Kochin's interview, it can be assumed that these grassroots structures serve as local contacts for the Foundation and receive its grants, sometimes in secret, even if the host country bans the Centres (as was the case in 2014 with Ukraine, when the Centres remained only on the territory of the occupied areas of Donetsk and Luhansk regions) (Kornatskii 2015).

3.2 From the "core" to the "periphery": the geographical dimension of "Russkiy Mir"

Geographic expansion through establishing and maintaining new Centres and Cabinets is one of the most important indicators of the Foundation's effectiveness. In March 2022, the Foundation had 104 active Centres in 52 countries, 128 Cabinets in 57 countries, and over 5700 friendly organisations in nearly 160 countries (including 2700 such friendly organisations in Russia).

The key geographical clusters of the "Russkiy Mir" network that correspond to the Foundation's stated priorities are depicted in Figure 13.

---

186 Fond "Russkiy Mir." "Katalog 'Ves Russkiy Mir'" [Catalogue "Whole Russian World"]. Information portal of the "Russkiy Mir" Foundation. n. d. http://web.archive.org/web/20220808094400/https://russkiymir.ru/catalogue/.
187 Ibid.

1. The former Soviet republics account for approximately 20% of the Centres, Cabinets, and 948 friendly organisations listed in the aforementioned "Russkiy Mir" catalogue.
2. Countries with strong Orthodox Churches (Bulgaria, Belarus, Greece, Georgia, Cyprus, Montenegro, Romania, Serbia, and Ukraine) are considered religiously connected to the "Russian world." They account for the catalogue's 54 Centres and Cabinets and 699 organisations. Given the relatively small population of these countries, this number is disproportionately high, highlighting the significance of the religious factor.
3. Countries with substantial Russian-speaking minorities (Brazil, Germany, Israel, the United States, the United Kingdom, Ukraine, and Kazakhstan) account for 23 Centres and Cabinets and 781 friendly organisations in the catalogue.
4. European (EU+EFTA) and North American countries host up to 86 Centres and Cabinets and 1216 friendly organisations listed in the catalogue.[188] These high numbers can be explained not only by the presence of countries like Italy, France, or Germany, with which Russia seeks to establish economic and political ties to secure foreign policy support, but also by the inclusion of a large number of former socialist countries, Orthodox-dominated countries, and countries with substantial Russian-speaking diasporas.

---

[188] For more details about some of the representations of "Russkiy Mir" Foundation in the countries of Europe, in particular in Great Britain and Italy, see Smagliy (2018, 22–27).

Figure 13. Key geographical clusters of the "Russkiy Mir" Foundation's network (as of March 2022)

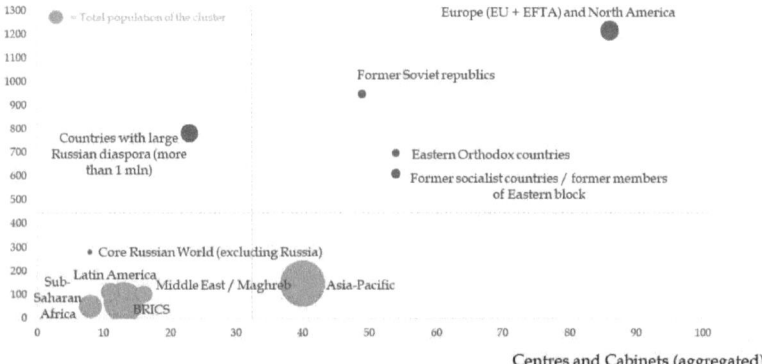

* Size of the circle corresponds to the overall population of each cluster of countries
Source: the database of the Centres, Cabinets and friendly organisations of the "Russkiy Mir" Foundation

In addition to the priority clusters listed above, the geographical representation of the "Russkiy Mir" Foundation is distinguished by a number of other essential characteristics. Using data published by the Foundation, Figure 14 illustrates the global distribution of Centres and Cabinets in various nations and regions. Additionally, Figure 15 includes friendly organisations. Table 5 evaluates the presence of the "Russkiy Mir" Foundation per one million inhabitants in every country worldwide.

Figure 14. The number of Centres and Cabinets of the "Russkiy Mir" Foundation in different countries of the world (as of March 2022)

Figure 15. The number of Centres, Cabinets, and friendly organisations of the "Russkiy Mir" Foundation in different countries of the world (as of March 2022)

Table 5. Number of Centres, Cabinets and friendly organisations of the "Russkiy Mir" Foundation per 1 million population (as of March 2022)

	Number of Centres and Cabinets per 1 million population	Number of organisations per 1 million population
Orthodox countries	0,476	6,16
Former Soviet republics	0,317	6,13
Former socialist/Eastern bloc countries	0,274	3,09
«Core» of the «Russian World» (excluding Russia)	0,150	5,30
Europe (EU + EFTA) and Northern America	0,107	1,51
Countries with a sizeable Russian diaspora (over 1 million)	0,033	1,12
Middle East and Maghreb	0,030	0,19
Latin America	0,018	0,18
Asia-Pacific	0,010	0,03
Sub-Saharan Africa	0,008	0,05
BRICS	0,004	0,02

Source: the database of the Centres, Cabinets, and friendly organisations of the "Russkiy Mir" Foundation obtained from the Foundation's website in March 2022

In general, the geographical distribution of the network of Cabinets and Centres of the Russian World and "Russkiy Mir"-friendly organisations corresponds to the Foundation's stated priorities and its interpretation of the "Russian World" concept. "Russkiy Mir" is well-represented in countries formerly a part of the Soviet Union or Eastern bloc and where Orthodox Christianity is the dominant religion. Numerous "Russkiy Mir"-supporting organisations can be found in nations with sizable Russian diasporas. Other countries, particularly in the Global South, have a relatively small number of Centres, Cabinets, and friendly organisations (but at least one such organisation can be found in every country in these regions).

Nonetheless, there are notable and significant deviations from the general tendency. Bulgaria, for instance, stands out in terms of the number of Centres and Cabinets. Not only is this country dominated by the Orthodox Church, but it was also a member of the socialist camp in the past. Due to linguistic similarity and regional peculiarities in international relations, it also has longstanding bilateral ties with Russia. Therefore, Bulgaria has a solid foundation for expanding the activities of the "Russkiy Mir" Foundation. Since Moscow has historically regarded Moldova as part of its sphere of influence, Moldova is another priority of the "Russkiy Mir." Among Western nations, the United States and Germany (to a lesser extent, Spain, Italy, and France) have the highest priority, and this is due to a combination of factors, including the presence of large Russian-speaking diasporas and political considerations in the case of EU nations.

Russia's foreign policy priorities are reflected in the Fund's active presence in China and Turkey, outside the Fund's typical geographic scope. Against a backdrop of increasingly strained relations with the West, Russia has sought to establish ties with these countries over the past decade. The case of Ukraine is explained by the fact that although the Centres and Cabinets were closed in it after 2014 and therefore continued to function only in the temporarily occupied territories of the Donetsk and Lugansk regions, the Catalogue of Friendly Organisations of the Foundation still lists 234 organisations promoting the "Russian world" on the territory of Ukraine. Only 111 of these organisations operate on government-controlled territory in Ukraine.[189] In terms of the density of organi-

---

[189] The "Russkiy Mir" Foundation ensures its presence on Russian-occupied territory and in unrecognised pseudo-republics supported by Russia. Thus, as of the spring of 2022, six centres and nine cabinets of "Russkiy Mir" were located in these territories: the temporarily occupied areas of the Donetsk and Luhansk regions in Ukraine, Transnistria in Moldova, and South Ossetia in Georgia. The Centre on V. Putin Street in Tskhinvali, the "capital" of self-proclaimed South Ossetia, is exemplary.

sations per 1 million inhabitants, the Baltic states stand out significantly (up to 93 organisations per 1 million people), which is primarily attributable to the extremely high proportion of Russians or Russian speakers (for example, up to a third of the entire population in Latvia). Meanwhile, the number of "Russkiy Mir" organisations in other countries is relatively low, indicating that the Fund may not have the resources to ensure its pervasive presence.

The second map illustrates how the "Russian World" is attempting to expand its geographic presence by partnering with organisations in the Global South. Significantly, the Foundation's presence on the African continent is practically non-institutionalized because, despite having friendly organisations in almost every African country (Figure 15), this presence is not confirmed by the "Russkiy Mir" network of Cabinets and Centres (Figure 14). Presumably lacking the resources to establish Cabinets and Centres in every country, it creates ties with a small number of partner organisations in each. This geographical trend may indicate the "Russian World's" desire to expand its influence in this region. As a result of the Foundation's limited activities in Western countries, African participation and attention will become increasingly important. Despite the Foundation's apparent global reach, the number of organisations in each country, except for those with the highest priority, is negligible concerning the population.

In conclusion, it is necessary to explain certain discrepancies between the actual geography and density of the Foundation's network presence and its declared work directions in Aleksey Gromyko's view. The assumption is that the original plans were modified as the organisation evolved (Gromyko's work was published in 2010) due to the shifting priorities of the Russian government, which is the Fund's primary client, and considering the opportunities available in different countries.

Establishing Cabinets and Centres of the "Russkiy Mir" Foundation in foreign countries differs from establishing branches of other Russian cultural diplomacy institutions. First, the Foundation's activities target individuals interested in learning Russian. While Rossotrudnichestvo almost always opens representative offices in the capitals of other nations, "Russkiy Mir" has "more room for manoeuvre": "[we] can work in remote regions of the country...> [our centres are] where there is an interest of local citizens, where there is their initiative and desire to study Russian, to teach it to their children" (Kornatskii 2015). These organisations complement one another in this way.

In 2022, 65 out of 104 active Centres and 83 out of 128 functional Cabinets (over sixty per cent) were located outside capital cities. This peculiarity of the Foundation's policy, which aims to be less visible in major metropolitan areas and academic hubs, is also noted by other researchers (Popovic, Jenne, and Medzihorsky 2020). If the Foundation's activities are not perceived favourably by host countries, it is believed that a low-profile presence will result in less resistance or public aggression.

By April 2023, the Foundation's Centres' presence on the world map had changed remarkably. The Foundation's website declared that only 82 Centres were functioning, as 23 had to be closed (see the table below). Only one new centre, based on the former Foundation's Cabinet at Luhansk university, opened. This wave of shutdowns occurred despite the immense number of reports about the Foundation's activity and its drastically increased funding. The geographic distribution of the closed Centres is rather predictable. It includes predominantly Western Europe (Austria, Netherlands, Spain, the United Kingdom), Eastern Europe and former Soviet Union republics (Bulgaria, the Czech Republic, Georgia, Estonia, Latvia, Poland), Japan, and the US.

Table 6. Russian Centres that were closed down after the Russian full-scale invasion of Ukraine

Russian Centre of the University of Salzburg	Austria
Russian Centre of the University of Innsbruck	Austria
Russian Centre of the University of Buenos Aires	Argentina
Russian Centre at the health and recreation complex "Kamchia"	Bulgaria
Russian Centre of the Municipal Cultural Institute "Metropolitan Library"	Bulgaria
Russian Centre of the University of Durham	United Kingdom

Russian Centre at the Russian-British Cultural Centre "Pushkin House"	United Kingdom
Russian Centre of the University of Edinburgh	United Kingdom
Centre of the Russian Language in Tbilisi "Azbuka"	Georgia
Russian Centre of the University of Guayaquil	Ecuador
Centre of the Russian Language at the Pushkin Institute	Estonia
Russian Centre of the "Russian House in Barcelona" Cultural Foundation	Spain
Russian Centre of the University of Daugavpils	Latvia
Russian Centre of the Baltic International Academy	Latvia
Russian Centre of the University of Groningen	Netherlands
Russian Centre of the University of Wrocław	Poland
Russian Centre of the Maria Curie-Skłodowska University	Poland
Russian Centre of the Municipal Public Library named after Maria Dąbrowska	Poland
Russian Centre of American Councils for International Education	USA
Russian Centre Bilingual Programs and Research Corp.	USA
Russian Centre of the Masaryk University	Czech Republic
Russian Centre of the University of West Bohemia	Czech Republic
Russian Centre of the Far Eastern Federal University Branch Campus in Hakodate	Japan

* The list was compiled by comparing the Russian Centre and Cabinets database obtained in March 2022 to the one on the Foundation's website in mid-April 2023. Therefore, the table does not represent any changes after April 2023.

Compared to the beginning of 2022, the number of Cabinets had almost not changed by the spring of 2023 and reached 126 active units. Only two Cabinets were closed down (in Argentina and in Poland), one was upgraded to a Centre (Luhansk), and one more was opened in Tajikistan.

3.3 All the money from "Russkiy Mir": distribution of grants by the Foundation

A significant portion of the Foundation's resources is devoted to supporting projects of non-governmental organisations, professional associations, academic and educational institutions, and the media through the provision of grants. According to the Foundation, these projects relate to two primary directions:

- Projects to promote the use and study of Russian (organisation of Russian language training, support for Russian-language schools abroad, preparation of methodological materials, competitions, and contests)
- Humanitarian and cultural projects (events dedicated to Russian culture and history, historical memory preservation, Russian-language media support, thematic festivals, and holidays).

In 2023, the webpage about the Fund's grants featured information about the priority of grant distribution for the representatives of the Commonwealth of Independent States, Shanghai Cooperation Organization, BRICS, Africa, Latin America, Asia, and the Middle East. This geographical orientation underlines once again Russian cultural diplomacy's big turn (at least as declared) towards the "seven billion people" who are not representing the "privileged West."[190]

Twice a year, grant applications are accepted. However, no official statistics or publicly available information regarding grant funding amounts exist. The actual amounts of grant funding are unknown. Still, comments from the Foundation's leaders about the need to increase funding and independent evaluations expressing doubts about the effectiveness of using these funds can be found in the media (Dmitriieva 2015). The official reports include information on the number of applications and grants awarded (see

---

190 Fond "Russkiy Mir." "Vyacheslav Nikonov: Idyot stolknovenie dvukh mirov za bushchee planety" [Vyacheslav Nikonov: There Is a Clash of Two Worlds for the Future of the Planet]. April 5, 2022. https://russkiymir.ru/news/299605/?sphrase_id=1230901.

chart below), but this data is inaccurate and contradicts other information from the Foundation.

No publicly available official information about the allocated grants is presented in the form of formal reports. The Fund talks about the grantees' activities only implicitly, the information is dosed as separate pieces of news, and it is rather challenging to build up a larger representation out of them. The striking rise of funding in 2022 again stresses the Fund's lack of transparency.

Figure 16. Annual amounts of funds allocated as grants by the "Russkiy Mir" Foundation, 2016-2020

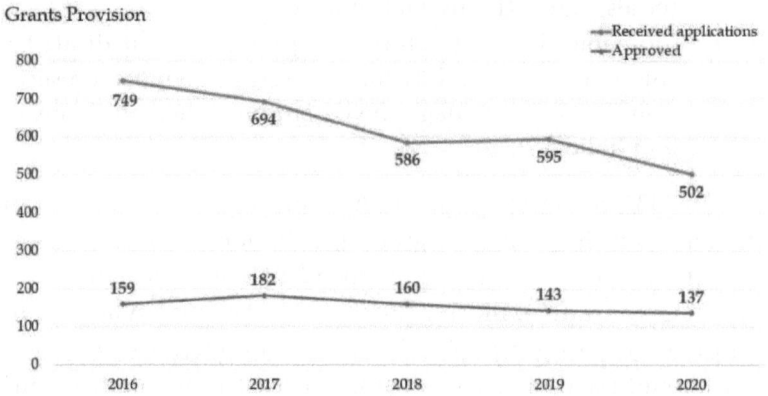

Source: annual reports of the "Russkiy Mir" Foundation, https://russkiymir.ru/fund/reports.php

According to this graph, approximately 25% of all grant applications are approved annually. However, according to executive director Kochin, only one in ten applications received grants in 2015 due to a lack of funds (Kornatskii 2015). Counting the number of approved grant applications for the most recent grant cycle (September 2021) yields a nearly identical result: 300 evaluated applications accounted for 38 approvals or approximately 13 per cent.[191]

---

[191] Fond "Russkiy Mir." "Proekty" [Projects]. n. d. https://russkiymir.ru/grants/proekt.php.

In addition, the information in the reports regarding the distribution of grants between organisations from the Russian Federation and other countries does not correspond to the website statistics. In the Foundation's official reports for 2016–2020, grants to Russian organisations account for one-third of all approved applications, ranging from 24 to 38 per cent annually. Analysis of the above-mentioned 300 applications submitted in September 2021 reveals that at least 22 of the 38 approved applications originated from Russian organisations (i.e., 58 per cent). This is considerably more than what official statistics indicate.

In 2016–2020, grants were distributed roughly equally between the "Promotion of the Russian Language" and "Cultural and Humanitarian Themes" categories (see Table 7). Nonetheless, the information regarding the number of projects in both directions over the past two years does not match the total number of projects. Inaccuracies in the statistics are probably not fatal, but they indicate that the Foundation's official information on its activities is not transparent.

Table 7. Distribution of grants provided by the "Russkiy Mir" Foundation by areas of activity

	2016	2017	2018	2019	2020	Total
Promotion of the Russian language	83	74	71	65	36	329 (45%)
Cultural and humanitarian projects	76	108	89	85	42	400 (55%)
Total	159	182	160	150	78	729 (100%)
Number of grants in the reports for 2016-2020	159	182	160	143	137	781
Difference	0	0	0	-7	59	52

Source: annual reports of the "Russkiy Mir" Foundation, https://russkiymir.ru/fund/reports.php.

3.4 Protecting linguistic and geopolitical supremacy: projects supported by the "Russkiy Mir" Foundation

In its annual reports, the "Russkiy Mir" Foundation details events, including those organised by other organisations with the Foundation's financial assistance. This information can be found on the

"Russkiy Mir" website, specifically in the catalogue of grant applications and photo reports on the implementation of these grants. The Foundation's grant funding supports several different areas on a thematic level.

1. *Projects promoting the study of the Russian language worldwide* are central to the Foundation's stated objectives. The Russian language competitions in Italy and Spain, the All-Russian Olympiad in Russian as a foreign language, the conference "We Will Preserve You, Russian Language!," the project "Russian Language in the Republic of Kazakhstan," the International Week of the Russian language in Sochi, and the Day of the Russian language in Colombo, Sri Lanka, as well as the event "We Speak Russian" in Tuva (a Siberian city in the Russian Federation), are examples of such projects that have taken place in recent years. According to Foundation reports, it is unclear what percentage of participants were foreign nationals, in other words, neither Russian immigrants nor people of Russian descent.
2. *Support for and promotion of Russian culture abroad* (literature, dance, music, theatre, etc.) Examples include the textbook "Russian Literature at the Lesson" (Austria), "Anthology of Short Prose of the Silver Age of Russian Literature" (China), theatrical musical performances (Portugal), New Year's performances for children (Ankara, Turkey), a tour of the Slavic studies students choir (Serbia), the festival "Tchaikovsky Is the Soul of Russia" (Mexico), the international festival of Russian romance "European Romansiada" (Hamburg, Germany), the Russian film festival "Russian Resurrection" (Australia), the festival-competition "Balkan Romansiada."
3. *Projects focused on the Russian understanding of the Second World War and the Soviet experience.* Professional literature describes in detail the centrality of the victory of the USSR in World War II and the postwar redistribution of areas of influence in the world and Europe to the ideology of the "Russian world" (see, for instance, Malinova 2017 and

Mann 2020). Since at least a decade ago, the Russian government has used "anti-fascism" language in its propaganda to mobilize the populace. The "Russkiy Mir" Foundation and its grant funding contributed to maintaining such tales in Russia and abroad. Thus, among the submitted and supported projects are a book on the "liberation of Belgrade from the fascists" (as of spring 2022, the application was being reviewed), a congress of scouting forces, "Guerrilla Glory," commemorating the anniversary of victory in the "Great Patriotic War," or "Restored military monuments in the Republic of Moldova" (the project was supported), as well as a youth camp under the auspices of the Communist Party of the Russian Federation in (2020). By the way, the camp was loaded with Soviet emblems and aspects of Soviet mythology: it was named "Molodaya Gvardiya" ("Young Guard") in honour of the Soviet underground organisation of the same name that operated in Ukraine during World War II. Participants attended a series of lectures by Russian academics on Russia's national interests, "the West's" "distortion" of Russia's history, and "Russia, Ukraine, Belorussia—the History of Divided Rus."[192]

3.5 Educational dimension: professors and students of "Russkiy Mir"

As the Russian language and literature are the principal instruments for spreading the "Russian world," it is only natural that the "Russkiy Mir" Foundation supports investments in education professionals. For this purpose, it organises and finances several programmes to unify the pedagogical community of Russian teachers

---

[192] NB: The event's organisers referred to Belarus by its traditional Russian name, "Belorussia." The use of the name "Belorussia," as well as "Moldavia" in relation to Moldova, "Kirghizia" in relation to Kyrgyzstan, and "Pribaltika" in relation to the Baltic States refers to the imperial tradition in Russian word usage and is perceived negatively by Russia's neighbours, especially in the light of its aggressive actions.

and educators and ensure their presence abroad to develop personal ties and spread the "Russian world" from Albania to Uruguay. Among these programmes are:

- The annual international pedagogical forum of "Russkiy Mir," where, according to the idea of the organizers, experts should discuss current aspects of teaching Russian and literature, ways to transfer Russia's cultural heritage to future generations, and practices for the pedagogical community to make consolidated decisions in teaching Russian, literature, and culture. At least eight forums have been held to date (the last forum took place online in December 2020). According to the Foundation's annual report, more than 600 people participated in this event in 2020, including representatives from thirty foreign countries and thirty regions of the Russian Federation. The platform unites the pedagogical community of Russianists in Russia and the rest of the world.
- Since 2018, *the "Professor of the Russian World" programme* has been in operation. The purpose of the initiative is to coordinate and promote the international travel of Russian educators, primarily to enhance the teaching of Russian in local educational institutions. According to information available to the public, a professor from Smolensk State University visited the Schottengymnasium in Vienna in 2019. Students participated in a series of Russian language classes taught by the professor. According to public information, the visit of Olga Sinyova, an associate professor of the linguistics department at Moscow State University, to Albania was extremely fruitful: the professor participated in Pushkin's readings and delivered at least 250 academic hours of lectures, seminars, and workshops.[193]
- *The "Student of the Russian World" programme* allows foreign students, notably those studying philology, history, and

---

[193] Obshchestvo rossiiskikh sootechestvennikov Albanii [Community of Russian Compatriots of Albania]. "Professor Russkogo mira v Albanii" [Professor of the Russian world in Albania]. August 7, 2019. http://rusobsina.al/профессор-русского-мира-в-албании/.

politics, to complete internships at Russian universities. However, the program's stated objective is to improve the motivation of overseas students to study Russian. Most of this program's efforts aim to promote studying the Russian language and literature in the Ukrainian territories of Donetsk and Luhansk, temporarily occupied by Russia.[194] For instance, in 2019, the municipality of Kolomna (Moscow region) hosted a ten-day school for students from these unrecognised "republics." According to the "Donetsk People's Republic" "Ministry of Education," similar summer schools for children from occupied Donetsk and Luhansk are periodically hosted in Russia.[195] According to the school's organisers, one of the purposes of such summer schools is to create bilateral ties with young people from the occupied regions and to mobilise them for the "Russian world."[196] However, the programme's geographic scope is not confined to the targeted bounds of Russia's "sphere of influence." At least in 2014, British interns at St. Petersburg State University participated in the course.[197]

Lastly, the Foundation supports the international competition of pedagogical talents "Kristalnaya chernilnitsa" ("Crystal Inkwell") and conferences of MAPRYAL, the International Association of Teachers of Russian Language and Literature. In general, the Foundation's own or supported activities focus on traditional and

---

194 Komsomolskaiia Pravda. "Letniie shkoly dlia studentov Russkogo mira" [Summer Schools for the Students of the Russian World]. August 1, 2019. https://www.kp.ru/daily/27010/4072275/.
195 Fond "Russkiy Mir." "V fonde 'Russkiy mir' proshla vstrecha s prepodavateliami Donetskogo natsionalnogo universiteta" [A Meeting with the Professors from Donetsk National University Was Held at the "Russkiy Mir" Foundation in Moscow]. September 29, 2021. https://russkiymir.ru/news/292813/.
196 "Novorossiia." "Sergei Panteleiev: Preodoleniie ukrainskikh raskolov — v mirovozzrenii russkogo edinstva" [Sergei Panteleev: Overcoming Ukrainian Splits Is in the Worldview of Russian Unity]. September 4, 2019. https://novorosin form.org/sergej-panteleevya-preodolenie-ukrainskih-raskolov-yayayayaya-v-mirovozzrenii-russkogo-edinstva-35002.html.
197 Fond "Russkiy Mir." "Studenty luchshikh vuzov Velikobritanii izuchaiut russkiy iazyk v SPbGU" [Students from the best universities in the UK study Russian at St Petersburg State University]. n. d. http://russkiymir.ru/fund/projects/student/155229/.

repetitive components of Russian culture, such as Pushkin, Dostoevsky, or Tchaikovsky; Russian folk costumes; militaristic themes from World War II; or direct imperial propaganda about "union" or "friendship." It seeks to consolidate Russia's dominance in regions it considers part of the "Russian world" or its spheres of influence.

3.6 Celebrations of unity: "Russkiy Mir" assemblies

The culmination of the celebration of the unity of the "Russian world" is the yearly grandiose Assemblies of "Russkiy Mir," which the Foundation itself refers to in its annual reports as the most important event of the year. The reporting materials of the Foundation always start with the outcomes of the most recent Assembly. The Assembly is traditionally held around the start of November, on the eve of the Day of National Unity in Russia, which was established as a national holiday following the reappropriation of Russia's imperial legacy.[198] They occurred from 2007 to 2020, and in 2021 it was planned offline, but it was cancelled owing to COVID-19 restrictions issued in late October (in 2020, due to the pandemic, the event was held online).[199]

The purpose of the assemblies is to summarise the Foundation's work. The presence of the Foundation's ideological sponsors among Russia's political elites also implies government support. During the concurrent panel discussions, participants would also share their experiences promoting the Russian language and cul-

---

[198] The celebration of the Day of National Unity in Russia was launched in 2004 to commemorate the liberation of Moscow from Polish intervention in 1612; these events have become a precondition for the end of a period of crisis and turmoil, known in Russian historiography as the "Time of Troubles." The Day of National Unity was intended to replace the celebration of the greatest holiday of the communist period, the day of the anniversary of the October Revolution. The celebration of the Day has apparently become a marker of belonging to the "Russian world": it is also celebrated in the self-proclaimed South Ossetia, "Donetsk-" and "Luhansk People's Republics," and Transnistria.

[199] Fond "Russkiy Mir." "XV Assambleiia Russkogo mira" [15th Assembly of "Russkiy Mir"]. n. d. https://web.archive.org/web/20211104114801/https://15assamb.russkiymir.ru/.

ture internationally. The Assembly is a gathering place for "compatriots" and all those who share the "Russkiy Mir" ideas and values.

As a rule, assemblies begin with a lavish opening ceremony, during which participants listen to an introduction by Vladimir Putin, who is not present in person, and greetings from several high-ranking officials. Typically, representatives of the presidential administration are present, and occasionally, other notable guests, such as Patriarch Kirill of the Russian Orthodox Church, attend. Several panel discussions, led by the Foundation's administration, and a "cultural programme" are held during the event. For instance, a video tour of the areas where Fyodor Dostoevsky lived and worked in St. Petersburg was scheduled for 2020. Participating in these debates are members of the Russian government, hierarchs of the Russian Orthodox Church, and representatives of the "Russian world" from around the world, especially academics from international universities.[200]

Conclusions

The "Russkiy Mir" Foundation was the first in a series of newly founded or restructured public and cultural diplomacy organisations intended to promote the revanchist goal of rectifying the consequences of the collapse of the Soviet Union. It used the vague conservative "Russkiy Mir" ideology to be promoted in the "near abroad" countries to gather them back culturally and politically. The definition of the "Russian world" is expansive and emphatically expansionist, even global: in the view of its ideologues, it is a kind of civilization that appears to encompass, with concentric circles of varying intensity, all people who are at least in some way related to the Russian language and culture, these relations ranging from the fact of birth in the Russian hinterland to accidental interest in some

---

200 Sochinskii institut Rossiiskogo universiteta druzhby narodov [Sochi Institute of Patrice Lumumba Peoples' Friendship University of Russia]. "Assambleiia Russkogo mira" [Assembly of the Russian World]. n. d. https://www.rudn-sochi.ru/центр-тестирования/44-анонсы/1434-ассамблея-русского-мира.

Russian cultural phenomenon. Such an understanding of the "Russian world" would necessitate the most open and contemporary discourse and cultural interchange, multidisciplinarity, and openness to the perspectives and values of the Other. Instead, the "Russian world" is founded on a relatively narrow, essentialist, and archaic interpretation of Russian culture centred on linguistic and religious unity principles, an archaic communality, and unwavering submission to power and fate.

In contrast to Western institutions of cultural diplomacy, which attract more and more adherents of their cultures through academic opportunities, language learning, and creating an appealing image, Russian cultural diplomacy is more focused on uniting the base of supporters, relying on the dispersed diaspora of ethnic Russians and "Russian-speakers" (often Russified members of other ethnic groups). Such "cementing" rarely affords the possibility of genuine debate or interaction on an equal footing with representatives of different cultures. Russian cultural diplomacy presents its own cultural and geopolitical paradigms of the "Russian world" in foreign countries. Under these conditions, it is unsurprising that inexpensive popular images of bears, kokoshniks, and balalaikas accompany the opening of Russian film festivals or illustrate the release of a very recent phenomenon of small prose from the Russian Silver Age translated into Chinese.

Horizontally, the Foundation is one of the primary nodes of the state-controlled ecosystem of organisations devoted to expanding Russia's influence abroad, including Rossotrudnichestvo, the Gorchakov Fund, universities and their departments, research centres and think tanks, smaller oligarchic foundations, state-supported NGOs, state-focused media, etc. Their leadership, members and common propagandists serve on one another's supervisory, trustee, and executive boards, collaborate on numerous joint projects, post on each other's websites, and coordinate activities in general. The direct inheritance of contemporary Russian elites over Soviet elites caps this system.[201] In the principal institutions of cultural

---

201 According to Snegovaya and Petrov (2022), a prominent feature of the Russian political regime after the 1990s is the fact that, as of 2020, 60 percent of the highest political leadership of Russia consisted of individuals from the old Soviet

diplomacy in Russia, descendants of the communist *nomenklatura* occupy crucial responsibilities. Thus, Vyacheslav Nikonov, grandson of the infamous Stalin's closest collaborator Vyacheslav Molotov, and Alexey Gromyko, grandson of the renowned Soviet foreign minister Andrey Gromyko, have exerted a considerable impact on "Russkiy Mir" since the organisation's inception.

Given its role and composition, it is not surprising that since the beginning of the war against Ukraine in 2014, and especially after the start of its most aggressive phase in 2022, the "Russkiy Mir" Foundation and its speakers have supported, disseminated, and possibly even created key narratives of Russian propaganda. In addition, a significant portion of their own "news of the Russian world" of the war period on the foundation's website concerns accelerated Russification in the occupied territories of Ukraine, where Ukrainian textbooks are burned, schools switch to Russian curricula, billboards about Russia's history are installed, and forced deportations are facilitated.

---

nomenclature (the other 40 percent are people from law enforcement agencies, the so-called "siloviki").

First Roubles, Then Guns
The Alexander Gorchakov Public Diplomacy Fund

Denys Tereshchenko, Nadiia Koval

1. In the Name of Chancellor Gorchakov: Russia Collecting Itself

> And he alone continued the brave battle, the unequal battle with Europe.
> —Fyodor Tyutchev, *For the Jubilee of Prince Alexander Gorchakov*

The Alexander Gorchakov Public Diplomacy Fund, founded in 2010, is the latest of the series of institutions created by the Russian regime to reassert Russian positions internationally with a combination of threat and effective deployment of military force (as witnessed already during the Russo-Georgian War of 2008). It is only marginally involved in cultural diplomacy proper. Still, taking into account the integrated nature of Russian humanitarian policy in general and the Fund's main aims of promoting Russian foreign policy goals directly, the Gorchakov Fund exemplifies a significant institutional and ideological pillar of new Russian revisionism and expansionism that has driven the Russian regime's military and propagandist adventures in its neighbourhood for several decades already. The Fund's primary target audience is the youth, and more specifically, young experts in the countries of specific interest to Russia, predominantly from the former Soviet states, which demonstrates an aim to create an intellectual environment that will be most conducive to further Russian policies intended to keep the respective countries within Russia's sphere of influence.

The choice of Gorchakov as a "patron" of the Fund is in no way coincidental. The figure of Alexander Gorchakov, imperial Russia's 19th-century foreign minister and "the last chancellor," has gained popularity among Russian international relations professionals since the early 2000s, in the wake of a rethinking of the Russian Empire's historical heritage and under the sway of the former Minister of Foreign Affairs and Prime Minister Yevgeny Primakov, Sr. (Braun 2009, 10). Since then, the regime has espoused Gorchakov and his doctrine multiple times. It was during Primakov's tenure as Russia's Minister for Foreign Affairs that the A. M. Gorchakov's commemorative medal was introduced (1997). The inauguration of the medal was dedicated to the 200th anniversary of Gorchakov himself. The medal was meant to dignify "Russian nationals and foreigners in recognition of their merits in the consolidation of peace and the promotion of international cooperation and universal ideals and humanitarian values, as well as for their accomplishments in diplomatic activity."[202] By 2008, the people awarded this highly prestigious medal included the first Russian President Boris Yeltsin, second President Vladimir Putin, Primakov himself, UN Secretary-General Kofi Annan, and Patriarch Alexy II of Moscow. The tradition of honouring the memory of Gorchakov remained after Primakov left his office. In 2012, Putin referred to Gorchakov's famous formula of "collecting oneself" in the title of his pre-election article, "Russia is collecting itself — challenges that have to be addressed" (Putin 2012). In 2014, as Russia was clearly on its path from collecting itself to aggressive reassertion, specifically in the Ukrainian Crimea, Sergei Lavrov helped unveil a monument to Gorchakov at MGIMO, Moscow State Institute of International Relations. During the event, Lavrov stressed again that it was "Gorchakov who laid down the principles of Russia's foreign policy, which this country is also following today."[203]

---

202 Ministry of Foreign Affairs of the Russian Federation. n. d. "Pamiatnaia medal A. M. Gorchakova." [Memorable medal of A. M. Gorchakov]. https://web.archive.org/web/20080403032207/http://www.mid.ru/nsite-sv.nsf/b3d4f4566a00e34343256cc4003a99fd/ee690ec3abfd889e43256cc5003ec0a1?OpenDocument (Accessed via WayBack Machine as of April 3, 2008).
203 Vesti. 2014. "Lavrov otkryl pamiatnik Gorchakovu vo vnutrennem dvore MGIMO" [Lavrov unveiled the monument to Gorchakov in the inner courtyard of MGIMO]. October 14, 2014. https://www.vesti.ru/article/1809320.

This appropriation of Gorchakov's legacy by the Russian elites can be explained by the fact that they found striking parallels between the context in which Gorchakov put forward his foreign policy concepts and the foreign policy challenges faced by Russia after the collapse of the Soviet Union (Splidsboel-Hansen 2002). Alexander Gorchakov became Minister of Foreign Affairs of the Russian Empire in 1856, immediately after Russia's humiliating defeat in the Crimean War and the signing of the Peace Treaty of Paris imposed by the Western powers. Under the Treaty's terms, Russia was losing influence in the Black Sea region and European affairs in general, which was a severe humiliation to Russia, which had just several decades ago become one of the most important European powers after its prominent role in the Napoleonic Wars concluded with the Vienna Congress. However, another major blow to its prestige was the forced disposal of the right to keep warships and arsenals in the Black Sea. After assuming the office, Gorchakov proposed a seemingly moderate but eventually revanchist foreign policy doctrine, summarised in one of his most cited quotations: "Russia is not sulking, Russia is collecting itself" (*La Russie ne boude pas. La Russie se recueille* as the original diplomatic dispatch, written in French, put it) (Splidsboel-Hansen 2002, 378–380).

"Collecting oneself" in the doctrine of Gorchakovism meant Russia's need for internal reforms to get prepared to demand a revision of the regional "security architecture" as soon as its restored power allows it. After the Crimean defeat, the Russian government realised that one of its most important causes was the economic backwardness that caused the Russian imperial army's inferiority on the battlefield and logistics. Overcoming Russia's international humiliation required modernization, which was coming around as Alexander II commenced necessary reforms in several key areas. Another vital aspect of Gorchakovism was the need to reduce the perception of a threat from Russia among other great powers (Splidsboel-Hansen 2002, 381). All of this became Russian official policy under Alexander II and Gorchakov. In the end, as early as 1870, Gorchakov oversaw the unilateral withdrawal from the post-

Crimean Treaty of Paris, which meant prospects for the remilitarization of the Black Sea and was subsequently so much appraised by Russian diplomat-cum-poet Fyodor Tyutchev.[204]

This success story resonated well with what some Russian elites felt and aspired to in the 1990s, after their former imperial project, the Soviet Union and, in Europe, the Warsaw Pact block, collapsed. Feeling humiliated as the U.S. was asserting itself as the only global power, especially after NATO interventions in the Balkans, Russian foreign policy circles employed the semantic framework of Gorchakovism to both reform and "collect itself" before reasserting their ambitious claims concerning the critical security questions. As mentioned, Russian foreign minister and eventually prime minister Yevgeny Primakov Sr. actively promoted the reappropriation of the Gorchakov doctrine for the post-Soviet Russian Federation (Skak 2016, 332). Primakov's tenure in office is closely associated with the famous episode in 1999 when he, after receiving the news that NATO was planning an airstrike operation in Serbia, ordered his plane to turn around over the Atlantic Ocean during the flight to the U.S., thus cancelling the planned official visit. It was also Primakov who put forward what can be called the Primakov doctrine, i.e., a set of foreign policy principles that emblematized Russia's turnaround from its attempts to integrate into Western international institutions unconditionally and to assert Russia's claim to parity among the "great powers" instead. Summed up, the doctrine can be laid out as the combination of the following mutually reinforcing principles:

1. The inevitable multipolarity in the world with outright denial of the right of the U.S. to assert the "global policeman" role. This seems to be one of the fundamental concerns of the Russian leadership, which also taps well into the grievances about American hegemony and "neo-colonialism" in the countries of the Global South.
2. Reaching the balance of power among the largest countries in the world, such as the U.S., Russia, India, and China.

---

[204] Tyutchev, Fyodor. "Kniaziu Gorchakovu" [To Prince Gorchakov]. *Kultura.rf*. https://www.culture.ru/poems/45808/knyazyu-gorchakovu.

3. This, in turn, leads to Russia's reorientation to the East as it strives to establish better relations with China and India as opposed to European and North American countries. This tendency proved even more remarkable after February 24, 2022.
4. As a would-be great power, Russia and its leadership struggled to remain a veto-player, keeping a critical voice on the crucial questions of international politics, which, according to this doctrine, should not and cannot be resolved without Russian input.
5. Multipolarity and Russia's desired great power status should also mean that Moscow retains exclusive rights to its "sphere of interest," which is first and foremost considered to be the countries of the former Soviet Union (FSU). While the foundation of the Commonwealth of Independent States was an early attempt to "earmark" this area for future Russian operations, this later developed into the doctrine of Eurasian integration embodied in the Union State of Russia and Belarus and the Eurasian Economic Union under Putin. Russia's sensitivity to the developments in the FSU countries is still visible, apart from the obvious examples of Ukraine and Belarus, through its numerous activities in Moldova, Georgia, Armenia, and Central Asia.
6. The last but not least pillar of the Primakov doctrine is the policy of deterring the West, as embodied in the attempts to prevent further NATO expansion and weaken transatlantic unity and liberal order, among other things, through the support of favourable political parties in European countries.[205]

The figure of Yevgeny Primakov himself became an emblematic one for this turn in Russian foreign policy and Russia's increasing assertiveness in the international arena and came to be officially endorsed by Putin himself. It is no surprise that the state-controlled TV channel Rossiya 1 produced a movie to mark Primakov's 85th anniversary in 2014, already after the Russian occupation of Crimea

---

[205] For an analysis of Yevgeny Primakov's influence on Russia's foreign policy from the late 1990s, please see Skak 2016.

(Brilyov 2014; for Putin's comment on Primakov, see minutes 48 to 50). After Primakov died in 2015, the Institute of World Economy and International Relations (IMEMO) organised a yearly international summit, *The Primakov Readings*, held in Moscow and dedicated to international security issues envisioned by Russian *mezhdunarodniki*.

It was not long before the Russian government began implementing the Primakov doctrine. Throughout the 2000s, but especially after Putin's 2007 Munich speech, Russia increasingly demanded a comprehensive review of the world order to negotiate a "new inclusive security architecture" while developing special bilateral political and economic relations with some Western countries, especially France and Germany. This was accompanied by attempts to split the transatlantic unity between the U.S. and the EU by actively supporting the idea of European strategic autonomy from the U.S. in its security and defence policies. Promoting these and related discourses has been at the heart of Putin's public diplomacy when working with Western political leaders, prominent researchers and analysts, and the youth who wanted to join those circles. The choice of Gorchakov as a patron for an organisation that should guide and fund this policy was quite logical.

As in the second half of the nineteenth century, Russian baculine arguments favouring a new revanchist order soon acquired a practical dimension with the Russo-Georgian war, the occupation of Ukrainian Crimea, the start of the war in the Donbas, and now the full-scale war against Ukraine (Splidsboel-Hansen 2002, 384). Notably, the instrumental adoption of the doctrine of "concentration" was de facto admitted by the Russian authorities. As early as 2009, Russia's long-time foreign minister Sergei Lavrov, as cited by Skak, claimed that "the chief conclusion which we draw for ourselves about the outcome of 2008 is that Russia completed the era of 'concentration'" (Skak 2011, 147–148). No wonder Vladimir Putin quoted Gorchakov's "Russia is not sulking, Russia is collecting itself" at a press conference on December 23, 2021, in response to a question about a possible war with Ukraine (Prezident Rossii 2021), just two months before the attack. Also, it became known only later that the transition from "collecting itself" to a much more assertive challenger posture had recently been non-publicly but communicated to the U.S. In the autumn of 2021, during one of the high-level meetings between the U.S. and Russian officials initiated by the White House in an attempt to prevent the Russian full-scale invasion of Ukraine, Nikolai Patrushev, the Secretary of the Security Council of the Russian Federation, told CIA director William Burns about the future "special military operation," "We can do this. We are back" (Schwirtz et al. 2022). On the eve of the invasion, the Russian leadership was quite sure that Russia had already "collected itself" and was ready to strike back with an assertive unilateral move. One could argue that the harbingers of this move were already present in the activity of organisations like the Gorchakov Fund, which espoused the Gorchakov doctrine as adopted and readjusted by Primakov. Gorchakov Fund's geography of immediate activity thus marked the Kremlin's foremost ambitions of keeping tight control over former Soviet satellites.

2. Inter Pares: Gorchakov Fund in The Ecosystem of (Pro-)Government Public Diplomacy Organisations

The Alexander Gorchakov Public Diplomacy Fund was established as a "non-governmental organisation" by order of Russian President Dmitry Medvedev dated February 2, 2010, No.60-RP, and is de-facto subordinated to the Russian Ministry of Foreign Affairs. Leonid Drachevsky, a former diplomat, former Deputy Minister of Foreign Affairs, and Minister for Commonwealth of Independent States Affairs has been the Fund's head since its foundation.

It is quite telling that more than a third of the budget of this "non-governmental organisation" is provided by the federal budget, and some unnamed individuals supply the rest. Moreover, as demonstrated below, Russian authorities oversee the Gorchakov Fund's activities closely. Thus, the Gorchakov Fund is an example of what social scientists call a *GONGO* (government-organised non-governmental organisation). Authoritarian regimes like Russia use *GONGOs* to promote the government's agenda in the civil sector while creating a semblance of legitimacy for these organisations as non-governmental structures. One of the two areas of the Gorchakov Fund's activities is the allocation of grants for NGO projects. Via this tool, as was planned (Petrov 2012), the Fund could closely coordinate the activities of Russian and foreign NGOs promoting Russia's public diplomacy efforts by defining priority areas of their work in strict accordance with government priorities (Simons 2018, 152, 157).

The official website states that the Fund aims to encourage Russian public diplomacy development and promote a favourable social, political, and business climate for Russia abroad.[206] The Fund's Executive Director also formulated it as "creating an *adequate image of Russia* and our national and cultural values for the global community" (italics are by us — Authors).[207] The goal had to be achieved via the support of Russian public diplomacy activities, the encouragement of Russian non-governmental organisations to cooperate with foreign counterparts, and the active involvement of civil society institutions in the foreign policy processes.[208] The Fund's target audience is young scholars and researchers from the "near abroad," i.e., in Kremlin parlance, Russia's neighbouring countries, with particular attention to those previously part of the USSR. The Fund's two major domains of activities are conducting its own events (public lectures, conferences, courses, and schools) and providing grant support for projects of Russian non-governmental organisations dealing with public diplomacy.

In fact, through the distribution of grants and its educational activities, the Fund has been creating an interconnected network of experts who are carriers of views and ideas about Russia that are

---

[206] Gorchakov Fund. n. d. "Mission and goals." https://en.gorchakovfund.ru/portal/page/2902cca9-09f4-4a53-b9ed-868b5977a57b.

[207] Gorchakov Fund. n. d. "Executive Director's Address." https://en.gorchakovfund.ru/portal/page/3f8e2877-2128-4d57-b6d4-c5da836b9e37.

[208] Russian Federation. President. Rasporiazhenie #60-rp Prezidenta Rossiiskoi Federatsii o sozdanii Fonda podderzhki publichnoi diplomatii imeni A. M. Gorchakova [Order #60-rp of the President of the Russian Federation on the establishment of the Alexander Gorchakov Public Diplomacy Fund]. Issued February 2, 2010. https://rulaws.ru/president/Rasporyazhenie-Prezidenta-RF-ot-02.02.2010-N-60-rp/.

complementary to the Kremlin and who, in the future, can spread these views in their countries. This network is institutionalised in the "Gorchakov Club" (see below the section on the Fund's projects). This scheme is supposed to facilitate adopting decisions favourable to Russia in foreign capitals.

The Gorchakov Fund is not the only non-governmental organisation closely associated with the government that promotes Kremlin discourses and narratives among Russian and foreign think-tanks and academic circles. The junction of the Fund with Russia's hierarchy of governance and the horizontal ecosystem of similar non-governmental organisations are its governing bodies: the Board, which carries out the operational management of activities, and the Board of Trustees, which holds the supervisory function. The Board also has an Expert Council that defines priority areas for the funds' allocation and prepares recommendations on grant applications. An Academic Council ensures the participation of the academic community in public diplomacy projects and "analyses the Fund's research projects." Together, as we assume, their task is to oversee the ideological compliance of the Fund's activities with the foreign policy goals of the country's leadership.

According to the order of the President of the Russian Federation establishing the Fund, its Board of Trustees is formed by persons recommended by the Russian Foreign Ministry, "interested federal executive bodies," the Federation Council of the Federal Assembly of the Russian Federation, the State Duma of the Federal Assembly of the Russian Federation, the Public Chamber of the Russian Federation, the Chamber of Commerce and Industry of the Russian Federation, the media, as well as civil society organisations.

As a result, the Fund's Board of Trustees, legally a non-governmental, non-profit organisation, is chaired by Russian Foreign Minister Sergey Lavrov, who personally attends its meetings. Moreover, the Fund receives allocations from the federal budget via the Ministry of Foreign Affairs budget programme. Furthermore, as of spring 2022, the Fund's Board included Konstantin Kosachev, an ideologue of Russian foreign policy, former director of Rossotrudnichestvo,' chairman of the Federation Council's Committee on International Affairs, and, since 2021, Deputy Head of the Federation Council of Russia (upper house of parliament).[209] The Russian hierarchy of governance is also represented in the Fund by the advisor to the President of Russia on foreign policy issues, Yuri Ushakov, and members of the Russian Parliament, Alexandr Karelin and Suleyman Kerimov.

The Board of Trustees also includes Yevgeny Primakov, Jr., head of Rossotrudnichestvo; Anatoly Torkunov, the rector of the Moscow State Institute of International Relations; and several Russian oligarchs, possibly financial supporters of the Fund (Smagliy 2018, 20).

Horizontal links with related organisations are represented through the mutual membership of their representatives in their counterparts' governing bodies. For instance, the Board of Trustees of the Gorchakov Fund brings together Igor Ivanov (the President of the Russian International Affairs Council, RIAC, a think-tank that disseminates Kremlin-friendly foreign policy narratives); Aleksandr Bessmertnykh, Head of the World Council of Former Foreign Ministers;[210] Viktor Kamyshanov, President of the Federation of Peace and Conciliation;[211] as well as Vladimir Yakunin, Head of the Board of Trustees of the Fund of St. Andrew the First-Called[212] and the Centre of National Glory of Russia. The links between the organisations are close and, importantly, reciprocal. Thus, for example, Leonid Drachevsky has also been a member of the Board of Trustees of the RIAC since 2011.

Even though the Russian state broadly supports the Gorchakov Fund, the share of allocations flowing directly from the

---

209 Konstantin Kosachev is, among other things, the author of an important text for Russia's foreign policy discourse, where he substantiates the importance of so-called "compatriots" for Russia's foreign policy in the "near abroad." See Kosachev (2004).
210 Russian International Affairs Council. n. d. "Aleksandr Bessmertnykh." https://russiancouncil.ru/en/aleksandr-bessmertnykh/.
211 Rossiiskii sovet po mezhdunarodnym delam. April 30, 2015. „Federatsiia mira i soglasiia" [Federation of Peace and Conciliation]. http://ir.russiancouncil.ru/organisations/ifpc/.
212 Fond Andreia Pervozvannogo [Fund of St. Andrew the First-Called]. n. d. https://fap.ru/.

federal budget is not very large compared to what other similar structures receive. Thus, according to the pro-government Russian media RBK that analysed the data obtained from the official government portal of the Russian Federation, *spending.gov.ru*, out of the Fund's budget of 102.1 million roubles (about 1.3 million US dollars),[213] only 48.4 million roubles (about 614 000 US dollars) came directly from federal funding in 2016. In that year, the Fund received 38.8 million roubles (492 000 US dollars), or 38%, from the unnamed "Russian organisations and citizens" (Tkachev et al. 2017). From 2014 to 2019, federal budgeting for the Fund remained at about 50 million roubles (634 000 US dollars) (Tkachev et al. 2017). Still, in 2020, according to *spending.gov.ru*, the Fund received a subsidy from the Russian Foreign Ministry of more than 171 million roubles (about 2.17 million US dollars).[214] In addition, it is noteworthy that at least in 2017, one of the Fund's key events, Dialogue for the Future, was held at least with a partial financial contribution from a grant from the President of the Russian Federation, which was provided by the Presidential Grants Fund "for civil society development."[215]

In 2015, the Fund's executive director boasted that the share of public funding in the organisation's budget was declining (Pilko 2015). However, non-state funding sources are unknown since the Fund does not publish donor information. Most likely, those are the oligarchs and heads of big state enterprises represented in the Fund's Board of Trustees. Those, as of spring 2022, included, for instance:

---

213 Hereinafter, the U.S. dollar equivalent of sums in roubles is calculated in accordance with the exchange rate of U.S. dollar to the rouble as of February 22nd, 2022, at the Wall Street Journal Markets website. https://www.wsj.com/market-data/quotes/fx/RUBUSD/historical-prices.
214 Gosraskhody. n. d. "Vse subsidii FONDA PODDERZHKI PUBLICHNOI DIPLOMATII IMENI A. M. GORCHAKOVA" [All subsidies of the Alexander Gorchakov Public Diplomacy Fund]. https://webcache.googleusercontent.com/search?q=cache:TAwHV1Ull60J:https://spending.gov.ru/subsidies/receivers/450%25D0%25951036/ (accessed via Google Cache July 13, 2023).
215 KSORSG. 2017. "V Moskve zavershilsia 'Dialog vo imia budushchego—2017'" [Dialogue for the Future 2017 has ended in Moscow]. November 23, 2017. http://korsovet.ge/international/dialog-2/.

- Vladimir Yevtushenkov, head of the Board of Directors of "Sistema" Investment Company,
- Dmitry Mazepin, head of the Board of Directors of "Uralkhim," one of the largest companies in the Russian mineral fertilisers market (under individual EU sanctions),
- Alexey Mordashov, head of the Board of Directors of "Severstal" Steel and Mining Company (under individual EU sanctions),
- Mikhail Prokhorov, President of "ONEXIM" Investment Group,
- Nikolay Tokarev, President of JSC "Transneft," which transports oil products (under individual EU sanctions),
- Alisher Usmanov, founder of "USM Holdings" Metallurgy and Mining Holding (under individual EU sanctions),
- Sergei Chemezov, Director General of "Rostekh," a state company in the field of high-tech industry (under individual EU sanctions),
- Mikhail Shelkov, deputy head of the Board of Directors of "VSMPO-Avisma" Metallurgical Company.[216]

The Gorchakov Fund is well integrated into the partnerships between the Russian regime and oligarchs. That system has been constructed and maintained to develop and promote the Kremlin's foreign policy narratives. This structure comprises closely related organisations and actors who exchange views and jointly organise and fund events. The regime presumably co-opted oligarchs and heads of large state-owned enterprises by including them in the Fund's Board of Trustees to provide resources for the Fund's activities. After the start of the full-scale Russian invasion of Ukraine on February 24th, 2022, some of these people, primarily those linked to large state natural resources enterprises that literally fund Russia's war effort, at least through paying taxes to the Russian state, came under individual sanctions from the European Union, the United States, and other countries opposing Russia's illegitimate war.

---

[216] The Gorchakov Fund. n. d. "Structure: Board of Trustees." https://gorchakovfond.com/en/about/structure/.

3. An Unequal Battle with Europe? The Fund's Own Activities and Projects

One of the ways the Fund disseminates the ideas and narratives of Russian foreign policy discourse to its target audiences is by organising its events. To this end, it holds several programmes aimed at initiating cooperation between young Russian and foreign researchers of international relations, often with the participation of the Russian leadership, including Russian Foreign Minister Sergey Lavrov. Such programmes include:

- *The "Dialogue for the Future" Forum*, one of the oldest (launched in 2011) annual programmes of the Fund for young researchers in international relations, political scientists, journalists, and analysts from Russia and other countries who spend several days in discussions in Moscow, visit the Russian Foreign Ministry and have the opportunity to converse with the Minister of Foreign Affairs of the Russian Federation (see the section on the Dialogue below).[217]
- *The Potsdam Meetings*, a bilateral Russian-German high-level conference attended by MPs from Germany and Russia (see the section on Meetings below).
- *The Youth Forum of the Potsdam Meetings*, an event accompanying the Potsdam Meetings, attended by younger participants from Germany and Russia.[218]
- *Diplomatic seminar for young specialists*, an annual programme of meetings between young professionals in international relations, journalism, political science, and history, representatives of public organisations, and well-known Russian political scientists, researchers of international relations, and government officials. The programme has been running since 2012, and as of 2021, 400 people from about

---

217 The Gorchakov Fund. n. d. "Dialogue for the Future." https://en.gorchakovfund.ru/portal/page/dialogueforthefuture.
218 The Gorchakov Fund. n. d. "Youth Forum of the Potsdam Meetings." https://en.gorchakovfund.ru/portal/page/youthpotsdam.

30 countries have participated (The Gorchakov Fund website: Diplomatic seminar for young specialists, n.d.).
- *The annual meetings of the Gorchakov Fund's Friends*, the informal meetings of Russian and foreign international relations professionals (mainly from "near abroad" countries), have been taking place since 2013 in Moscow. These professionals are members of the "Gorchakov Club," an alumni association, and the Fund's "most active young participants in academic and educational programs." In 2021, the "Gorchakov Club" had more than 250 members.[219]
- The *Arctic*,[220] *Balkan*,[221] and *Caucasian dialogues*[222] are regular programmes offering meetings between Russian and foreign experts and young professionals in international relations, economics, and security from the respective regions to discuss the most pressing issues related to Russia's foreign policy developments there. The Arctic Dialogue is held biennially, and the Balkan and Caucasian dialogues are held annually. All three regions are strategically interesting to Russia, as reflected in its 2016 Foreign policy concept.
- *The School on Central Asia* is the Fund's annual educational program that brings interested experts together to discuss "issues of comprehensive development of relations between Central Asia and Russia." Since 2016, the event has been held alternately in one of the region's countries.[223]
- *The International Youth Media School* is an educational programme of the Fund, which offers master classes on media projects for young journalists but also for political scientists

---

[219] The Gorchakov Fund. n. d. "Annual Meetings of the Gorchakov Club's Members." https://en.gorchakovfund.ru/portal/page/thegotchakovclubmeetings.
[220] The Gorchakov Fund. n. d. "The Arctic Dialogue." The Gorchakov Fund website. https://en.gorchakovfund.ru/portal/page/thearcticdialogue.
[221] The Gorchakov Fund. n. d. "The Balkan Dialogue." The Gorchakov Fund website. https://en.gorchakovfund.ru/portal/page/thebalkandialogue.
[222] The Gorchakov Fund. n. d. "The Caucasian Dialogue." The Gorchakov Fund website. https://en.gorchakovfund.ru/portal/page/thecaucasusdialogue.
[223] The Gorchakov Fund. n. d. "The School on Central Asia." https://en.gorchakovfund.ru/portal/page/schoolcentralasia.

and international relations professionals from Russia and other countries.[224]
- *The Russian-Slovak Expert Forum*, one of the Fund's events dedicated to specific European countries, and the Potsdam Meetings. The Forum has been held since 2016. It is attended by Russian and Slovak experts who discuss topics of common interest selected from prior consultations.[225] In 2019, for instance, the subject of discussion was "cooperation within the OSCE, the impact of external factors on bilateral relations, and the results of the EU Eastern Partnership policy."[226]
- The *Expert Mobility* and *Russian Perspective* programmes offer trips for Russian scholars and experts to participate in international conferences abroad and to speak at universities and research centres.[227] The Fund has not updated public information about these programmes on its website, so we do not know whether they are still operational as of early 2022. The expert mobility projects included the
- "InteRussia" research internship programme for foreign specialists, but information about it is available only on the website of the partner organisation of the Fund, the Russian International Affairs Council.[228]

---

224 The Gorchakov Fund. n. d. "International Youth Media School." https://en.gorchakovfund.ru/portal/page/mediaschool.
225 Fond Gorchakova. n. d. "Rossiisko-slovatskii ekspertnyi forum" [The Russian-Slovak Expert Forum]. https://gorchakovfund.ru/portal/page/rossiyskoslovatskiyekspertnyyforum.
226 Fond Gorchakova. 2019. "IV Rossiisko-slovatskii ekspertyi forum" [The 4th Russian-Slovak Expert Forum]. Facebook, October 8, 2019. https://www.facebook.com/media/set/?set=a.2551920611497956&type=3.
227 Fond Gorchakova. 2020. "2 fevralia Fondu Gorchakova ispolniaietsia 10 let!" [On February 2nd, the Gorchakov Fund Turns 10 Years Old!]. February 2, 2020. http://web.archive.org/web/20201021072203/https://gorchakovfund.ru/news/view/2-fevralya-fondu-gorchakova-ispolnyaetsya-10-let/.
228 RSMD. 2021. "Gleb Ivashentsov vystupil s lektsiei dlia uchastnikov programmy InteRussia Fonda Gorchakova" [Gleb Ivashentsov Delivered a Lecture for the Participants of the InteRussia Gorchakov Fund Programme]. November 18, 2021. https://russiancouncil.ru/news/gleb-ivashentsov-vystupil-s-lektsiey-dlya-uchastnikov-programmy-interussia-fonda-gorchakova/.

3.1 Dialogue with an Eye to the Future

"Dialogue for the Future" is one of the first programmes of the Gorchakov Fund, defined as "key" by the Fund itself. It is a discussion platform attracting young (25 to 35) journalists, political scientists, and think-tank representatives from the Commonwealth of Independent States and Baltic states for meetings with and lectures from senior officials, including Russian Foreign Minister Sergey Lavrov. In addition, the Fund invites the "most experienced participants" to the Dialogue, that is, its alumni and those to whom the Fund and its management are assumably most sympathetic given their foreign policy views.

The "Dialogue" is usually dedicated to discussing Russia's foreign policy. Since 2014 the representatives of Iran, Turkey, China, and the self-proclaimed republics of Abkhazia, South Ossetia, and Transnistria have also been invited to participate (Smagliy 2018, 19).

In a few instances, Western politicians have participated in the "Dialogue" and thus legitimised the event by promoting pro-Kremlin narratives. For example, in 2017, the "Dialogue" meeting was opened by Franco Frattini (Smagliy 2018, 19), a former Italian foreign minister who sat in Silvio Berlusconi's cabinet. At the meeting, he urged Europeans and Russians to resume strategic relations immediately.[229]

The "Dialogue" has also gathered pro-Russian or Russian-curious political scientists, international relations researchers, and experts such as Hanna Notte or Alexander Rahr, who, at a meeting in December 2021, expressed concern that the EU "did not pay attention" to the Eurasian project of Russia, in order not to "allow it to become a strong player", and that is why no one was working on the shared space "from Lisbon to Vladivostok."[230] In yet another

---

[229] KSORSG. 2017. "V Moskve zavershilsia 'Dialog vo imia budushchego – 2017'" [Dialogue for the Future 2017 has ended in Moscow]. November 23, 2017. http://korsovet.ge/international/dialog-2/.

[230] Fond Gorchakova. 2021. "XI 'Dialog vo imia budushchego,' den pervyi: o novom miroporiadke i epokhe nestabilnosti" [11th "Dialogue for the Future," Day One: about the New World Order and the Era of Turmoil]. December 1, 2021. http://web.archive.org/web/20220123091021/https://gorchakovfund.ru/

iteration of promotion efforts for Russia-controlled integration projects, the 2022 "Dialogue" meeting, held in December, was dedicated to the 100th anniversary of the foundation of the USSR.[231] Participants, among other things, lauded the Soviet Union for allegedly being a progressive project and mused over the reasons it failed.

However, the event's target audience is students, young academics, and professionals from Russia and other countries. The Fund pays for the participants' accommodation in Moscow, food, cultural programme, and transportation through the city.[232]

Like most events of the Fund, this programme attracts young professionals interested in international relations, including those pursuing graduate studies, and, presumably, will influence the prevailing narratives among political decision-makers in Russia and abroad in the future.

3.2 On the Approaches to Berlin: The Potsdam Meetings

The Potsdam Meetings were initiated in 1999 by German President Roman Herzog as a regular conference of German and Russian high-ranking officials, including representatives of the German Bundestag and the Federal Assembly of Russia.[233] They were held jointly under the German-Russian Forum's auspices to discuss topics of common interest related to science and culture.[234] Since then,

---

news/xi-dialog-vo-imya-budushchego-den-pervyy-o-novom-miroporyadke-i-epokhe-nestabilnosti/.

231 The conference's chosen title was "100 years of the USSR: the future in common creation." Fond Gorchakova. 2022. "Dialog vo imya budushchego-2022: otkryt priiom zaiavok na glavnuiu programmu Fonda Gorchakova" [Dialogue for the Future 2022: The Call for Applications for the Main Program of the Gorchakov Fund Has Been Launched]. October 8, 2022. https://gorchakovfund.ru/portal/news/view/dialog_vo_imia_budushchego2022_otkryt_priem_zaiavok_na_glavnuiu_programmu_fonda_gorchakova_61137.

232 The Gorchakov Fund. n. d. "Dialogue for the Future." https://en.gorchakovfund.ru/portal/page/dialogueforthefuture.

233 Deutsch-Russisches Forum e.V. [German-Russian Forum]. n. d. „Potsdamskiie vstrechi" [The Potsdam Meetings]. https://www.deutsch-russisches-forum.de/ru/o-nas/sfery-deyatelnosti/potsdamskie-vstrechi.

234 Deutsch-Russisches Forum e.V. [German-Russian Forum]. n. d. "O nas" [About Us]. https://www.deutsch-russisches-forum.de/ru/o-nas.

the Meetings have taken place annually and even biannually in recent years, despite the growing aggressiveness of Russia's foreign policy over the past decade. From the very beginning, one of the event's partners has been the Konrad Adenauer Foundation, affiliated with the Christian Democratic Union of Germany (CDU).[235]

The person who oversaw the organisation of the Meetings and headed the German-Russian Forum for over a decade was Matthias Platzeck, a controversial former East German politician. Platzeck was an environmental activist in the German Democratic Republic who, in late 1989, participated in the Central Round Table, the GDR's de facto transition committee, and eventually got a seat in the first multiparty East German government under former SED party boss-cum-reformist Hans Modrow. After a brief career in the Green Party, Platzeck switched to the Social Democrats, occupying important positions while serving in local and state governments.[236] Since 2014, Platzeck has been active in the German-Russian Forum, which co-organised the Potsdam Meetings, a position he occupied until March 2022. For a long time, Platzeck was known for his mediating and conciliatory approach, especially vis-à-vis Russia. As if to prove this, in 2020, he published a book, *We Need a New Ostpolitik: Russia as a Partner* (in German, *Wir brauchen eine neue Ostpolitik: Russland als Partner*), where he argued, in a neo-Brandtian move, that Germany "has to finally accept Russia as a partner and take its interests seriously [...] acknowledging that the also West, in the recent decades, committed crucial mistakes."[237]

Meetings are usually attended by several dozen representatives from both sides (the total number of participants can reach 60

---

235 Konrad Adenauer Stiftung. 2020. "Am 25. Mai 2020 finden die XVIII. Potsdamer Begegnungen per Video-Konferenz statt" [On May 25, 2020, The 8th Potsdam Meetings Are Taking Place]. Konrad-Adenauer-Stiftung. May 25, 2020. https://www.kas.de/de/veranstaltungen/detail/-/content/am-25-mai-2020-finden-die-xviii-potsdamer-begegnungen-per-video-konferenz-statt.

236 Open-Air-Ausstellung Revolution und Mauerfall. n. d. "Matthias Platzeck." https://revolution89.de/en/people/details?tx_news_pi1%5Baction%5D=detail&tx_news_pi1%5Bcontroller%5D=News&tx_news_pi1%5Bnews%5D=280&cHash=eee98247eedd3f236ab7ced9f02020bc.

237 Ullstein Buchverlage. n. d. "Wir brauchen eine neue Ostpolitik" [We Need a New Ostpolitik]. https://www.ullstein.de/werke/wir-brauchen-eine-neue-ostpolitik/hardcover/9783549100141.

people), including ordinary MPs, heads of parliamentary committees, and representatives of various factions, including the opposition. Unfortunately, information on the cost of the event is not publicly available.

Although the Gorchakov Fund was established much later after the Potsdam Meetings launched in 1999, it has been actively involved in its funding and organisation since 2010, when the Fund's Executive Director began participating in the meetings.

It is clear from the topics of annual conferences and press releases that what began as a series of discussions on relatively narrow and somewhat abstract issues eventually became a platform for discussing geopolitics and foreign policy interests. After 2014, fewer and fewer press releases mentioned exhibitions, literary readings, or film screenings previously used to accompany the Meetings. Moreover, after the beginning of Russia's aggression against Ukraine in 2014, there has been an increasing securitisation and politicisation of discussions, despite the initial focus of the Potsdam Meetings on culture and science. The last few meetings were held under the personal patronage of the Foreign Ministers of Germany and Russia, who opened the conferences with welcoming speeches.[238]

The tendency is eloquently evidenced by the change in the topics of meetings: from cultural identity (2000), urban cultures (2002), values (2006), the problem of ageing (2007), discussions on water (2011), the Internet (2012) to such foreign policy and security-related topics as:

- "Europe from Lisbon to Vladivostok: An unalterable path to European stability" (2016),
- "Russia and the West: Ways of political and economic exit from the crisis" (2017),

---

238 Baranovskaia, Marina. "'Potsdamskiie vstrechi': kak FRG i RF vybratsia iz eskalatsii." [The Potsdam Meetings: How Germany and Russia Can Get Out of the Spiral of Escalation]. *Deutsche Welle*. May 18, 2021. https://www.dw.com/ru/potsdamskie-vstrechi-kak-germanii-i-rossii-vybratsja-iz-spirali-jeskalacii/a-57573920.

- "New Governments in Germany and Russia: The Road to Mutual Understanding in Politics and Economics" (2018).[239]

In 2013, Russia's rhetoric concerning Europe was relatively peaceful. During a discussion on identities and interpretations of history, one of the participants, Konstantin Asadovsky, quoted Russian historian Nikolay Karamzin while appealing to Russia's unalterably European future.[240]

But since 2014, the Russian representatives have started to openly politicise the Meetings, while the German ones have been stressing the Meetings' importance for continuing the dialogue. In 2015, the topic covered was the Helsinki Accords and considerations of possible new security architecture in the European region. One year after the attempted annexation of Crimea and the launch of Russia's war against Ukraine in Donetsk and Luhansk oblasts, the participants discussed the possibility of a new "pan-European unity" through OSCE renewal and the implementation of the "Helsinki-2" process.[241] This had to ensure the prospects of establishing a free trade zone "from Lisbon to Vladivostok" (i.e., between the European Union and the Eurasian Economic Union) and eliminate the urgency of the question of Ukraine's belonging to either Western or Eastern Europe. The search for "common narratives" for Germany and Russia continued in 2016.[242] Even in 2019, German politicians, such as Dirk Wiese (a member of the Bundestag from the

---

239 Deutsch-Russisches Forum e.V. [German-Russian Forum]. n. d. „Potsdamskiie vstrechi" [The Potsdam Meetings]. https://www.deutsch-russisches-forum.de/ru/o-nas/sfery-deyatelnosti/potsdamskie-vstrechi.
240 Deutsch-Russisches Forum e.V. [German-Russian Forum]. 2013. "XV. Potsdamer Begegnungen" [15th Potsdam Meetings]. https://www.deutsch-russisches-forum.de/xv-potsdamer-begegnungen/394.
241 Deutsch-Russisches Forum e.V. [German-Russian Forum]. 2015. "XVII. Potsdamer Begegnungen" [17th Potsdam Meetings]. https://www.deutsch-russisches-forum.de/xvii-potsdamer-begegnungen/504.
242 Deutsch-Russisches Forum e.V. [German-Russian Forum]. 2016. "Potsdamer Begegnungen mit Sergej Lawrow am 8. November 2016 in Moskau" [Potsdam Meetings with Sergei Lavrov in Moscow on November 8, 2016]. Deutsch-Russisches Forum e.V. https://www.deutsch-russisches-forum.de/potsdamer-begegnungen-mit-sergej-lawrow-am-8-november-in-moskau/2907.

Social Democratic Party), insisted that international issues could be resolved "only together with Russia."[243]

The rhetoric of the German representatives has also somewhat evolved. In May 2021, the 25th Potsdam Meetings were opened with a welcoming speech by German Foreign Minister Heiko Maas. He called for dialogue but criticised Russia for suppressing civil society, "sabre-rattling on the border with Ukraine," and organising covert special operations in Germany and Europe.[244]

The last conference of the Potsdam meetings took place in December 2021. The Russians continued to insist on their agenda, namely the need for a European-Russian dialogue without the participation of the US and questioning Europe's Atlantic orientation, which Russia deems problematic.[245]

Eventually, Russia's open and large-scale war against Ukraine, which began on February 24th, 2022, forced the German co-organisers of the meetings to announce the Meetings' suspension in early March 2022. The head of the German-Russian forum, Matthias Platzeck, who was responsible for organising the meetings, resigned.[246]

However, the Potsdam meetings had already assisted in developing bilateral ties between parliamentarians and, conse-

---

243 Deutsch-Russisches Forum e.V. [German-Russian Forum]. 2019. "XXII Potsdamer Begegnungen in Berlin" [22th Potsdam Meetings in Berlin]. https://www.deutsch-russisches-forum.de/xxii-potsdamer-begegnungen-in-berlin/1760936.
244 Predstavitelstva Germanii v Rossii [Representations of Germany in Russia]. 2021. "Privetstvennoie slovo Federalnogo ministra Haiko Maasa po sluchaiu XXV Potsdamskikh vstrech" [Welcoming Remarks by Federal Minister Heiko Maas on the Occasion of the 25th Potsdam Meetings]. May 18, 2021. https://germania.diplo.de/ru-ru/aktuelles/-/2460146.
245 Grigoriev, Viktor. "Nachniom s razoruzheniia iazyka! O chem govorili na 'Potsdamskikh vstrechakh' v Moskve" ["Let's Start by Disarming the Language!" What Was Discussed at the Potsdam Meetings in Moscow]. *Kommersant*. December 20, 2021. https://www.kommersant.ru/doc/5099082.
246 Deutsch-Russisches Forum e.V. [German-Russian Forum]. 2022. „Zum angekündigten Rücktritt Matthias Platzecks" [On the announced resignation of Matthias Platzeck]. March 3, 2022. https://www.deutsch-russisches-forum.de/zum-angeku-ndigten-ru-cktritt-matthias-platzecks-vom-amt-des-vorsitzenden/5603361.

quently, the political elites of both countries, bringing more understanding of each other's political demands. This rapprochement of German and Russian politicians was mutual, as both foreign ministers attended the latest meetings, and it was only the Russian invasion of 2022 made the German side reconsider its attitude towards this interaction platform.

4. Grants à la Russe: Financial Support of Individual Projects

The grant allocations for public sector projects from the Gorchakov Fund, as the Executive Director himself acknowledged, were intended to serve as "transmission gear" between the state and the NGOs dealing with public diplomacy.[247] There is a consensus that the Fund must function as a "system-forming" («системообразующая») GONGO that helps systematise the activities of individual NGOs via a system of grant distribution (Burlinova 2022, 14). The Fund seems to treat its grant recipients as proper stakeholders, providing assistance and training in preparing applications, using digital technologies, organising project work, and orienting in foreign policy.[248]

The Fund's work is typically organised in two grant cycles during the year, one extending from January 15 to February 15, the other from July 15 to August 15. Both Russian and foreign NGOs can compete for grants.[249]

An organisation needs to apply on the Fund's website, after which it undergoes an examination, that is, an assessment of feasibility and ideological compliance, in an Expert Council headed by RIAC President and former Russian Foreign Minister Igor Ivanov. After that, grant offers are finalised at the meeting of the Board of Trustees. According to the Fund's Executive Director, as of 2015,

---

247 Petrov, Sergei. 2012. "U obshchestvennoi diplomatii bolshie vozmozhnosti" [Public diplomacy offers great opportunities]. Rosbalt. June 7, 2012. https://www.rosbalt.ru/main/2012/06/07/990104.html (accessed July 13, 2023).
248 See Fond Gorchakova. 2022. "Kursy NKO Fonda Gorchakova" [NGO Classes of the Gorchakov Fund]. December 12, 2022. https://gorchakovfund.ru/portal/news/view/kursy_nko_fonda_gorchakova_24595.
249 Fond Gorchakova. n. d. "Granty" [Grants]. https://gorchakovfund.ru/portal/events-and-news.

only about 17–20% of applications received a positive response due to the large number of submitted proposals. According to another representative of the Fund, quoted in one of the studies, the Fund annually conducts about 260 projects in 20 thematic areas (Vendil Pallin and Oxenstierna 2017, 27).

Funds are distributed according to priority areas. In 2022, all of those corresponded to Russia's foreign policy vectors as defined in the Concept of Foreign Policy of the Russian Federation, approved by Vladimir Putin in 2016. Among them are strengthening relations with former Soviet states and other neighbouring states, regional policies in Asia-Pacific, the Middle East, and Africa, the Arctic policy in the context of Russia's chairmanship in the Arctic Council, possible geopolitical configurations in the Balkans, a "constructive agenda" in relations between Russia and the Euro-Atlantic region, "integrative processes," and "shaping Russia's objective image abroad."[250] Thus a presumably non-governmental organisation, established by order of the President of Russia and de facto subordinate to the Ministry of Foreign Affairs of Russia, distributes the funds strictly following government priorities.

Unlike Western grant-giving organisations, the Gorchakov Fund does not publish information on the number of allocated funds and support activities, even though the Fund is one of the most extensive grant organisations of such kind in the Russian Federation. As the Fund representatives explain themselves, this is due to security considerations since they do not want to expose their recipients to the authorities in Western countries (Burlinova 2022, 30). However, information about the activities sponsored by the Fund can be found either in the Fund's materials or on its partners' websites. For instance, some are mentioned in the Fund's presentation published on its website, and others on the Fund's page on Timepad.[251]

---

250 Russian Federation. President. "Kontseptsiia vneshnei politiki Rossiiskoi Federatsii" [Concept of Foreign Policy of the Russian Federation]. Approved on 31 March 2023. https://www.mid.ru/ru/detail-material-page/1860586/.
251 Timepad. n. d. "Fond podderzhki publichnoi diplomatii imeni A. M. Gorchakova" [The Alexander Gorchakov Public Diplomacy Fund]. https://fond-gorchakova.timepad.ru/events/.

The activities supported by the Fund could be categorised into those related to international relations and those targeting the field of culture. For instance, the Gorchakov Fund endorsed the awarding of the "East-West. Golden Arch" film prize in 2021 (the Fund's Executive Director headed the Board of Trustees),[252] an international educational school, a youth conference of Russian compatriots in Great Britain, a series of workshops by film industry professionals,[253] and an international film festival in Serbia (Reid 2020, 128).

Some foreign organisations could be considered the Fund's regular partners since they have received grants for organising events more than once. For instance, several events were held in collaboration with the Italian Institute for Eurasian Studies, chaired by former Italian Foreign Minister Franco Frattini (see above about his participation in the Dialogue for the Future), such as the online discussion "Between Centrifugal and Inertial: The Future of European Integration During the Pandemic Times" (November 30, 2020),[254] online lecture by Italian Ambassador to Russia Pasquale Terracciano (December 4, 2020),[255] and the online discussion "Afghanistan After the Withdrawal of US Troops: Who Will Help Create a Strong State?" (August 3, 2021).[256] Other foreign organisations

---

252 "Vostok—Zapad. Zolotaiia arka" [East-West. Golden Arch]. n. d. http://web.archive.org/web/20220625072642/https://www.eurasiacinema.org/.
253 Timepad. 2021. "'Kino i Literatura. Kadr i slovo.' Master-klass Vadima Abdrashytova"[Cinema and Literature. Frame and Word." Workshop by Vadim Abdrashitov]. November 26, 2021. https://fond-gorchakova.timepad.ru/event/1850967/.
254 Timepad. 2020. "Onlain-diskussiia 'Mezhdu tsentrobezhnoi siloi i siloi inertsii: budushchhee ievrointegratsii vo vremia pandemii'" [Online discussion "Between Centrifugal and Inertial: The Future of European Integration During the Pandemic Times"]. November 30, 2020. https://fond-gorchakova.timepad.ru/event/1491848/.
255 Timepad. 2020. "Onlain-lektsiia posla Italii v RF Pasquale Terracciano" [Online lecture by Italian Ambassador to Russia Pasquale Terracciano]. December 4, 2020. https://fond-gorchakova.timepad.ru/event/1497432/.
256 Timepad. 2021. "Onlain-diskussiia 'Afganistan posle vyvoda voisk SShA: kto pomozhet sozdat silnoie gosudarstvo?'" [Online discussion "Afghanistan After the Withdrawal of US Troops: Who Will Help Create a Strong State?"]. August 3, 2021. https://fond-gorchakova.timepad.ru/event/1722843/.

that can boast close cooperation with the Fund are the "Franco-Russian Dialogue" Association, chaired by pro-Russian politician Thierry Mariani (online discussions "Security in Europe: The Role of Russia and France"[257] and "Gaullist Europe of Nations. Significance of the Concept for Soviet and Modern European Policy"),[258] and the Scottish group "Friends of Russia" (online discussion "Russian-British Relations 2020: Expert Opinion").[259]

Among the Fund's financial support recipients are its long-term domestic partners: the Diplomatic Academy of the Russian Federation, the Institute of World Economy and International Relations, and the Council on Foreign and Defence Policy. In addition, the Fund promotes conferences,[260] international summer schools,[261] and open lectures with the participation of similar Russian pro-government or peri-governmental organisations, which is another evidence of a whole ecosystem of such organisations aimed at spreading pro-Kremlin foreign policy narratives. Sometimes even reputable Western think tanks, like the German Council on Foreign Relations, co-organised events in cooperation with the Fund, but such

---

257 Timepad. 2021. "Onlain-diskussia 'Bezopasnost v Evrope: rol RF i Frantsii'" [Online discussion "Security in Europe: The Role of Russia and France"]. November 2, 2021. https://fond-gorchakova.timepad.ru/event/1829437/. Interestingly, an investigation by The Insider identified that the "Franco-Russian Dialogue" Association has two registered addresses in France. One of them coincides with the address of the representation of the Russian Railways, the other is exactly where the Russian House of Science and Culture in Paris, a Rossotrudnichestvo branch, is located. See more in Fishman 2023.
258 Timepad. 2021. "Gollistskaiia Evropa otechestv. Znachimost kontseptsii dlia sovetskoi i sovremennoi evropeiskoi politiki" [Gaullist Europe of Nations. Significance of the Concept for Soviet and Modern European Policy]. April 14, 2021. https://fond-gorchakova.timepad.ru/event/1607938/.
259 Timepad. 2020. "Rossiisko-britanskiie otnosheniia 2020: ekspertnyi vzgliad" [Russian-British Relations 2020: Expert Opinion]. December 29, 2020. https://fond-gorchakova.timepad.ru/event/1515479/.
260 RIAS. 2020 "Middle East Issues Discussed at the Diplomatic Academy Conference." October 10, 2020. https://russiancouncil.ru/news/problemy-blizhnego-vostoka-obsudili-na-konferentsii-v-diplomaticheskoy-akademii-/?sphrase_id=89423586.
261 HSE. n. d. "International Russian-Chinese Summer School on International Relations." https://we.hse.ru/ruschn/.

cases have not been too frequent.[262] In 2022, events supported by the Fund included the "Eurasian School of Integration Law" for young law specialists, held in Moscow, the UN Model in Pyatigorsk, or an event aimed to bolster contacts between youth representatives of Russia and Russia-supported non-recognized enclaves like "Abkhazia," "DPR," "LPR," and "South Ossetia" called "International Youth Forum "Creating Future Together," initiated by an employee of the Centre for Strategic Studies of "Abkhazia," Kamug Gabrava. Gabrava received 300,000 roubles from the Fund to carry it out.[263]

By offering grants to NGOs' projects that meet Russia's foreign policy goals and bringing together activists, experts, and researchers in the framework of the Gorchakov Fund's Friends Club, the Fund, together with similar pro-government organisations, actively promotes Russian interpretations of the current state of international relations and Russian understandings of its geopolitical interests. The spread of these understandings was intended to eventually reach the decision-making circles of foreign governments, including European ones, and influence their policies, particularly those towards Eastern Europe and Ukraine.

However, the Fund has a relatively limited budget for an institution that aims to ensure Russia's "soft power" and public diplomacy efficiency. Its budget amounts to just a little more than a million euros. The size of individual grants distributed by the Fund can reach 200–300 thousand roubles (around 2,500–3,800 US dollars, meaning those are relatively small-scale activities). Some alumni of the Fund's programmes have claimed that the Fund's activities exhibited a "lack of money, attitude, infrastructure, and

---

262 DGAP. 2015 „Deutsch-Russische Beziehungen 25 Jahre Nach Dem Zwei-Plus-Vier-Vertrag: Historische und aktuell-politische Perspektiven" [German-Russian Relations 25 Years after Two Plus Four Agreement]. September 25, 2015. https://dgap.org/de/veranstaltungen/deutsch-russische-beziehungen-25-jahre-nach-dem-zwei-plus-vier-vertrag.
263 Apsadgyl. 2022. "Proekt Kamuga Gabrava vyigral grant Fonda Gorchakov na forume 'Evraziia Global'" [Kamug Gabrava`s project won the Gorchakov Fund grant at the "Eurasia Global" forum]. June 14, 2022. https://apsadgil.info/news/society/proekt-kamuga-gabrava-vyigral-grant-fonda-gorchakova-na-forume-evraziya-global/.

comfortable conditions," which was combined with an overload of ideological propaganda, which makes it less attractive when compared to American and European counterparts (Gussarova 2017, 13).

5. Limited Geography, Modest Achievements: Representative Offices Abroad

Unlike the extensive networks of the "Russkiy Mir" Foundation or Rossotrudnichestvo, the Gorchakov Fund has only two affiliated institutions abroad: the Centres in Tbilisi and Minsk. Between 2013 and 2015, the Fund's Information Centre also operated in Kyiv, but it was closed by the Security Service of Ukraine. Information on the budget and staff of individual centres in Tbilisi and Minsk is not publicly available. The geography of the Fund's representations is meant to "earmark" the Kremlin's foreign influence ambitions, as witnessed by the developments in Belarus and Georgia in the recent decade.

The Georgian-Russian Public Centre, named after Evgeny Primakov Sr. in Tbilisi,[264] was established in 2013 based on an institution friendly to the Gorchakov Fund, the Georgian Institute of International Relations in Tbilisi.[265] The Fund relied on pro-Russian politicians who were also members of the Gorchakov Fund's Friends Club.[266] These were Zaza Abashidze, the founder and first director of the Centre (2013–2015), former and current directors Berkhan Khurtsidze (2015–2018) (Dzvelishvili and Kupreishvili 2015, 5, 43–44), and Dimitri Lortkipanidze (2018–present), as well

---

[264] Fond Gorchakova. n. d. "Gruzino-Rossiiskii obshchestvennyi tsentr imeni E.M. Primakova" [Russian-Georgian Public Centre named after Evgeny Primakov]. https://gorchakovfund.ru/portal/page/dfeb6403-0b1a-4d21-b49e-c3291c95e2a8.

[265] Obshchestvennyi tsentr Primakova [Primakov Public Centre]. 2022. "Gruzino-rossiiskii obshchestvennyi tsentr imeni E.M. Primakova – teper onlain!" [The Georgian-Russian Public Centre named after Evgeny Primakov – Now in Instagram!]. February 10, 2022. https://www.instagram.com/p/CZyoX74Iuxy/.

[266] Federalnaia Gruzinskaia natsionalno-kulturnaia avtonomiia v Rossii [Federal Georgian national and cultural autonomy in Russia]. 2018. "Dmitrii Lortkipanidze: 'Otnosheniia mezhdu Rossiiei i Gruziiei – platsentarnyie'" [Dimitri Lortkipanidze: "Relations between Russia and Georgia are Placental"]. December 15, 2018. http://kartvelebi.ru/sobytiya/9/149726/.

as project coordinator Natalia Tsereteli and co-worker Nino Kiziku-rashvili.[267] They have generally supported and promoted Russia's foreign policy priorities in Georgian public discourse.

The Centre operates in two main activity domains. The first is free Russian language courses (operational since 2015), designed for nine months, as of 2020–2021 (i.e., during the pandemic). At the Centre, there were four study groups in which 50 people studied Russian.[268] According to "Ekho Kavkaza" (Echo of the Caucasus), in 2018, 80 people took these Russian language courses (Paresishvili 2019).

Other tracks include conferences, seminars, and lectures (including online) with the participation of Georgian and Russian professionals in international relations. For example, in February 2022, shortly before the full-scale war between Russia and Ukraine, the Centre organised a lecture by Doctor of Psychology Alexander Rusetsky, "Issues of Scientific and Practical Support of the Georgian-Russian Peace Process." A few months before the event, the Centre began posting videos of the lectures on its YouTube channel. The Primakov Centre apparently became one of the springboards for Russian activities in the country. The Centre's Instagram page, one of its few media outlets, was created only in February 2022 and became highly active throughout the year as the Gorchakov Fund's Georgia-related events abounded. One of the organisations with which the Gorchakov Fund frequently cooperated in Georgia turned out to be Alt Info. This media outlet is associated with supporting pro-Russian protests in Tbilisi in 2022 (Gabritchidze 2022).

The Centre for Analysis and Forecasting of Union Integration Processes in Minsk was established in 2020. As of May 2023, the Centre's director is Sergey Palagin. Its main task is postulated as "the organisation of educational and scientific-practical activities,

---

267 IMEMO. 2018. "VI Ezhegodnaia vstrecha chlenov Kluba Fonda Gorchakova. Programma." [Programme of the 6th Annual Meeting of the Members of the Gorchakov Fund Club] December 2018. https://www.imemo.ru/files/File/ru/events/2018/14122018/14122018-PROG-FG-002.pdf.

268 Obshchestvennyi tsentr Primakova [Primakov Public Centre]. 2022. "Kursy russkogo iazyka" [Russian language courses]. February 16, 2022. https://www.instagram.com/p/CaB7xEUK7ZE/.

participants of which can get full information about the current integration processes of Russia and Belarus."[269] Among the partners of the Fund are key state academic and analytical organisations in the Republic of Belarus.

The Centre in Minsk seems less interesting than the Georgian one, as Russia's both hard and soft power in Belarus is visibly stronger, and especially since 2020, Russia's leadership exerts much leverage over Minsk. Moreover, unlike Georgia, Belarus has not had an armed conflict with Russia in the recent past. Consequently, Russia has not had such a negative image that it should be corrected through public diplomacy.

The Information Centre of the Gorchakov Fund operated in Kyiv from 2013 to 2015 at the Institute of International Relations of the National Aviation University of Ukraine (IIR of the NAU).[270] As in the case of the Georgian Centre, the Fund established its branch within a university Department of International Relations. The timing of the Centre's creation was hardly coincidental: in November 2013, the Ukrainian government announced a decision not to sign Ukraine's Association Agreement with the European Union, which Moscow apparently imposed, and Russia could prepare to deploy a propaganda infrastructure to promote its integration projects instead. Employees of the IIR of the NAU and some of the Gorchakov Fund's Friends Club members[271] began actively supporting this agenda in December 2013. In late December, the Centre was visited by Ukrainian Foreign Minister Leonid Kozhara, who promised

---

269 Fond Gorchakova. n. d. "Tsentr analiza i prognozirovaniia soiuznykh integratsionnykh protsessov" [The Centre for Analysis and Forecasting of Union Integration Processes]. https://gorchakovfund.ru/portal/page/9bc8f70b-d5ca-416f-b4b3-adaac941f95e.
270 Ukrinform. 2015. "Ukrainski studenty zdaly v SBU rosiyskykh psevdodyplomativ" [Ukrainian Students Handed Over Russian Pseudo-Diplomats to the Security Service of Ukraine]. February 2, 2015. https://www.ukrinform.ua/rubric-society/1810521-ukraiinski_studenti_zdali_v_sbu_rosiyskih_psevdodiplomativ_2017008.html.
271 Milovanova, Olha. 2013. "Dyplomatychnyi seminar molodykh spetsialistiv" [Diplomatic Seminar for Young Experts]. *Hazeta Natsionalnoho Aviatsiinoho Universytetu "Aviator"* [Newspaper of the National Aviation University "Aviator"], No. 28 (1473). https://www.pdf-archive.com/2014/01/07/28/28.pdf. P. 6.

support from the Ministry of Foreign Affairs and announced his intention to hold an expert roundtable on "Russian-Ukrainian relations with high-ranking guests from both countries" in the spring of 2014.[272]

In February 2015, the Security Service of Ukraine closed the Centre after a request from students who complained that it was conducting subversive activities.[273] According to the executive director of the Gorchakov Fund, the branch continued to operate without any reference to the "parent" structure in Moscow (Pilko 2015). However, we could not find any mention of its operations after 2015.

Unlike Rossotrudnichestvo or the "Russkiy Mir" Foundation, the Gorchakov Fund does not have an extensive network of representative offices abroad, which might be hindered by its limited budget and the type of its activities, mainly centred around grant distribution. However, the Fund managed to establish representations in Georgia, a country Russia attacked in 2008, and Belarus, a country engaged in a Union State integration project with Russia. An attempt to open the branch in Ukraine happened at the beginning of the Revolution of Dignity in December 2013. In Georgia and Ukraine, branches were established at some university departments. The scale of these branches' activities is relatively insignificant, at least at first sight. Those activities primarily include lectures and seminars, and in the case of the Georgian Centre, Russian language courses for several dozen people a year.

---

272 Fond Gorchakova. 2013. "Glava MID Ukrainy posetil Informtsentr Fonda Gorchakova v Kieve" [The Ukrainian Foreign Minister Visited the Information Centre of the Gorchakov Fund in Kyiv]. December 26, 2013. https://gorchakovfund.ru/news/view/glava-mid-ukrainy-posetil-informtsentr-fonda-gorchakova-v-kieve/.

273 Ukrinform. 2015. "Ukrainski studenty zdaly v SBU rosiyskykh psevdodyplomativ" [Ukrainian Students Handed Over Russian Pseudo-Diplomats to the Security Service of Ukraine]. February 2, 2015. https://www.ukrinform.ua/rubric-society/1810521-ukraiinski_studenti_zdali_v_sbu_rosiyskih_psevdodiplomativ_2017008.html.

6. Priorities and Activities of the Gorchakov Fund After the Full-Scale Invasion of Ukraine

After the beginning of the full-scale invasion of the Russian Federation against Ukraine, the Gorchakov Fund continued its activities. The grant cycles and internships continued like before the war. The Fund organised and advertised its lectures and published articles about Russian cultural figures. The Fund's Facebook page was still active even a year after the ban of this social network in Russia. Moreover, on February 21, 2023, the Fund launched its English-speaking Telegram channel.[274] In its communications, the Fund, though being part and parcel of the Russian international relations environment entangled with the war effort, still seemed to have preserved its quiet, moderate and analysis-oriented rhetoric, using carefully picked phrases and avoiding full-blown propaganda effort that "Russkiy Mir" Foundation and Rossotrudnichestvo were pursuing. The Fund and Russian foreign policy circles, its key stakeholder, probably did not want to ruin the bridges that could link them to the Western professional environment.

The all-out invasion appears to have prompted increased difficulty for the Fund's clients to seek foreign funding or to continue cooperation with their partners from abroad. Russia's "foreign influence" legislation had already labelled any Russian NGO that received funding from foreign sources as a "foreign agent." Still, the new 2022 law has intensified the rules and made some domestic Russian experts worry whether the legislator now expected Russian NGOs, even those working in the field of public diplomacy, to abandon all cooperation with any partners abroad. This issue, according to the report of the Russian Council on Foreign Affairs, is fundamentally hindering their operations, which the report's author suggested bringing forth in communication with the authorities (Burlinova 2022, 26).

The Fund seems flexible in adapting its activity to the new geopolitical reality that Russia and its elites found themselves in after

---

274 The Gorchakov Fund. n. d. Telegram. https://t.me/TheGorchakovFund.

February 24, 2022. Within the first months after the full-scale invasion, the Fund attempted to address the most pressing issues, such as the implications of the new Russian aggression for security in Europe, the sanctions regime, and relations with the West, in its public events. For instance, on February 26th, 2022, the Fund announced a youth session on "Security in Europe: Finding Spaces for Dialogue," where one of the topics was the crisis of the security architecture in Europe and the possibility of de-escalation of the confrontation between Russia and NATO.[275] Later, on March 2nd, the Fund organised a lecture on the consequences of removing Russian banks from SWIFT.[276] At the same time, the Fund had to announce the "suspension" of applications for participation in the Potsdam Meetings Youth Forum.[277] On March 4th, the page rebroadcasted an interview with Russian Foreign Minister Sergey Lavrov on the war against Ukraine and economic sanctions against Russia.[278] On March 10th, another expert lectured on the history of sanctions, a pressing issue for today's Russia).[279] As before the war, the Fund

---

275 Fond Gorchakova. 2022. "Tsentr Primakova i Sovet molodykh uchenykh i aspirantov IMEMO RAN pod egidoi mezhdunarodnogo foruma 'Primakovskiie chteniia' organizuiut molodezhnuiu sessiiu na temu 'Bezopasnost v Evrope: poisk prostranstv dialoga'" [Under the auspices of the Primakov Readings International Forum, the Primakov Centre and the IMEMO Council of Young Scientists and Specialists are organizing a Youth Session of the Primakov Readings-2022 on the topic "Security in Europe: Looking for Dialogue Opportunities"]. Facebook, February 26, 2022. https://www.facebook.com/FondGorcakova/posts/5019940021362657.
276 Fond Gorchakova. 2022. "O sisteme SWIFT i ieie znachenii v sovremennoi mirovoi ekonomike" [On the SWIFT System and Its Significance in the Modern World Economy. Facebook page of the Gorchakov Fund]. Facebook, March 2, 2022. https://www.facebook.com/FondGorcakova/posts/5031525366870789.
277 Fond Gorchakova. 2022. "Priem zaiavok na IX Molodezhnyi forum 'Potsdamskikh vstrech' vremenno priostanovlen" [The 9th Potsdam Meetings Youth Forum—Applications Suspended. Facebook page of the Gorchakov Fund]. Facebook, March 2, 2022. https://www.facebook.com/FondGorcakova/posts/5031921890164470.
278 Fond Gorchakova. 2022. "Videozapis i tekstovaia versiia interviu glavy Russian Foreign Ministry—MID Rossii Sergeia Lavrova" [Video recording and text version of the interview of the Russian Foreign Minister Sergey Lavrov]. Facebook, March 4, 2022. https://www.facebook.com/FondGorcakova/posts/5036805319676127.
279 Fond Gorchakova. 2022. "'Mneniie eksperta': Igor Semenovskii ob istorii primeneniia sanktsii v mirovoi ekonomike" ["Expert Opinion": Igor Semenovsky on

continued to forward messages from the country's political leadership on foreign policy, which now had to adapt to the new reality.

However, by the summer of 2022, the Fund came up with a new, more "positive" agenda that better corresponded to Russia's new wave of intensification of its Eurasian integrationist efforts as well as increased attention to the countries of the Global South and its partners such as China or Iran, which both are expected to function as an alternative to former cooperation with the West.

The changes are noticeable in the de facto geographical priorities that the Fund pursued in 2022, which corresponded squarely with the Kremlin's integrationist ambitions. One remarkable development is the introduction of programmes in or related to Georgia, as there were growing fears that this country was again falling under Moscow's heavy political and economic influence. The Fund launched a whole array of new events and programmes in 2022, including the Georgian-Russian Dialogue held in July 2022,[280] the bilateral Russian-Georgian Forum attended by officials from both countries[281] and the accompanying Russian-Georgian Youth Forum (both held consecutively in December 2022).[282] The intensity of such activities was outstanding and unprecedented, arguably pointing to the rising interest of Russian elites in Georgia after the failure to hold control in Ukraine and Moldova. The issues discussed on these fora included Georgian neutrality vis-à-vis Russia in the Russian-

---

    the History of the Application of Sanctions in the Global Economy]. Facebook, March 10, 2022. https://www.facebook.com/watch/live/?ref=watch_permalink&v=456442316169346.

280 Fond Gorchakova. 2022. "V Moskve zavershilsia Gruzino-rossiiskii dialog 2022" [The Georgian-Russian Dialogue 2022 Ended in Moscow]. July 9, 2022. https://gorchakovfund.ru/portal/news/view/v_moskve_zavershilsia_gruzinorossiiskii_dialog_2022_60465.

281 Fond Gorchakova. 2022. "Pri podderzke Fonda Gorchakova sostoialsia dvustoronnii rossiisko-gruzinskii forum" [Bilateral Russian-Georgian Forum was held with the support of the Gorchakov Fund]. December 9, 2022. https://gorchakovfund.ru/portal/news/view/pri_podderzhke_fonda_gorchakova_sostoialsia_dvustoronnii_rossiiskogruzinskii_forum__61693.

282 Fond Gorchakova. 2022. "Rossiisko-Gruzinskii Molodezhnyi forum v Peterburge: priem zaiavok otkryt" [Russian-Georgian Youth Forum in St. Petersburg: the call for applications is open]. November 17, 2022. https://gorchakovfund.ru/portal/news/view/rossiiskogruzinskii_molodiozhnyi_forum_v_peterburge_priiom_zaiavok_otkryt_61541.

Ukrainian war, economic cooperation and development, especially in the context of Russian migration to Georgia after the launch of the big war and mobilisation (which is sometimes framed as "tourism"), visa regime, and flight connections between the two countries, i.e., their hypothetical resume on Russian requests. All of this was highly alarming in light of Georgia's application for EU membership status in the spring of 2022. It reflected Russian efforts to bring Georgia back into its sphere of influence with a combination of incentives and the threat of force.

It is telling that despite Moscow's ambitions, Moldova, on the contrary, remained outside of the scope of the Fund's activities. One possible explanation may be that the Georgian government proved more permissive concerning the Russian-Georgian rapprochement than the much more pro-European Moldovan authorities. Indeed, Maia Sandu's party and government made several significant steps to align their foreign policies with the EU's, while Georgia remained reluctant to do so.

Various configurations of projects for Russia-led integration of the former Soviet Union countries remained high on the Gorchakov Fund's agenda in 2022. There was high attention paid to Belarus, Armenia, and Central Asia. Some events were dedicated to Russian-Belarusian and Eurasian integration and included high-ranking officials. The Fund continued to facilitate the integration of Belarus and Russia with a number of events that attempted to relate topics of integration to various spheres of activity, including even seemingly distant issues of music. Thus, in November 2022, the Fund's Minsk Centre organised a meeting of experts who were going to discuss, among other things, whether there are "single musical origins of the Union State" of Russia and Belarus.[283] However,

---

[283] Fond Gorchakova. 2022. "Tsentr analiza i prognozirovaniia soiuznykh integratsionnykh protsessov provedet ekspertnuiu vstrechu o muzyke Rossii i Belorussii" [The Centre for Analysis and Forecasting of Union Integration Processes in Minsk to hold an expert meeting on music in Russia and in Belarus]. November 18, 2022. https://gorchakovfund.ru/portal/news/view/tsentr_an aliza_i_prognozirovaniia_soiuznykh_integratsionnykh_protsessov_provediot _ekspertnuiu_vstrechu_o_muzyke_rossii_i_belorussii_61552.

experts invited by the Fund convened to discuss more serious issues, such as whether there is a place for the Bologna Process in the educational systems of Russia and Belarus and whether there is a need to unify the two countries' educational systems.[284] In an even more ambitious integrationist move, participants of the 10th Belarusian-Russian Youth Forum held in 2022 determined to reframe this platform into a Youth Forum of Regions of the Union State. Meanwhile, the 2022 forum addressed questions about the two states' common historical and cultural heritage. The forum is part of a ministry-level integrationist effort between the Russian Federation and the Republic of Belarus.[285]

Another prominent example of the observation that the Fund's activities go hand in hand with the rapprochement of official relations between the countries is the case of Serbia. Put into an ambiguous position after the beginning of the full-scale invasion, the Serbian government did not join the EU-led sanctions regime against Russia (at least until March 2023). Simultaneously, the Fund seemed to launch another youth forum, the Russian-Balkan Youth Forum, held in Novi Sad, Serbia.[286] During the year, the Gorchakov Fund published numerous comments by Serbian experts or pundits on the role of the West, Russia's benevolent policies in the Balkans, etc. Predictably, Iran and China had a noticeable presence in the

---

[284] Fond Gorchakova. 2022. "Pri sodeistvii Fonda Gorchakova proydet rossiiskobelorusskaia vstrecha o vysshem obrazovanii Soiuznogo gosudarstva" [A Russian-Belarusian meeting on the higher education in the Union State will be held with the support of the Gorchakov Fund]. August 23, 2022. https://gorc hakovfund.ru/portal/news/view/pri_sodeistvii_fonda_gorchakova_proidiot _rossiiskobelorusskaia_vstrecha_o_vysshem_obrazovanii_soiuznogo_gosudar stva_60850.

[285] Fond Gorchakova. 2022. "V 2023 godu vpervye proydet Molodezhnyi fourm regionov Soiuznogo gosudarstva" [In 2023, the Youth Forum of the Regions of the Union State to be held for the first time]. June 21, 2022. https:// gorchakovfund.ru/portal/news/view/v_2023_godu_vpervye_proidet_molo dezhnyi_forum_regionov_soiuznogo_gosudarstva_60303.

[286] Fond Gorchakova. 2022. "V Riazani pri uchastii Fonda Gorchakova otkrylsia Rossiisko-Balkanskii molodezhnyi forum" [Russian-Balkan Youth Forum was opened in Ryazan' with participation of the Gorchakov Fund]. December 14, 2022. https://gorchakovfund.ru/portal/news/view/v_riazani_pri_uchastii_ fonda_gorchakova_otkrylsia_rossiiskobalkanskii_molodiozhnyi_forum_6172 2.

topics of the events organised or funded by the Gorchakov Fund, exploring opportunities for closer cooperation between these countries and Russia.

Thematically, the Fund's events centred on topics closely corresponding to the main pillars of the Primakov doctrine. Among the issues addressed was the question of multipolarity and the anticipation, among international relations experts, of the future resolution of the growing tensions between major competing powers in the world.[287] Also, the Fund seemed to underline the alliances with Russia's participation as a hypothetical counterweight to the U.S.-led projects, such as BRICS, the Shanghai Cooperation Organization, and the Eurasian Economic Union. Only a few discussions were held in 2022 that addressed topics related to Ukraine, Europe, or North America. One of the rare exceptions was a publication under the rubric "Expert's opinion" with a comment about the reunification of Germany, putting in doubt the legal aspects of East Germany's post-1989 incorporation into the FRG, as well as the successes of contemporary Germany's integration thirty years after its commencement.[288] Otherwise, at least in the Gorchakov Fund and in terms of topics of events, Russia's great re-orientation to the East seemed to have been accomplished.

Conclusions

Founded in 2010 on a wave of economic boom and increasing Russian federal budget revenues driven by rising global energy prices, the Gorchakov Fund GONGO has become part and parcel of an

---

[287] Fond Gorchakova. 2022. "'Staraiia sistema rushitsia, novaiia eshche ne prishla': v Fonde Gorchakova proshla konferentsiia '2022: Predvaritelnyie itogi'" [The old system is collapsing, the new one has not come yet: the conference '2022: Preliminary results' was held at the Gorchakov Fund]. December 30, 2022. https://gorchakovfund.ru/portal/news/view/_staraia_sistema_rushitsia_no vaia_eshche_ne_prishla_v_fonde_gorchakova_proshla_konferentsiia_2022_pr edvaritelnye_itogi_61831.

[288] Fond Gorchakova. 2022. "'Mnenie eksperta': Artyom Sokolov — ob ocherednoi godovshchine obiedineniia Germanii" ['An expert's opinion': Artyom Sokolov — on another anniversary of the reunification of Germany]. October 6, 2022. https://gorchakovfund.ru/portal/news/view/mnenie_eksperta_artio m_sokolov__ob_ocherednoi_godovshchine_obedineniia_germanii_61116.

ecosystem of interconnected state pro-government organisations promoting the Kremlin's long-established foreign policy narratives, formed along the key principles established already by Evgeny Primakov Sr. and inspired by the symbolic figure of the chancellor Aleksander Gorchakov. Since the end of the 1990s, these narratives have been revolving around the idea of Russia re-collecting itself economically and politically after the defeat in the Cold War and the subsequent collapse of the Soviet Union to re-incorporate the lost territories and reassure the leading position of Russia through reformatting the world order towards multipolarity in cooperation with the ascending powers of the Global South.

Such an openly revanchist ideology needed some sugar-coating and presentation as Russia's "objective" foreign policy interests to be promoted in the professional communities of other countries; thus, the Fund has been a helpful instrument in this regard, enabling different types of dialogues in and about the regions of interest to Russian foreign policy. The Fund has a long-term strategy approach, as its activities are focused on creating lasting ties and consolidating the Russian narratives between young researchers and experts from Russia and foreign countries, although it also supports and promotes the key Russian foreign policy pundits and their ideas. The Gorchakov Fund's key aim seems to be forming a circle of friends among future foreign policy elites in Western and non-Western countries.

The Fund's primary modus operandi was to (co)-hold a variety of self-designed priority dialogue platforms and to simultaneously invest in non-governmental organisations and their representatives from the different corners of the world for projects that promote Russia-beneficial foreign policy ideas. Although tightly controlled by the government, the status of a non-governmental organisation has probably been intended to enable the Fund to provide grants to foreign nationals and organisations. Still, it could also serve the purpose of hiding the sources for over 50% of its revenues and reporting as little as possible on its expenditures. On the surface, the Fund seemed to emulate, at least pro forma, the activities of Western funds and donor organisations, while in essence, it had reverted to mere ideological indoctrination with the Kremlin's narratives (Tafuro 2014, 5).

Interestingly, of all the three Russian soft power institutions analysed in this book, the Gorchakov Fund has taken the most reserved position during the all-out war with Ukraine and, unlike Rossotrudnichestvo and the "Russkiy Mir" Foundation, avoids direct propaganda and war effort support, still trying to present Russian foreign policy ideas analytically and adjusting to the wartime reality (doubling, for instance, on its activities in Georgia).

Conclusions
Russian Cultural Diplomacy after 2022

Nadiia Koval, Denys Tereshchenko

Three newly founded or restructured Russian public and cultural diplomacy organisations that have been analysed in this book were designed to promote the revanchist goals of overcoming the "greatest catastrophe of the twentieth century," i.e., the collapse of the Soviet Union, and were tasked with restoring or perhaps establishing Russian "soft power" to maintain the attraction and affection for Russian culture on the global stage. This ambitious endeavour was made possible by the availability of the necessary financial resources, partly due to the dramatic rise in energy costs worldwide in the early 2000s and Russia's economic recovery after the crises of the 1990s.

However, two decades later, the results of these organisations' activities are somewhat contradictory. On the one hand, global studies and opinion polls indicate that attitudes toward Russia, particularly in the West, have not improved or have even worsened, most dramatically after the 2022 invasion (Gramlich 2023; Brand Finance 2022) and Russia's key state cultural diplomacy organisations were first designated as propaganda machines (2016) and then sanctioned, together with their leadership (2022), limiting their capacities and credibility in a number of key (Western) regions and countries. The inner drivers of Russian cultural diplomacy, e. g., the direct subordination of cultural diplomacy to the political rationale, its firm integration into the state apparatus, its almost total reliance on the state budget, and the focus on revanchist and conservative values of the "Russian world," all suggest that Russia's cultural policy is currently being used for political goals, which might influence the usual approaches to building cultural relations with authoritarian countries.

On the other hand, by imitating *pro forma* the activities of global institutions of public and cultural diplomacy, including the creation of representative offices abroad, the provision of grants for artistic projects, the organisation of Russian language studies, and the hosting of cultural events, these organisations have been long spinning the narratives that were taken at face value, promoting the current Russian regime's understanding of the world order and supporting Russian-centred versions of history and politics of the whole Eastern European region, influencing indirectly or directly the decision-making processes in different countries. For instance, revising and reassessing these ideas and narratives in Russian and Eastern European studies has only started and does not go without hurdles.

There is still a number of political leaders and academic and think-tank intellectuals who accept the logic of spheres of influence, believe in the close cultural and historical affinity between Ukrainians and Russians that affects the sovereignty of Ukraine and its parts, and find the Russian logic of restructuring the current world order appealing or even worth attempting, etc. For several reasons, these beliefs are more widespread in the Global South. Not surprisingly, as Russian aggression came to be condemned in the West with the respective actions taken against its propaganda and "soft power" organisations, this is where Russia claims to at least partially relocate its representative offices and cultural diplomacy efforts in general.[289]

How did the war challenge the premises of Russia's cultural diplomacy? At least, as long as Russia still believes that its victory is possible, nothing has changed in essence. Russia continuously instrumentalises culture politically in two ways: promoting a cultural background for reassembling the "Russian civilisation," mainly in the post-Soviet countries, and using its key cultural diplomacy institutions for war propaganda and war effort support, as elaborated in the previous chapters.

---

289 Rossotrudnichestvo. 2022. „Itogi raboty Rossotrudnichestva v 2022 godu: novyie usloviia gumanitarnoi politiki" [Results of Rossotrudnichestvo's activities in 2022: new conditions for humanitarian policy], December 21, 2022, https://rs.gov.ru/news/itogi-raboty-rossotrudnichestva-v-2022-godu-novye-usloviya-gumanitarnoj-politiki/.

The key foreign policy documents now postulate directly that Russia is a civilisation in itself, centred around the Russkiy Mir ideology and its values. Promoting and assembling this "Russian world," with a particular emphasis on the compatriots as a group and former Soviet states as a geographical focus, including through (re)education and Russian language learning promotion, remains the task at hand. Thus, amid the war, the Pushkin Institute has produced a new edition of their yearly Index on the condition and status of the Russian language worldwide, both globally and in the former USSR republics (see Arefiev et al. 2022) and the year 2023 has been declared the year of the Russian language in the CIS, charging the freshly created Russian MFA Department for Multilateral Humanitarian Cooperation and Cultural Relations (DMHCCR) to coordinate all the activities of the state programme of promotion of the Russian language abroad.[290]

Interestingly, some cultural diplomacy bureaucrats, especially those with Western-style expertise in project management, are very well aware of the weak sides of Russian cultural diplomacy, but mainly from the organisational side, not so much on the level of the essence and goals. The study case is Dmitry Polikanov, the deputy head of Rossotrudnichestvo, one of the most outspoken representatives with a solid background in the NGO sector. In his most recent evaluation of the state and prospects of Russia's cultural diplomacy, one year after the all-out invasion of Ukraine started, his personal and organisation's open support for the war remained unchanged and not reflected upon. He framed the war as the battle between good and evil, meaning Russia and the "collective West," and thus emphasised the importance of the "fields of mental battles" and the imminent necessity of propaganda and informational warfare.

---

290 Redaktsiia portala "Russkiy Mir" [Editorial office of the "Russkiy Mir" portal]. 2023. "Departament MID stanet operatorom kompleksnoj programmy po prodvizheniyu russkogo yazyka za rubezhom" [Department of MFA will become an operator of a comprehensive programme for the promotion of the Russian language abroad]. 15.02.2023, https://russkiymir.ru/news/310406/.

> The key battles today are not fought on the battlefields but rather in news feeds, the metaverse of social networks, and communities united by a personal interest in a particular subject and providing a clear sense of "friend or foe" identification, i.e., in fact, in people's consciousness. In an environment of informational noise, facts become distorted by multiple perceptions, lose their value, and drown in a stream of interpretations, including interpretations through the lens of ideology. Thus, trust issues and technologies for manipulating public opinion come to the fore. In a world where news only lasts one day (or even less), most users have no time to figure out the truth about the stories of the Malaysian Boeing, Novichok, or Donbas events. In this case, the first mode of thought (according to Nobel laureate Daniel Kahneman's classification) is used, employing templates and stereotypes based on fundamental ideas of "right or wrong." This should become the object of influence for the effective dissemination of significant meanings for a particular country. (Polikanov 2023)

Thus, he only bemoans the instruments and the organisational peculiarities that make those goals less achievable and even boasts that the exceptional conditions of the war have created a unique momentum for introducing changes that had been resisted by the more conservative circles before. With his experience and expertise in NGO, he does not shy away from espousing distinctly anti-Western rhetoric while deploying Western instruments of effective project management and evaluation, involving a more thorough ranging and prioritisation of the goals, connecting them to national development goals, answering all why and what, quantifying KPIs and more effectively targeting audiences and the influence on them, criticising overreliance on traditional audiences and preaching to the choir, and the demands of more targeted work with local media and not only Russian media designed for international broadcasting. He criticised the overlapping functions and lack of coordination between numerous "soft power" institutions, and in particular, the tensions between the embassies in foreign countries and Rossotrudnichestvo representations there as to the preferred activities and formats, especially the traditionalist and inflexible top-down approaches of the former.

Another meaningful change, considering the tactic of Russian soft power after the war, is the will and willingness to function via creating new GONGOs and other "non-state actors," as well as seeking new, more flexible models for state institutions to establish their presence in foreign countries. This provides more flexibility and authenticity and allows to avoid cumbersome public procurement procedures as well as circumvent the limitations of the traditional Russian Houses, which on the one hand, have protected diplomatic status and function as parts of the embassies, but also have significant restrictions as to financing foreign partners, accepting non-state money, establishing commercial services, and in general, providing people-friendly services.

Russia's cultural diplomacy prospects are still contingent and depend upon various factors. The first, i.e., the results of the current Russo-Ukrainian war, are still undetermined and hard to foresee as the war is far from its end in its second year. Its outcomes, especially if Russia's armed forces come out of it severely damaged, might significantly hinder any subsequent Russian effort at promoting its "soft power." This estimate has already been partly proven in Moldova, where Russia's outright aggression forced the Moldovan elites to reconsider the country's neutrality and bid for EU membership together with Ukraine.

In the West, the discussion already centres on culture's everless credible neutrality, its independence from politics, and the (in)admissibility of its "cancelling." Here, the very obvious politicization of culture inherent in Russian policies might change lots of long-established *idées reçues* not only about Russian culture per se but also about the political and cultural peculiarities of numerous states of Eastern Europe, the Caucasus, and Central Asia that Russocentric perceptions and explanations have often overshadowed.

Another crucial question is how Russia will manage its declared turn towards the so-called "Global South" in its cultural diplomacy activities. Although Rossotrudnichestvo has already opened several new offices in several African countries, it remains to be seen whether it will succeed in finding a common conceptual framework to institutionalise this cooperation and establish a sustainable positive image of Russia on that continent. It is essential that the Russian language still retains political and cultural attractiveness in a number of societies in the Global South. In those regions, Russia relativizes its aggressive policies using the "fight against imperialism" rhetoric of the Western states, raises hopes for economic investment and military support, builds alliances with other anti-Western states, and enjoys a low level of basic awareness of Russia and Russian culture, making these countries susceptible to propaganda clichés. Seeking things in common, Russia puts forward undistinguished "traditional values," which could provide part of the appeal for Russian cultural diplomacy among authoritarian regimes espousing antiliberal values worldwide.

Thus, countering Russian ambitions within Europe and on other continents is one of the major challenges for the years to come, as Russia is likely to keep forcing its geopolitical ambitions and imperialist aims through soft power instruments. Nevertheless, as Joseph Nye, the leading theorist of "soft power," wrote in 2013, "For a declining power like Russia (or Britain before it), a residual soft power helps to cushion the fall" (Nye 2013).

Bibliography

Arefiev et al. *Indeks polozheniia russkogo iazyka v mire. 30 let Sodruzhestvu nezavisimykh gosudarstv. Vypusk 2* [Index of the status of the Russian language in the world. 30 years of the Commonwealth of Independent States. Issue #2]. Gosudarstvennyi institut russkogo iazyka im. A. S. Pushkina [The Pushkin State Russian Language Institute], Moskva, 2022. https://cis.minsk.by/img/news/24669/63bfff90826a3.pdf.

Atasuntsev, Aleksandr, Natalia Galimova, and Polina Khimshiashvili. 2020. "Vlasti pristupili k reforme rossiiskoi 'miagkoi sily'. Zachem obsuzhdaietsia ideia sozdania goskorporatsii po prodvizheniu interesov Moskvy" [The authorities have launched the reform of Russian 'soft power.' Why is the idea of establishing a state corporation aimed at promoting Moscow's interests is discussed]. *RBK.* July 13, 2020. https://www.rbc.ru/politics/13/07/2020/5f05a8079a79477c4c39bfa5.

Baranovskaia, Marina. "'Potsdamskiie vstrechi': kak FRG i RF vybratsia iz eskalatsii." [The Potsdam Meetings: How Germany and Russia Can Get Out of the Spiral of Escalation]. *Deutsche Welle.* May 18, 2021. https://www.dw.com/ru/potsdamskie-vstrechi-kak-germanii-i-rossii-vybratsja-iz-spirali-jeskalacii/a-57573920.

Brand Finance. 2022. "Nation Brands 2022. Russia's nation brand value takes $150 billion hit as invasion of Ukraine backfires." https://brandirectory.com/rankings/nation-brands/2022.

Braun, Aurel. "NATO and Russia: Post-Georgia Threat Perceptions". *IFRI Russia/NIS Center,* 2009. https://www.ifri.org/sites/default/files/atoms/files/ifrirussianatobraunengavril09.pdf.

Brilyov, Sergei. "Yevgeny Primakov. 85." 2014. Video, 51:40. https://smotrim.ru/brand/58622.

British Council. n. d. "2020-21 Annual Report and Accounts." https://www.britishcouncil.org/sites/default/files/annualreport_2020-21.pdf.

Burlinova, Natalia, Polina Vasilenko, Viktoria Ivanchenko, and Oleg Shakirov. "10 shagov na puti k effektivnoi publichnoi diplomatii Rossii. Ekspertnyi obzor rossiiskoi publichnoi diplomatii v 2018-2019 gg." [10 steps towards Russia's effective public diplomacy. An expert review of Russian public diplomacy in 2018-2019]. *RSMD* #52 (2020). https://russiancouncil.ru/papers/RussianPublicDiplomacy-Report52-Rus.pdf.

Burlinova, Nataliia. "Rossiiskiie NPO-mezhdunarodniki v sisteme publichnoi diplomatii Rossii: tipologiia, problemy vzaimodeistviia s gosudarstvom i vneshnii obraz v usloviiakh sanktsii" [Russian NGOs dealing with international relations in the system of Russia's public diplomacy: typology, problems of interaction with the state, and their external image under sanctions]. *RSMD* #81 (2022). https://russian council.ru/activity/publications/rossiyskie-npo-mezhdunarodniki-v-sisteme-publichnoy-diplomatii-rossii-tipologiya-problemy-vzaim odeys/.

Chernenko, Yelena. 2013. "'Miagkuiu silu' snabzhaiiut sredstvami" ["Soft power" is provided with means]. *Kommersant*. June 5, 2013. https://www.kommersant.ru/doc/2204815.

Dergachev, Vladimir, Irina Babloian, Dmitry Nikitin, and Yury Kukin. 2022. "'Gradus napriazhennosti stikh.' Zamglavy Rossotrudnichestva—o 'volnakh rusofobii,' uyekhavshykh artistakh i vzryve v TsAR" ["The degree of tension has decreased." Rossotrudnichestvo's Deputy Head about the "waves of Russophobia," the artists who have left and the explosion in CAR]. *RTVI*. December 20, 2022. https://rtvi.com/news/gradus-napryazhennosti-stih-zamglavy-ros sotrudnichestva-o-volnah-rusofobii-uehavshih-artistah-i-vzryve-v-c zar/.

Ditkovska, S. "Peredumovy stvorennia ta pochatky diialnosti Ukrainskoho tovarystva druzhby ta kulturnoho zviazku z zarubizhnymy krainamy" [The background and early work of the Ukrainian Society of Friendship and Cultural Relations with Foreign Countries]. *Hrani* 5 (2014), 102–108. http://nbuv.gov.ua/UJRN/Grani_2014_5_21.

Dmitriieva, Olga. 2015. "Dorogiie 'sootechestvenniki'" [Dear/Expensive "Compatriots"]. *Novoie vremia*. September 29, 2015. https://new times.ru/articles/detail/102183/.

Dosie [Dossier]. 2021. "Chto takoie i zachem nuzhno Rossotrudnichestvo" [What is Rossotrudnichestvo and its purpose?]. February 24, 2021. https://dossier.center/rossotr/.

Dosie [Dossier]. 2023. "V 2021 godu Kreml planiroval zakhvatit ne tolko Ukrainu, no i Belarus—pravda postepenno" [In 2021, Kremlin was planning to seize not only Ukraine but also Belarus, however, gradually]. February 20, 2023. https://dossier.center/union-br/.

Dzvelishvili, Nata and Tazo Kupreishvili. "Russian impact on Georgian media and NGOs." *Damoukidebloba.com*. June 2015. https://idfi.ge/en/russian-influence-of-georgian-ngos-and-media.

Fediakina, Anna. 2014. "Konstantin Kosachev: Raskola 'russkogo' iz-za sobytii na Ukraine net" [Konstantin Kosachev: There is no split of Russkiy Mir as a result of the developments in Ukraine]. *RG.ru*. August 19, 2014. https://rg.ru/2014/08/20/kosachev.html.

Fishman, Diana. 2022. "Ura-kompatrioty. Kak rossiiskaiia diaspora v SShA obsluzhivaiet interesy Kremlia" [Hurrah-compatriots. How the Russian diaspora in the U.S.A. serves the Kremlin's interests]. *The Insider*. November 8, 2022. https://theins.ru/politika/256770.

Fishman, Diana. 2023. "Ura-kompatrioty-3. Kak potomki beloemigrantov stali glavnymi agentami vliianiia Kremlia vo Frantsii" [Hurrah-compatriots-3. How the descendants of white émigrés became the Kremlin's main agents of influence in France]. *The Insider*. February 18, 2023. https://theins.ru/politika/259028.

Foxall, Andrew. *The Kremlin's Sleight of Hand: Russia's Soft Sower Offensive in the UK*. Policy paper no. 3. Russia Studies Centre at The Henry Jackson Society, 2015. https://henryjacksonsociety.org/wp-content/uploads/2019/01/HJS-The-Kremlins-Sleight-of-Hand-Report-NEW-web.pdf.

Gabritchidze, Nini. 2022. "Rise of Georgian alt-right group sparks fear of unrest." *Eurasianet*. March 23, 2022. https://eurasianet.org/rise-of-georgian-alt-right-group-sparks-fear-of-unrest.

Goethe Institut. „Jahrbuch/Annual Report 2020/2021." 2021. https://www.goethe.de/resources/files/pdf266/gi_jahrbuch_2021_web.pdf.

Gramlich, John. 2023. "What public opinion surveys found in the first year of the war in Ukraine." *Pew Research Center*. February 23, 2023. https://www.pewresearch.org/short-reads/2023/02/23/what-public-opinion-surveys-found-in-the-first-year-of-the-war-in-ukraine/.

Gubernatorov, Yegor. 2019. "Chislo izuchaiiushchikh russkii iazyk v mire upalo v 2 raza so vremen raspada SSSR" [The number of Russian learners in the world halves since the collapse of the Soviet Union]. *RBK*. November 28, 2019. https://www.rbc.ru/society/28/11/2019/5ddd18099a79473d0d9b0ab1.

Gussarova, Anna. "Russian Soft Power in Kazakhstan (and Central Asia): Taken for Granted?" *Central Asia Institute for Strategic Studies*. 2017. https://library.fes.de/pdf-files/bueros/kasachstan/14108.pdf.

Horbulin, Volodymyr. *The World Hybrid War: Ukrainian Forefront*. National Institute for Strategic Studies. Kharkiv: Folio, 2017. https://www.worldcat.org/title/world-hybrid-war-ukrainian-forefront/oclc/1000298302.

Hrupa z analizu hibrydnykh zahroz [Group for the Analysis of Hybrid Threats]. 2020. "Yak Kreml vykorystovuie 'miaku sylu' dlia hibrydnoho vplyvu: keis Rosspivrobitnytstva v Ukraiini" [How the Kremlin exploits soft power for hybrid influence: The case of Rossotrudnichestvo in Ukraine]. *Ukraine Crisis Media Center.* September 9, 2020. https://uacrisis.org/uk/how-kremlin-uses-soft-power-for-malign-influence-case-of-rossotrudnichestvo-in-ukraine.

Iliuk, T. "Transformatsiia publichnoi ta kulturnoi dyplomatii Rosii na suchasnomu etapi: diialnist 'Rosspivrobitnytstva'" [Transformation of Russia's public and cultural diplomacy at the present stage: The activities of Rossotrudnichestvo]. In Bulvinskyi, A. (ed.) *Krainy postradianskoho prostoru: vyklyky modernizatsii: zbirnyk naukovykh prats* []. Countries of the post-Soviet space: Challenges of modernisation]. Derzhavna ustanova "Instytut vsesvitnioi istorii NAN Ukrainy," Kyiv, 2016: 19–32. https://elibrary.ivinas.gov.ua/310/1/postrad 2016_-20-33.pdf.

Institut français [French Institute]. « Rapport d'activité » [Report on the activities]. 2020. https://www.institutfrancais.com/sites/default/files/medias/documents/if_ra_2020.pdf.

Khamraiev, Viktor. 2015. "Minobrnauki nuzhny dengi na 'Russkiy mir'" [Ministry of Education and Science in need of money for the "Russian world"]. *Kommersant.* June 24, 2015. https://www.kommersant.ru/doc/2753934.

Khimshiashvili, Polina. 2014. "'V krizis v razy povysilas poseshchaiemost kursov baleta,'—Konstantin Kosachev, rukovoditel Rossotrudnichestva" [Rossotrudnichestvo Head Konstantin Kosachev: "Attendance of ballet courses increased severalfold during the crisis"]. *Vedomosti.* March 13, 2014. https://www.vedomosti.ru/newspaper/articles/2014/03/13/v-krizis-v-razy-povysilas-poseschaemost-kursov-baleta.

Khimshiashvili, Polina. 2018. "Glava Rossotrudnichestva—RBK: 'My na latinitse pisat ne budem'" [Head of Rossotrudnichestvo to RBC: "We will not write in the Latin script"]. *RBK.* September 12, 2018. https://www.rbc.ru/interview/politics/12/09/2018/5b90ee6f9a794768296 7bd0a.

Kochin, Vladimir. "Russkiy iazyk—predmet politicheskii" [The Russian Language is a Political Subject]. *Strategiia Rossii* 6 (June 2016): 21–28. https://istina.msu.ru/media/publications/article/93c/16e/225240 72/str_6_2016.pdf.

Kornatskii, Nikolaii. 2015. "Esli nam dadut bolshiie biudzhety—vezde budet russkiy flag" [If We Are Given Big Budgets, the Russian Flag Will Be Everywhere]. *Izvestiia.* July 22, 2015. https://iz.ru/news/589034.

Kosachev, Konstantin. "Vneshnepoliticheskaia vertikal" [Foreign Policy Vertical]. *Russia in Global Politics*, No.3 (2004). https://globalaffairs.ru/articles/vneshnepoliticheskaya-vertikal/.

Kosachev, Konstantin. 2023. "Rossotrudnichestvo: istoki, realii, perspektivy" [Rossotrudnichestvo: origins, realities, perspectives]. *RSMD*. November 15, 2023. https://russiancouncil.ru/analytics-and-comments/comments/rossotrudnichestvo-istoki-realii-perspektivy/.

Koval, Nadiia, Maryna Irysova, Serhii Tytiuk, and Denys Tereshchenko. *Rossotrudnichestvo: The Unbearable Harshness of Soft Power*. Ukrainian Institute, Kyiv, 2022. https://ui.org.ua/en/sectors-en/rossotrudnichestvo-the-unbearable-harshness-of-soft-power-2/.

Kozdra, Michał. "The Boundaries of Russian Identity Analysis of the Concept of Russkiy MIR in Contemporary Russian Online Media." *Lingua Cultura* 12, no. 1 (February 28, 2018): 61–66. https://doi.org/10.21512/lc.v12i1.2004.

Kuzmin, Vladimir. 2019. "Rossotrudnichestvo poluchit sredstva na znachimyie zakhoroneniia za rubezhom" [Rossotrudnichestvo will receive funds for important burials abroad]. *RG.ru*, June 14, 2019. https://rg.ru/2019/06/14/rossotrudnichestvo-poluchit-sredstva-na-znachimye-zahoroneniia-za-rubezhom.html.

Laamanen, Ville. "VOKS, Cultural Diplomacy and the Shadow of the Lubianka: Olavi Paavolainen's 1939 Visit to the Soviet Union." *Journal of Contemporary History* 52, no. 4 (2017): 1022–41. https://www.jstor.org/stable/26416652.

Laru, Dmitrii. 2022. "'My vidim ostorozhnye signaly o tom, chto psikhoz budet svorachivat'sya' Glava Rossotrudnichestva Yevgeniy Primakov—ob otmene russkoy kul'-tury, natsionalisticheskikh nastroeniyakh za rubezhom i rabote v novykh usloviyakh" ['We are seeing very cautious positive signals that this psychosis will wind down.' Yevgeny Primakov, head of Rossotrudnichestvo, about the cancelling of the Russian culture, nationalistic feelings abroad, and working in new conditions] *Izvestiia*, June 16, 2022. https://iz.ru/1350596/dmitrii-laru/my-vidim-ostorozhnye-signaly-o-tom-chto-psikhoz-budet-svorachivatsia

Laruelle, Marlene. *The "Russian World": Russia's Soft Power and Geopolitical Imagination*. Center for Global Interests, 2015.

Lutsevych, Orysia. *Agents of the Russian World: Proxy Groups in the Contested Neighbourhood Research Paper*. Royal Institute of International Affairs, 2016. https://www.chathamhouse.org/sites/default/files/publications/research/2016-04-14-agents-russian-world-lutsevych.pdf.

Malinova, Olga. "Political Uses of the Great Patriotic War in Post-Soviet Russia from Yeltsin to Putin." In: Fedor, Julie, Kangaspuro, Markku, Lassila, Jussi, Zhurzhenko, Tatiana (eds) *War and Memory in Russia, Ukraine and Belarus*. Palgrave Macmillan Memory Studies. Palgrave Macmillan, Cham, 2017. https://doi.org/10.1007/978-3-319-66523-8_2

Mann, Yan. "(Re)Cycling the Collective Memory of the Great Patriotic War." *Journal of Slavic Military Studies* 33, no. 4 (October 1, 2020): 508–13. https://doi.org/10.1080/13518046.2020.1845080.

Masiyenko, Yulia, Kateryna Zahryvenko, Nadiia Koval, and Denys Tereshchenko. *"The Russian flag will be flown wherever Russian is spoken": "Russkiy Mir" Foundation*. Ukrainian Institute, Kyiv, 2022. https://ui.org.ua/en/sectors-en/russkiy-mir-foundation-2/.

Meister, Stefan. *Isolation and Propaganda. The Roots and Instruments of Russia's Disinformation Campaign*. DGAP, Transatlantic Academy Paper Series, 2016. https://dgap.org/system/files/article_pdfs/meister_isolationpropoganda_apr16_web_1.pdf.

Nevezhyn, V. "Sovetskaia politika i kulturnyiie szviazi s Germaniei (1939–1941 gg.)" [Soviet politics and cultural relations with Germany (1939–1941)]. *Otechestvennaiia istoriia* 1, 1993: 18–34. https://российская-история.рф/archive/1993-1.

Nikolskaya, Polina, Mari Saito, Maria Tsvetkova, and Anton Zverev. 2023. "Pro-Putin operatives in Germany work to turn Berlin against Ukraine." *Reuters*. January 3, 2023. https://www.reuters.com/investigates/special-report/ukraine-crisis-germany-influencers/.

Nikonov, Vyacheslav (ed.). *Smysly i tsennosti Russkogo mira. Sbornik statei i materialov kruglykh stolov, organizovannykh fondom "Russkiy mir"* [Meanings and Values of the Russian World. Collection of Articles and Materials of Round Tables Organized by the "Russkiy Mir" Foundation]. Moscow, 2010. https://russkiymir.ru/events/docs/Смыслы%20и%20ценности%20Русского%20мира%202010.pdf.

Novyie izvestiia. 2019. "Yevgeny Primakov: 'Khvatit nam balalaiek v gumanitarnoi politike!'" [Yevgeny Primakov: "Enough with balalaikas in humanitarian policy!"]. *Novyie izvestiia*. April 8, 2019. https://newizv.ru/article/general/08-04-2019/evgeniy-primakov-hvatit-nam-balalaek-v-gumanitarnoy-politike.

Nye Jr. J. S. 2013. "What China and Russia Don't Get About Soft Power." *Foreign Policy*. April 29, 2013. https://foreignpolicy.com/2013/04/29/what-china-and-russia-dont-get-about-soft-power/.

Paresishvili, Mziia. 2019. "Russkii tsents v stakane vody" [Russian Centre in a Glass of Water]. *Ekho Kavkaza*. December 9, 2019. https://www.ekhokavkaza.com/a/30316411.html.

Petrov, Sergei. 2012. "U obshchestvennoi diplomatii bolshie vozmozhnosti" [Public diplomacy offers great opportunities]. *Rosbalt*. June 7, 2012. https://www.rosbalt.ru/main/2012/06/07/990104.html.

Pilko, Alexey. 2015. "Leonid Drachevskii: Fond Gorchakova gotov k rasshireniiu sfery deiatelnosti" [Leonid Drachevsky: 'The Gorchakov Fund Is Ready to Expand the Scope of Its Activities]. *Fond podderzhki i zashchity prav sootechestvinnikov, prozhivaiushchikh za rubezhom* [Foundation for the Suppor and Protection of Compatriots Living Abroad]. July 28, 2015. https://pravfond.ru/press-tsentr/stati/leonid_drachevskiy_fond_gorchakova_gotov_k_rasshireniyu_sfery_deyatelnosti_1377/.

Polikanov, Dmitry. 2023. "Rol' 'miagkoi sily' v mezhdunarodnykh otnosheniakh: sovremennyi rossiiskii opyt i perspektivy." [The role of 'soft power' in international relatios: contemporary Russian experience and perspectives]. *RSMD*. April 17, 2023. https://russiancouncil.ru/analytics-and-comments/analytics/rol-myagkoy-sily-v-mezhdunarodnykh-otnosheniyakh-sovremennyy-rossiyskiy-opyt-i-perspektivy/.

Popovic, Milos R., Erin K. Jenne, and Juraj Medzihorsky. "Charm Offensive or Offensive Charm? An Analysis of Russian and Chinese Cultural Institutes Abroad." *Europe-Asia Studies* 72, no. 9 (July 31, 2020): 1445–67. https://doi.org/10.1080/09668136.2020.1785397.

Prezident Rossii [President of Russia]. 2014. "Obrashcheniie Prezidenta Rossiiskoi Federatsii" [Address of the President of the Russian Federation]. March 18, 2014. http://kremlin.ru/events/president/news/20603.

Prezident Rossii [President of Russia]. 2021. "Bolshaia press-konferentsiia Vladimira Putina" [Big press conference of Vladimir Putin]. December 23, 2021. http://kremlin.ru/events/president/news/67438.

Putin, Vladimir. 2012. "Rossiia sosredotachivaietsia — vyzovy, na kotoryie my dolzhny otvetit" [Russia collecting itself — challenges we must address]. *Izvestiia*. January 16, 2012. https://iz.ru/news/511884.

Reid, Ernest. "Moscow's Public Diplomacy and Russophilia in Serbia 2012–2019." *Godišnjak FPN*, no. 23 (January 1, 2020): 119–39. https://www.ceeol.com/search/article-detail?id=903685.

Rossotrudnichestvo. 2021. "Doklad o rezultatakh deiatelnosti Rossotrudnichestva po realizatsii vozlozhennykh na nego polnomochii za 2020 god" [Report on the Results of Rossotrudnichestvo's Activities in Realization of its Mandate]. https://rs.gov.ru/app/uploads/2022/12/doklad-o-rezultatah-deyatelnosti-rossotrudnichestva-2020-g..pdf.

Rossotrudnichestvo. 2023. "2022 Rossotrudnichestvo." https://rs.gov.ru/app/uploads/2023/03/rossotrudnichestvo-2023-kopiya-4.pdf.

Russkiy Arkhipelag. 2001. "Russkiy Mir: vosstanovleniie konteksta" [Russian World: Reconstructing the Context]. September 2001. https://archipelag.ru/ru_mir/history/history01/shedrovitsky-russmir/.

Schwirtz, Michael, Anton Troianovski, Yousur Al Hlou, Masha Froliak, Adam Entous, and Thomas Gibbons-Neff. 2022. "How Putin's War in Ukraine Became a Catastrophe for Russia." *New York Times*. December 16, 2022. https://www.nytimes.com/interactive/2022/12/16/world/europe/russia-putin-war-failures-ukraine.html.

Simons, Greg. "The Role of Russian NGOs in New Public Diplomacy," *Journal of Political Marketing*, 17, 2 (2018), 137–160, https://doi.org/10.1080/15377857.2018.1447755.

Sirena. 2022a. "Kreml' otdal na propagandu voiny eshche milliard. Pomozhet li emu eto?" [Kremlin has spent one more billion on war propaganda. Will it help?]. November 7, 2022. https://telegra.ph/Kreml-otdal-na-propagandu-vojny-eshche-milliard-Pomozhet-li-emu-ehto-11-07.

Sirena. 2022b. "Prezidentskii fond propagandy: komu Putin razdal milliard na podderzhku voiny. Rassledovanie 'Sireny'" [The presidential fund of propaganda: Who received billion for the support of war from Putin]. September 14, 2022. https://fund.sirena.news/.

Skak, Mette. "Russia's New 'Monroe Doctrine.'" In *Russian Foreign Policy in the 21st Century*, edited by Roger E. Kanet, 138–154. Palgrave Macmillan, 2011.

Skak, Mette. "Russian strategic culture: the role of today's *chekisty*," *Contemporary Politics* 22, 3 (2016): 324–341, https://doi.org/10.1080/13569775.2016.1201317.

Smagliy, Kateryna. *Hybrid Analytica: Pro-Kremlin Expert Propaganda in Moscow, Europe and the U.S. A Case Study on Think Tanks and Universities*. The Institute of Modern Russia, 2018. https://www.underminers.info/publications/hybridanalytica.

Snegovaya, Maria, and Kirill V Petrov. "Long Soviet Shadows: The Nomenklatura Ties of Putin Elites." *Post-Soviet Affairs* 38, no. 4 (April 11, 2022): 329–48. https://doi.org/10.1080/1060586x.2022.2062657.

Solovyov, Vladimir. 2012. "Protiv Rossii deistvuiut osoznanno i tselenapravlenno, no na eto nelzia obizhatsia" [Russia is facing intentional and targeted action against it. But it cannot take offence]. *Kommersant*. April 7, 2012. https://www.kommersant.ru/doc/1911330.

Sorokina, Elena. 2021. "Ot 'Kalinki' do Donbassa. Elena Sorokina—o kontseptsii 'Russkogo mira'" [From "Kalinka" to Donbas. Elena Sorokina—on the Concept of the "Russian World"]. Radio Svoboda. September 4, 2021. https://www.svoboda.org/a/ot-kalinki-do-don bassa-elena-sorokina-o-kontseptsii-russkogo-mira/31428922.html.

Splidsboel-Hansen, Flemming. "Past and Future Meet: Aleksandr Gorchakov and Russian Foreign Policy." *Europe-Asia Studies*, 54(3) (2002): 377-396. http://www.jstor.org/stable/826482.

Steshin, Dmitrii. 2021. "Yevgeny Primakov: Te, kto uchastvoval v travle russkikh, gostit i uchitsia v Rossii ne budut" [Evgeny Primakov: Those who participated in bullying Russians will not visit or study in Russia]. *Komsomolskaia pravda*. October 18, 2021. https://www.kp.ru/daily/28344/4491261/.

Surowiec, Paweł. "Post-Truth Soft Power: Changing Facets of Propaganda, Kompromat, and Democracy." *Georgetown Journal of International Affairs* 18, no. 3 (January 1, 2017): 21-27. https://doi.org/10.1353/gia.2017.0033.

Suslov, Mikhail. "'Russian World' Concept: Post-Soviet Geopolitical Ideology and the Logic of 'Spheres of Influence.'" *Geopolitics* 23, no. 2 (January 25, 2018): 330-53. https://doi.org/10.1080/14650045.2017.1407921.

Svystovych, S. "Vsesoiuzne tovarystvo kulturnykh zviazkiv iz zakordonom ta zovnishni kontakty ukrainskoi hromadskosti u 1924-1928 rokakh" [The All-Union Society for Cultural Relations with Foreign Countries and foreign contacts of the Ukrainian community in 1924-1928]. *"Gileya: naukovyi visnyk": Zbirnyk naukovykh prats*. Kyiv, 2011, 116-124. http://gileya.org/index.php?ng=library&cont=long&id=62.

Tafuro, Eleonora. "Fatal Attraction? Russia's Soft Power in Its Neighbourhood." *FRIDE Policy Brief*, No.181 (May 2014). https://www.files.ethz.ch/isn/180660/Fatal%20attraction_%20Russia%E2%80%99s%20soft%20power%20in%20its%20neighbourhood.pdf.

Tereshchenko, Denys and Nadiia Koval. *First Roubles, Then Guns: The Alexander Gorchakov Public Diplomacy Fund*. Ukrainian Institute, Kyiv, 2022. https://ui.org.ua/en/sectors-en/en-projects/en-research-anal ytics/gorchakov-diplomacy-fund-2/.

Tereshkova, Valentina. Valentina Tereshkova to Boris Yeltsin, October 25, 1991. *Yeltsin Tsentr*. https://yeltsin.ru/archive/paperwork/49393/.

Tkachev, Ivan, Pavel Koshkin, Oleg Makarov, Anton Fainberg. 2017. "Ekonomiia na 'miagkoi sile': Rossiia sokratit raskhody na vneshnepoliticheskuiu povestku" [Saving on the 'soft power': Russia will cut down the expenditures on the foreign policy agenda]. *RBK*. July 24, 2017. https://www.rbc.ru/newspaper/2017/07/24/59723c879a794741088d42d8.

Van Herpen, Marcel H. *Putin's Propaganda Machine: Soft Power and Russian Foreign Policy*. Rowman & Littlefield, 2015.

Vendil Pallin, Carolina, and Susanne Oxenstierna. *Russian Think Tanks and Soft Power*. Swedish Defence Research Agency, 2017. https://www.foi.se/rest-api/report/FOI-R--4451--SE.

Viperson. 2007. "Vyacheslav Nikonov: Sozdaniie Fonda 'Russkiy Mir'" [Vyacheslav Nikonov: the Creation of the "Russkiy Mir" Foundation]. June 29, 2007. https://viperson.ru/articles/vyacheslav-nikonov-sozdanie-fonda-russkiy-mir.

Yermolov, Mikhail. 2021. "Granitsy i masshtaby rossiiskogo sodeistviia mezhdunarodnomu razvitiiu" [Limits and scope of Russian international development assistance]. *RSMD*, August 3, 2021, https://russiancouncil.ru/analytics-and-comments/analytics/granitsy-i-masshtaby-rossiyskogo-sodeystviya-mezhdunarodnomu-razvitiyu/.

Zakem, Vera, Paul Saunders, and Daniel Antoun. "Mobilizing Compatriots: Russia's Strategy, Tactics, and Influence in the Former Soviet Union." *CNA*, November 2015. https://www.cna.org/archive/CNA_Files/pdf/dop-2015-u-011689-1rev.pdf.

Zhao, Xin. "Institut Konfutsiia i Fond 'Russkiy Mir' v kontekste globalizatsii: sravnitelnyi analiz" [Confucius Institute and the Russkiy Mir Foundation in the Context of Globalization: A Comparative Analysis]. *Obshchestvo: Filosofiia, Istoriia, Kultura*, Культура, September 25, 2020. https://doi.org/10.24158/fik.2020.9.25.

SOVIET AND POST-SOVIET POLITICS AND SOCIETY
Edited by Dr. Andreas Umland | ISSN 1614-3515

1   Андреас Умланд (ред.) | Воплощение Европейской конвенции по правам человека в России. Философские, юридические и эмпирические исследования | ISBN 3-89821-387-0

2   Christian Wipperfürth | Russland – ein vertrauenswürdiger Partner? Grundlagen, Hintergründe und Praxis gegenwärtiger russischer Außenpolitik | Mit einem Vorwort von Heinz Timmermann | ISBN 3-89821-401-X

3   Manja Hussner | Die Übernahme internationalen Rechts in die russische und deutsche Rechtsordnung. Eine vergleichende Analyse zur Völkerrechtsfreundlichkeit der Verfassungen der Russländischen Föderation und der Bundesrepublik Deutschland | Mit einem Vorwort von Rainer Arnold | ISBN 3-89821-438-9

4   Matthew Tejada | Bulgaria's Democratic Consolidation and the Kozloduy Nuclear Power Plant (KNPP). The Unattainability of Closure | With a foreword by Richard J. Crampton | ISBN 3-89821-439-7

5   Марк Григорьевич Меерович | Квадратные метры, определяющие сознание. Государственная жилищная политика в СССР. 1921 – 1941 гг | ISBN 3-89821-474-5

6   Andrei P. Tsygankov, Pavel A. Tsygankov (Eds.) | New Directions in Russian International Studies | ISBN 3-89821-422-2

7   Марк Григорьевич Меерович | Как власть народ к труду приучала. Жилище в СССР – средство управления людьми. 1917 – 1941 гг. | С предисловием Елены Осокиной | ISBN 3-89821-495-8

8   David J. Galbreath | Nation-Building and Minority Politics in Post-Socialist States. Interests, Influence and Identities in Estonia and Latvia | With a foreword by David J. Smith | ISBN 3-89821-467-2

9   Алексей Юрьевич Безугольный | Народы Кавказа в Вооруженных силах СССР в годы Великой Отечественной войны 1941-1945 гг. | С предисловием Николая Бугая | ISBN 3-89821-475-3

10 Вячеслав Лихачев и Владимир Прибыловский (ред.) | Русское Национальное Единство, 1990-2000. В 2-х томах | ISBN 3-89821-523-7

11 Николай Бугай (ред.) | Народы стран Балтии в условиях сталинизма (1940-е – 1950-е годы). Документированная история | ISBN 3-89821-525-3

12 Ingmar Bredies (Hrsg.) | Zur Anatomie der Orange Revolution in der Ukraine. Wechsel des Elitenregimes oder Triumph des Parlamentarismus? | ISBN 3-89821-524-5

13 Anastasia V. Mitrofanova | The Politicization of Russian Orthodoxy. Actors and Ideas | With a foreword by William C. Gay | ISBN 3-89821-481-8

14 Nathan D. Larson | Alexander Solzhenitsyn and the Russo-Jewish Question | ISBN 3-89821-483-4

15 Guido Houben | Kulturpolitik und Ethnizität. Staatliche Kunstförderung im Russland der neunziger Jahre | Mit einem Vorwort von Gert Weisskirchen | ISBN 3-89821-542-3

16 Leonid Luks | Der russische „Sonderweg"? Aufsätze zur neuesten Geschichte Russlands im europäischen Kontext | ISBN 3-89821-496-6

17 Евгений Мороз | История «Мёртвой воды» – от страшной сказки к большой политике. Политическое неоязычество в постсоветской России | ISBN 3-89821-551-2

18 Александр Верховский и Галина Кожевникова (ред.) | Этническая и религиозная интолерантность в российских СМИ. Результаты мониторинга 2001-2004 гг. | ISBN 3-89821-569-5

19 Christian Ganzer | Sowjetisches Erbe und ukrainische Nation. Das Museum der Geschichte des Zaporoger Kosakentums auf der Insel Chortycja | Mit einem Vorwort von Frank Golczewski | ISBN 3-89821-504-0

20 Эльза-Баир Гучинова | Помнить нельзя забыть. Антропология депортационной травмы калмыков | С предисловием Кэролайн Хамфри | ISBN 3-89821-506-7

21 Юлия Лидерман | Мотивы «проверки» и «испытания» в постсоветской культуре. Советское прошлое в российском кинематографе 1990-х годов | С предисловием Евгения Марголита | ISBN 3-89821-511-3

22 Tanya Lokshina, Ray Thomas, Mary Mayer (Eds.) | The Imposition of a Fake Political Settlement in the Northern Caucasus. The 2003 Chechen Presidential Election | ISBN 3-89821-436-2

23 Timothy McCajor Hall, Rosie Read (Eds.) | Changes in the Heart of Europe. Recent Ethnographies of Czechs, Slovaks, Roma, and Sorbs | With an afterword by Zdeněk Salzmann | ISBN 3-89821-606-3

24 *Christian Autengruber* | Die politischen Parteien in Bulgarien und Rumänien. Eine vergleichende Analyse seit Beginn der 90er Jahre | Mit einem Vorwort von Dorothée de Nève | ISBN 3-89821-476-1

25 *Annette Freyberg-Inan with Radu Cristescu* | The Ghosts in Our Classrooms, or: John Dewey Meets Ceauşescu. The Promise and the Failures of Civic Education in Romania | ISBN 3-89821-416-8

26 *John B. Dunlop* | The 2002 Dubrovka and 2004 Beslan Hostage Crises. A Critique of Russian Counter-Terrorism | With a foreword by Donald N. Jensen | ISBN 3-89821-608-X

27 *Peter Koller* | Das touristische Potenzial von Kam"janec'–Podil's'kyj. Eine fremdenverkehrsgeographische Untersuchung der Zukunftsperspektiven und Maßnahmenplanung zur Destinationsentwicklung des „ukrainischen Rothenburg" | Mit einem Vorwort von Kristiane Klemm | ISBN 3-89821-640-3

28 *Françoise Daucé, Elisabeth Sieca-Kozlowski (Eds.)* | Dedovshchina in the Post-Soviet Military. Hazing of Russian Army Conscripts in a Comparative Perspective | With a foreword by Dale Herspring | ISBN 3-89821-616-0

29 *Florian Strasser* | Zivilgesellschaftliche Einflüsse auf die Orange Revolution. Die gewaltlose Massenbewegung und die ukrainische Wahlkrise 2004 | Mit einem Vorwort von Egbert Jahn | ISBN 3-89821-648-9

30 *Rebecca S. Katz* | The Georgian Regime Crisis of 2003-2004. A Case Study in Post-Soviet Media Representation of Politics, Crime and Corruption | ISBN 3-89821-413-3

31 *Vladimir Kantor* | Willkür oder Freiheit. Beiträge zur russischen Geschichtsphilosophie | Ediert von Dagmar Herrmann sowie mit einem Vorwort versehen von Leonid Luks | ISBN 3-89821-589-X

32 *Laura A. Victoir* | The Russian Land Estate Today. A Case Study of Cultural Politics in Post-Soviet Russia | With a foreword by Priscilla Roosevelt | ISBN 3-89821-426-5

33 *Ivan Katchanovski* | Cleft Countries. Regional Political Divisions and Cultures in Post-Soviet Ukraine and Moldova | With a foreword by Francis Fukuyama | ISBN 3-89821-558-X

34 *Florian Mühlfried* | Postsowjetische Feiern. Das Georgische Bankett im Wandel | Mit einem Vorwort von Kevin Tuite | ISBN 3-89821-601-2

35 *Roger Griffin, Werner Loh, Andreas Umland (Eds.)* | Fascism Past and Present, West and East. An International Debate on Concepts and Cases in the Comparative Study of the Extreme Right | With an afterword by Walter Laqueur | ISBN 3-89821-674-8

36 *Sebastian Schlegel* | Der „Weiße Archipel". Sowjetische Atomstädte 1945-1991 | Mit einem Geleitwort von Thomas Bohn | ISBN 3-89821-679-9

37 *Vyacheslav Likhachev* | Political Anti-Semitism in Post-Soviet Russia. Actors and Ideas in 1991-2003 | Edited and translated from Russian by Eugene Veklerov | ISBN 3-89821-529-6

38 *Josette Baer (Ed.)* | Preparing Liberty in Central Europe. Political Texts from the Spring of Nations 1848 to the Spring of Prague 1968 | With a foreword by Zdeněk V. David | ISBN 3-89821-546-6

39 *Михаил Лукьянов* | Российский консерватизм и реформа, 1907-1914 | С предисловием Марка Д. Стейнберга | ISBN 3-89821-503-2

40 *Nicola Melloni* | Market Without Economy. The 1998 Russian Financial Crisis | With a foreword by Eiji Furukawa | ISBN 3-89821-407-9

41 *Dmitrij Chmelnizki* | Die Architektur Stalins | Bd. 1: Studien zu Ideologie und Stil | Bd. 2: Bilddokumentation | Mit einem Vorwort von Bruno Flierl | ISBN 3-89821-515-6

42 *Katja Yafimava* | Post-Soviet Russian-Belarussian Relationships. The Role of Gas Transit Pipelines | With a foreword by Jonathan P. Stern | ISBN 3-89821-655-1

43 *Boris Chavkin* | Verflechtungen der deutschen und russischen Zeitgeschichte. Aufsätze und Archivfunde zu den Beziehungen Deutschlands und der Sowjetunion von 1917 bis 1991 | Ediert von Markus Edlinger sowie mit einem Vorwort versehen von Leonid Luks | ISBN 3-89821-756-0

44 *Anastasija Grynenko in Zusammenarbeit mit Claudia Dathe* | Die Terminologie des Gerichtswesens der Ukraine und Deutschlands im Vergleich. Eine übersetzungswissenschaftliche Analyse juristischer Fachbegriffe im Deutschen, Ukrainischen und Russischen | Mit einem Vorwort von Ulrich Hartmann | ISBN 3-89821-691-8

45 *Anton Burkov* | The Impact of the European Convention on Human Rights on Russian Law. Legislation and Application in 1996-2006 | With a foreword by Françoise Hampson | ISBN 978-3-89821-639-5

46 *Stina Torjesen, Indra Overland (Eds.)* | International Election Observers in Post-Soviet Azerbaijan. Geopolitical Pawns or Agents of Change? | ISBN 978-3-89821-743-9

47 *Taras Kuzio* | Ukraine – Crimea – Russia. Triangle of Conflict | ISBN 978-3-89821-761-3

48 *Claudia Šabić* | „Ich erinnere mich nicht, aber L'viv!" Zur Funktion kultureller Faktoren für die Institutionalisierung und Entwicklung einer ukrainischen Region | Mit einem Vorwort von Melanie Tatur | ISBN 978-3-89821-752-1

49　*Marlies Bilz* | Tatarstan in der Transformation. Nationaler Diskurs und Politische Praxis 1988-1994 | Mit einem Vorwort von Frank Golczewski | ISBN 978-3-89821-722-4

50　*Марлен Ларюэль (ред.)* | Современные интерпретации русского национализма | ISBN 978-3-89821-795-8

51　*Sonja Schüler* | Die ethnische Dimension der Armut. Roma im postsozialistischen Rumänien | Mit einem Vorwort von Anton Sterbling | ISBN 978-3-89821-776-7

52　*Галина Кожевникова* | Радикальный национализм в России и противодействие ему. Сборник докладов Центра «Сова» за 2004-2007 гг. | С предисловием Александра Верховского | ISBN 978-3-89821-721-7

53　*Галина Кожевникова и Владимир Прибыловский* | Российская власть в биографиях I. Высшие должностные лица РФ в 2004 г. | ISBN 978-3-89821-796-5

54　*Галина Кожевникова и Владимир Прибыловский* | Российская власть в биографиях II. Члены Правительства РФ в 2004 г. | ISBN 978-3-89821-797-2

55　*Галина Кожевникова и Владимир Прибыловский* | Российская власть в биографиях III. Руководители федеральных служб и агентств РФ в 2004 г.| ISBN 978-3-89821-798-9

56　*Ileana Petroniu* | Privatisierung in Transformationsökonomien. Determinanten der Restrukturierungs-Bereitschaft am Beispiel Polens, Rumäniens und der Ukraine | Mit einem Vorwort von Rainer W. Schäfer | ISBN 978-3-89821-790-3

57　*Christian Wipperfürth* | Russland und seine GUS-Nachbarn. Hintergründe, aktuelle Entwicklungen und Konflikte in einer ressourcenreichen Region| ISBN 978-3-89821-801-6

58　*Togzhan Kassenova* | From Antagonism to Partnership. The Uneasy Path of the U.S.-Russian Cooperative Threat Reduction | With a foreword by Christoph Bluth | ISBN 978-3-89821-707-1

59　*Alexander Höllwerth* | Das sakrale eurasische Imperium des Aleksandr Dugin. Eine Diskursanalyse zum postsowjetischen russischen Rechtsextremismus | Mit einem Vorwort von Dirk Uffelmann | ISBN 978-3-89821-813-9

60　*Олег Рябов* | «Россия-Матушка». Национализм, гендер и война в России XX века | С предисловием Елены Гощило | ISBN 978-3-89821-487-2

61　*Ivan Maistrenko* | Borot'bism. A Chapter in the History of the Ukrainian Revolution | With a new Introduction by Chris Ford | Translated by George S. N. Luckyj with the assistance of Ivan L. Rudnytsky | Second, Revised and Expanded Edition ISBN 978-3-8382-1107-7

62　*Maryna Romanets* | Anamorphosic Texts and Reconfigured Visions. Improvised Traditions in Contemporary Ukrainian and Irish Literature | ISBN 978-3-89821-576-3

63　*Paul D'Anieri and Taras Kuzio (Eds.)* | Aspects of the Orange Revolution I. Democratization and Elections in Post-Communist Ukraine | ISBN 978-3-89821-698-2

64　*Bohdan Harasymiw in collaboration with Oleh S. Ilnytzkyj (Eds.)* | Aspects of the Orange Revolution II. Information and Manipulation Strategies in the 2004 Ukrainian Presidential Elections | ISBN 978-3-89821-699-9

65　*Ingmar Bredies, Andreas Umland and Valentin Yakushik (Eds.)* | Aspects of the Orange Revolution III. The Context and Dynamics of the 2004 Ukrainian Presidential Elections | ISBN 978-3-89821-803-0

66　*Ingmar Bredies, Andreas Umland and Valentin Yakushik (Eds.)* | Aspects of the Orange Revolution IV. Foreign Assistance and Civic Action in the 2004 Ukrainian Presidential Elections | ISBN 978-3-89821-808-5

67　*Ingmar Bredies, Andreas Umland and Valentin Yakushik (Eds.)* | Aspects of the Orange Revolution V. Institutional Observation Reports on the 2004 Ukrainian Presidential Elections | ISBN 978-3-89821-809-2

68　*Taras Kuzio (Ed.)* | Aspects of the Orange Revolution VI. Post-Communist Democratic Revolutions in Comparative Perspective | ISBN 978-3-89821-820-7

69　*Tim Bohse* | Autoritarismus statt Selbstverwaltung. Die Transformation der kommunalen Politik in der Stadt Kaliningrad 1990-2005 | Mit einem Geleitwort von Stefan Troebst | ISBN 978-3-89821-782-8

70　*David Rupp* | Die Rußländische Föderation und die russischsprachige Minderheit in Lettland. Eine Fallstudie zur Anwaltspolitik Moskaus gegenüber den russophonen Minderheiten im „Nahen Ausland" von 1991 bis 2002 | Mit einem Vorwort von Helmut Wagner | ISBN 978-3-89821-778-1

71　*Taras Kuzio* | Theoretical and Comparative Perspectives on Nationalism. New Directions in Cross-Cultural and Post-Communist Studies | With a foreword by Paul Robert Magocsi | ISBN 978-3-89821-815-3

72　*Christine Teichmann* | Die Hochschultransformation im heutigen Osteuropa. Kontinuität und Wandel bei der Entwicklung des postkommunistischen Universitätswesens | Mit einem Vorwort von Oskar Anweiler | ISBN 978-3-89821-842-9

73 Julia Kusznir | Der politische Einfluss von Wirtschaftseliten in russischen Regionen. Eine Analyse am Beispiel der Erdöl- und Erdgasindustrie, 1992-2005 | Mit einem Vorwort von Wolfgang Eichwede | ISBN 978-3-89821-821-4

74 Alena Vysotskaya | Russland, Belarus und die EU-Osterweiterung. Zur Minderheitenfrage und zum Problem der Freizügigkeit des Personenverkehrs | Mit einem Vorwort von Katlijn Malfliet | ISBN 978-3-89821-822-1

75 Heiko Pleines (Hrsg.) | Corporate Governance in post-sozialistischen Volkswirtschaften | ISBN 978-3-89821-766-8

76 Stefan Ihrig | Wer sind die Moldawier? Rumänismus versus Moldowanismus in Historiographie und Schulbüchern der Republik Moldova, 1991-2006 | Mit einem Vorwort von Holm Sundhaussen | ISBN 978-3-89821-466-7

77 Galina Kozhevnikova in collaboration with Alexander Verkhovsky and Eugene Veklerov | Ultra-Nationalism and Hate Crimes in Contemporary Russia. The 2004-2006 Annual Reports of Moscow's SOVA Center | With a foreword by Stephen D. Shenfield | ISBN 978-3-89821-868-9

78 Florian Küchler | The Role of the European Union in Moldova's Transnistria Conflict | With a foreword by Christopher Hill | ISBN 978-3-89821-850-4

79 Bernd Rechel | The Long Way Back to Europe. Minority Protection in Bulgaria | With a foreword by Richard Crampton | ISBN 978-3-89821-863-4

80 Peter W. Rodgers | Nation, Region and History in Post-Communist Transitions. Identity Politics in Ukraine, 1991-2006 | With a foreword by Vera Tolz | ISBN 978-3-89821-903-7

81 Stephanie Solywoda | The Life and Work of Semen L. Frank. A Study of Russian Religious Philosophy | With a foreword by Philip Walters | ISBN 978-3-89821-457-5

82 Vera Sokolova | Cultural Politics of Ethnicity. Discourses on Roma in Communist Czechoslovakia | ISBN 978-3-89821-864-1

83 Natalya Shevchik Ketenci | Kazakhstani Enterprises in Transition. The Role of Historical Regional Development in Kazakhstan's Post-Soviet Economic Transformation | ISBN 978-3-89821-831-3

84 Martin Malek, Anna Schor-Tschudnowskaja (Hgg.) | Europa im Tschetschenienkrieg. Zwischen politischer Ohnmacht und Gleichgültigkeit | Mit einem Vorwort von Lipchan Basajewa | ISBN 978-3-89821-676-0

85 Stefan Meister | Das postsowjetische Universitätswesen zwischen nationalem und internationalem Wandel. Die Entwicklung der regionalen Hochschule in Russland als Gradmesser der Systemtransformation | Mit einem Vorwort von Joan DeBardeleben | ISBN 978-3-89821-891-7

86 Konstantin Sheiko in collaboration with Stephen Brown | Nationalist Imaginings of the Russian Past. Anatolii Fomenko and the Rise of Alternative History in Post-Communist Russia | With a foreword by Donald Ostrowski | ISBN 978-3-89821-915-0

87 Sabine Jenni | Wie stark ist das „Einige Russland"? Zur Parteibindung der Eliten und zum Wahlerfolg der Machtpartei im Dezember 2007 | Mit einem Vorwort von Klaus Armingeon | ISBN 978-3-89821-961-7

88 Thomas Borén | Meeting-Places of Transformation. Urban Identity, Spatial Representations and Local Politics in Post-Soviet St Petersburg | ISBN 978-3-89821-739-2

89 Aygul Ashirova | Stalinismus und Stalin-Kult in Zentralasien. Turkmenistan 1924-1953 | Mit einem Vorwort von Leonid Luks | ISBN 978-3-89821-987-7

90 Leonid Luks | Freiheit oder imperiale Größe? Essays zu einem russischen Dilemma | ISBN 978-3-8382-0011-8

91 Christopher Gilley | The 'Change of Signposts' in the Ukrainian Emigration. A Contribution to the History of Sovietophilism in the 1920s | With a foreword by Frank Golczewski | ISBN 978-3-89821-965-5

92 Philipp Casula, Jeronim Perovic (Eds.) | Identities and Politics During the Putin Presidency. The Discursive Foundations of Russia's Stability | With a foreword by Heiko Haumann | ISBN 978-3-8382-0015-6

93 Marcel Viëtor | Europa und die Frage nach seinen Grenzen im Osten. Zur Konstruktion ‚europäischer Identität' in Geschichte und Gegenwart | Mit einem Vorwort von Albrecht Lehmann | ISBN 978-3-8382-0045-3

94 Ben Hellman, Andrei Rogachevskii | Filming the Unfilmable. Casper Wrede's 'One Day in the Life of Ivan Denisovich' | Second, Revised and Expanded Edition | ISBN 978-3-8382-0044-6

95 Eva Fuchslocher | Vaterland, Sprache, Glaube. Orthodoxie und Nationenbildung am Beispiel Georgiens | Mit einem Vorwort von Christina von Braun | ISBN 978-3-89821-884-9

96 Vladimir Kantor | Das Westlertum und der Weg Russlands. Zur Entwicklung der russischen Literatur und Philosophie | Ediert von Dagmar Herrmann | Mit einem Beitrag von Nikolaus Lobkowicz | ISBN 978-3-8382-0102-3

97 Kamran Musayev | Die postsowjetische Transformation im Baltikum und Südkaukasus. Eine vergleichende Untersuchung der politischen Entwicklung Lettlands und Aserbaidschans 1985-2009 | Mit einem Vorwort von Leonid Luks | Ediert von Sandro Henschel | ISBN 978-3-8382-0103-0

98   *Tatiana Zhurzhenko* | Borderlands into Bordered Lands. Geopolitics of Identity in Post-Soviet Ukraine | With a foreword by Dieter Segert | ISBN 978-3-8382-0042-2

99   *Кирилл Галушко, Лидия Смола (ред.)* | Пределы падения – варианты украинского будущего. Аналитико-прогностические исследования | ISBN 978-3-8382-0148-1

100 *Michael Minkenberg (Ed.)* | Historical Legacies and the Radical Right in Post-Cold War Central and Eastern Europe | With an afterword by Sabrina P. Ramet | ISBN 978-3-8382-0124-5

101 *David-Emil Wickström* | Rocking St. Petersburg. Transcultural Flows and Identity Politics in the St. Petersburg Popular Music Scene | With a foreword by Yngvar B. Steinholt | Second, Revised and Expanded Edition | ISBN 978-3-8382-0100-9

102 *Eva Zabka* | Eine neue „Zeit der Wirren"? Der spät- und postsowjetische Systemwandel 1985-2000 im Spiegel russischer gesellschaftspolitischer Diskurse | Mit einem Vorwort von Margareta Mommsen | ISBN 978-3-8382-0161-0

103 *Ulrike Ziemer* | Ethnic Belonging, Gender and Cultural Practices. Youth Identitites in Contemporary Russia | With a foreword by Anoop Nayak | ISBN 978-3-8382-0152-8

104 *Ksenia Chepikova* | ‚Einiges Russland' - eine zweite KPdSU? Aspekte der Identitätskonstruktion einer postsowjetischen „Partei der Macht" | Mit einem Vorwort von Torsten Oppelland | ISBN 978-3-8382-0311-9

105 *Леонид Люкс* | Западничество или евразийство? Демократия или идеократия? Сборник статей об исторических дилеммах России | С предисловием Владимира Кантора | ISBN 978-3-8382-0211-2

106 *Anna Dost* | Das russische Verfassungsrecht auf dem Weg zum Föderalismus und zurück. Zum Konflikt von Rechtsnormen und -wirklichkeit in der Russländischen Föderation von 1991 bis 2009 | Mit einem Vorwort von Alexander Blankenagel | ISBN 978-3-8382-0292-1

107 *Philipp Herzog* | Sozialistische Völkerfreundschaft, nationaler Widerstand oder harmloser Zeitvertreib? Zur politischen Funktion der Volkskunst im sowjetischen Estland | Mit einem Vorwort von Andreas Kappeler | ISBN 978-3-8382-0216-7

108 *Marlène Laruelle (Ed.)* | Russian Nationalism, Foreign Policy, and Identity Debates in Putin's Russia. New Ideological Patterns after the Orange Revolution | ISBN 978-3-8382-0325-6

109 *Michail Logvinov* | Russlands Kampf gegen den internationalen Terrorismus. Eine kritische Bestandsaufnahme des Bekämpfungsansatzes | Mit einem Geleitwort von Hans-Henning Schröder und einem Vorwort von Eckhard Jesse | ISBN 978-3-8382-0329-4

110 *John B. Dunlop* | The Moscow Bombings of September 1999. Examinations of Russian Terrorist Attacks at the Onset of Vladimir Putin's Rule | Second, Revised and Expanded Edition | ISBN 978-3-8382-0388-1

111 *Андрей А. Ковалёв* | Свидетельство из-за кулис российской политики I. Можно ли делать добро из зла? (Воспоминания и размышления о последних советских и первых послесоветских годах) | With a foreword by Peter Reddaway | ISBN 978-3-8382-0302-7

112 *Андрей А. Ковалёв* | Свидетельство из-за кулис российской политики II. Угроза для себя и окружающих (Наблюдения и предостережения относительно происходящего после 2000 г.) | ISBN 978-3-8382-0303-4

113 *Bernd Kappenberg* | Zeichen setzen für Europa. Der Gebrauch europäischer lateinischer Sonderzeichen in der deutschen Öffentlichkeit | Mit einem Vorwort von Peter Schlobinski | ISBN 978-3-89821-749-1

114 *Ivo Mijnssen* | The Quest for an Ideal Youth in Putin's Russia I. Back to Our Future! History, Modernity, and Patriotism according to Nashi, 2005-2013 | With a foreword by Jeronim Perović | Second, Revised and Expanded Edition | ISBN 978-3-8382-0368-3

115 *Jussi Lassila* | The Quest for an Ideal Youth in Putin's Russia II. The Search for Distinctive Conformism in the Political Communication of Nashi, 2005-2009 | With a foreword by Kirill Postoutenko | Second, Revised and Expanded Edition | ISBN 978-3-8382-0415-4

116 *Valerio Trabandt* | Neue Nachbarn, gute Nachbarschaft? Die EU als internationaler Akteur am Beispiel ihrer Demokratieförderung in Belarus und der Ukraine 2004-2009 | Mit einem Vorwort von Jutta Joachim | ISBN 978-3-8382-0437-6

117 *Fabian Pfeiffer* | Estlands Außen- und Sicherheitspolitik I. Der estnische Atlantizismus nach der wiedererlangten Unabhängigkeit 1991-2004 | Mit einem Vorwort von Helmut Hubel | ISBN 978-3-8382-0127-6

118 *Jana Podßuweit* | Estlands Außen- und Sicherheitspolitik II. Handlungsoptionen eines Kleinstaates im Rahmen seiner EU-Mitgliedschaft (2004-2008) | Mit einem Vorwort von Helmut Hubel | ISBN 978-3-8382-0440-6

119 *Karin Pointner* | Estlands Außen- und Sicherheitspolitik III. Eine gedächtnispolitische Analyse estnischer Entwicklungskooperation 2006-2010 | Mit einem Vorwort von Karin Liebhart | ISBN 978-3-8382-0435-2

120 *Ruslana Vovk* | Die Offenheit der ukrainischen Verfassung für das Völkerrecht und die europäische Integration | Mit einem Vorwort von Alexander Blankenagel | ISBN 978-3-8382-0481-9

121 *Mykhaylo Banakh* | Die Relevanz der Zivilgesellschaft bei den postkommunistischen Transformationsprozessen in mittel- und osteuropäischen Ländern. Das Beispiel der spät- und postsowjetischen Ukraine 1986-2009 | Mit einem Vorwort von Gerhard Simon | ISBN 978-3-8382-0499-4

122 *Michael Moser* | Language Policy and the Discourse on Languages in Ukraine under President Viktor Yanukovych (25 February 2010–28 October 2012) | ISBN 978-3-8382-0497-0 (Paperback edition) | ISBN 978-3-8382-0507-6 (Hardcover edition)

123 *Nicole Krome* | Russischer Netzwerkkapitalismus Restrukturierungsprozesse in der Russischen Föderation am Beispiel des Luftfahrtunternehmens „Aviastar" | Mit einem Vorwort von Petra Stykow | ISBN 978-3-8382-0534-2

124 *David R. Marples* | 'Our Glorious Past'. Lukashenka's Belarus and the Great Patriotic War | ISBN 978-3-8382-0574-8 (Paperback edition) | ISBN 978-3-8382-0675-2 (Hardcover edition)

125 *Ulf Walther* | Russlands „neuer Adel". Die Macht des Geheimdienstes von Gorbatschow bis Putin | Mit einem Vorwort von Hans-Georg Wieck | ISBN 978-3-8382-0584-7

126 *Simon Geissbühler (Hrsg.)* | Kiew – Revolution 3.0. Der Euromaidan 2013/14 und die Zukunftsperspektiven der Ukraine | ISBN 978-3-8382-0581-6 (Paperback edition) | ISBN 978-3-8382-0681-3 (Hardcover edition)

127 *Andrey Makarychev* | Russia and the EU in a Multipolar World. Discourses, Identities, Norms | With a foreword by Klaus Segbers | ISBN 978-3-8382-0629-5

128 *Roland Scharff* | Kasachstan als postsowjetischer Wohlfahrtsstaat. Die Transformation des sozialen Schutzsystems | Mit einem Vorwort von Joachim Ahrens | ISBN 978-3-8382-0622-6

129 *Katja Grupp* | Bild Lücke Deutschland. Kaliningrader Studierende sprechen über Deutschland | Mit einem Vorwort von Martin Schulz | ISBN 978-3-8382-0552-6

130 *Konstantin Sheiko, Stephen Brown* | History as Therapy. Alternative History and Nationalist Imaginings in Russia, 1991-2014 | ISBN 978-3-8382-0665-3

131 *Elisa Kriza* | Alexander Solzhenitsyn: Cold War Icon, Gulag Author, Russian Nationalist? A Study of the Western Reception of his Literary Writings, Historical Interpretations, and Political Ideas | With a foreword by Andrei Rogatchevski | ISBN 978-3-8382-0589-2 (Paperback edition) | ISBN 978-3-8382-0690-5 (Hardcover edition)

132 *Serghei Golunov* | The Elephant in the Room. Corruption and Cheating in Russian Universities | ISBN 978-3-8382-0570-0

133 *Manja Hussner, Rainer Arnold (Hgg.)* | Verfassungsgerichtsbarkeit in Zentralasien I. Sammlung von Verfassungstexten | ISBN 978-3-8382-0595-3

134 *Nikolay Mitrokhin* | Die „Russische Partei". Die Bewegung der russischen Nationalisten in der UdSSR 1953-1985 | Aus dem Russischen übertragen von einem Übersetzerteam unter der Leitung von Larisa Schippel | ISBN 978-3-8382-0024-8

135 *Manja Hussner, Rainer Arnold (Hgg.)* | Verfassungsgerichtsbarkeit in Zentralasien II. Sammlung von Verfassungstexten | ISBN 978-3-8382-0597-7

136 *Manfred Zeller* | Das sowjetische Fieber. Fußballfans im poststalinistischen Vielvölkerreich | Mit einem Vorwort von Nikolaus Katzer | ISBN 978-3-8382-0757-5

137 *Kristin Schreiter* | Stellung und Entwicklungspotential zivilgesellschaftlicher Gruppen in Russland. Menschenrechtsorganisationen im Vergleich | ISBN 978-3-8382-0673-8

138 *David R. Marples, Frederick V. Mills (Eds.)* | Ukraine's Euromaidan. Analyses of a Civil Revolution | ISBN 978-3-8382-0660-8

139 *Bernd Kappenberg* | Setting Signs for Europe. Why Diacritics Matter for European Integration | With a foreword by Peter Schlobinski | ISBN 978-3-8382-0663-9

140 *René Lenz* | Internationalisierung, Kooperation und Transfer. Externe bildungspolitische Akteure in der Russischen Föderation | Mit einem Vorwort von Frank Ettrich | ISBN 978-3-8382-0751-3

141 *Juri Plusnin, Yana Zausaeva, Natalia Zhidkevich, Artemy Pozanenko* | Wandering Workers. Mores, Behavior, Way of Life, and Political Status of Domestic Russian Labor Migrants | Translated by Julia Kazantseva | ISBN 978-3-8382-0653-0

142 *David J. Smith (Eds.)* | Latvia – A Work in Progress? 100 Years of State- and Nation-Building | ISBN 978-3-8382-0648-6

143 *Инна Чувычкина (ред.)* | Экспортные нефте- и газопроводы на постсоветском пространстве. Анализ трубопроводной политики в свете теории международных отношений | ISBN 978-3-8382-0822-0

144 *Johann Zajaczkowski* | Russland – eine pragmatische Großmacht? Eine rollentheoretische Untersuchung russischer Außenpolitik am Beispiel der Zusammenarbeit mit den USA nach 9/11 und des Georgienkrieges von 2008 | Mit einem Vorwort von Siegfried Schieder | ISBN 978-3-8382-0837-4

145 *Boris Popivanov* | Changing Images of the Left in Bulgaria. The Challenge of Post-Communism in the Early 21st Century | ISBN 978-3-8382-0667-7

146 *Lenka Krátká* | A History of the Czechoslovak Ocean Shipping Company 1948-1989. How a Small, Landlocked Country Ran Maritime Business During the Cold War | ISBN 978-3-8382-0666-0

147 *Alexander Sergunin* | Explaining Russian Foreign Policy Behavior. Theory and Practice | ISBN 978-3-8382-0752-0

148 *Darya Malyutina* | Migrant Friendships in a Super-Diverse City. Russian-Speakers and their Social Relationships in London in the 21st Century | With a foreword by Claire Dwyer | ISBN 978-3-8382-0652-3

149 *Alexander Sergunin, Valery Konyshev* | Russia in the Arctic. Hard or Soft Power? | ISBN 978-3-8382-0753-7

150 *John J. Maresca* | Helsinki Revisited. A Key U.S. Negotiator's Memoirs on the Development of the CSCE into the OSCE | With a foreword by Hafiz Pashayev | ISBN 978-3-8382-0852-7

151 *Jardar Østbø* | The New Third Rome. Readings of a Russian Nationalist Myth | With a foreword by Pål Kolstø | ISBN 978-3-8382-0870-1

152 *Simon Kordonsky* | Socio-Economic Foundations of the Russian Post-Soviet Regime. The Resource-Based Economy and Estate-Based Social Structure of Contemporary Russia | With a foreword by Svetlana Barsukova | ISBN 978-3-8382-0775-9

153 *Duncan Leitch* | Assisting Reform in Post-Communist Ukraine 2000–2012. The Illusions of Donors and the Disillusion of Beneficiaries | With a foreword by Kataryna Wolczuk | ISBN 978-3-8382-0844-2

154 *Abel Polese* | Limits of a Post-Soviet State. How Informality Replaces, Renegotiates, and Reshapes Governance in Contemporary Ukraine | With a foreword by Colin Williams | ISBN 978-3-8382-0845-9

155 *Mikhail Suslov (Ed.)* | Digital Orthodoxy in the Post-Soviet World. The Russian Orthodox Church and Web 2.0 | With a foreword by Father Cyril Hovorun | ISBN 978-3-8382-0871-8

156 *Leonid Luks* | Zwei „Sonderwege"? Russisch-deutsche Parallelen und Kontraste (1917-2014). Vergleichende Essays | ISBN 978-3-8382-0823-7

157 *Vladimir V. Karacharovskiy, Ovsey I. Shkaratan, Gordey A. Yastrebov* | Towards a New Russian Work Culture. Can Western Companies and Expatriates Change Russian Society? | With a foreword by Elena N. Danilova | Translated by Julia Kazantseva | ISBN 978-3-8382-0902-9

158 *Edmund Griffiths* | Aleksandr Prokhanov and Post-Soviet Esotericism | ISBN 978-3-8382-0963-0

159 *Timm Beichelt, Susann Worschech (Eds.)* | Transnational Ukraine? Networks and Ties that Influence(d) Contemporary Ukraine | ISBN 978-3-8382-0944-9

160 *Mieste Hotopp-Riecke* | Die Tataren der Krim zwischen Assimilation und Selbstbehauptung. Der Aufbau des krimtatarischen Bildungswesens nach Deportation und Heimkehr (1990-2005) | Mit einem Vorwort von Swetlana Czerwonnaja | ISBN 978-3-89821-940-2

161 *Olga Bertelsen (Ed.)* | Revolution and War in Contemporary Ukraine. The Challenge of Change | ISBN 978-3-8382-1016-2

162 *Natalya Ryabinska* | Ukraine's Post-Communist Mass Media. Between Capture and Commercialization | With a foreword by Marta Dyczok | ISBN 978-3-8382-1011-7

163 *Alexandra Cotofana, James M. Nyce (Eds.)* | Religion and Magic in Socialist and Post-Socialist Contexts. Historic and Ethnographic Case Studies of Orthodoxy, Heterodoxy, and Alternative Spirituality | With a foreword by Patrick L. Michelson | ISBN 978-3-8382-0989-0

164 *Nozima Akhrarkhodjaeva* | The Instrumentalisation of Mass Media in Electoral Authoritarian Regimes. Evidence from Russia's Presidential Election Campaigns of 2000 and 2008 | ISBN 978-3-8382-1013-1

165 *Yulia Krasheninnikova* | Informal Healthcare in Contemporary Russia. Sociographic Essays on the Post-Soviet Infrastructure for Alternative Healing Practices | ISBN 978-3-8382-0970-8

166 *Peter Kaiser* | Das Schachbrett der Macht. Die Handlungsspielräume eines sowjetischen Funktionärs unter Stalin am Beispiel des Generalsekretärs des Komsomol Aleksandr Kosarev (1929-1938) | Mit einem Vorwort von Dietmar Neutatz | ISBN 978-3-8382-1052-0

167 *Oksana Kim* | The Effects and Implications of Kazakhstan's Adoption of International Financial Reporting Standards. A Resource Dependence Perspective | With a foreword by Svetlana Vlady | ISBN 978-3-8382-0987-6

168 *Anna Sanina* | Patriotic Education in Contemporary Russia. Sociological Studies in the Making of the Post-Soviet Citizen | With a foreword by Anna Oldfield | ISBN 978-3-8382-0993-7

169 *Rudolf Wolters* | Spezialist in Sibirien Faksimile der 1933 erschienenen ersten Ausgabe | Mit einem Vorwort von Dmitrij Chmelnizki | ISBN 978-3-8382-0515-1

170 *Michal Vít, Magdalena M. Baran (Eds.)* | Transregional versus National Perspectives on Contemporary Central European History. Studies on the Building of Nation-States and Their Cooperation in the 20th and 21st Century | With a foreword by Petr Vágner | ISBN 978-3-8382-1015-5

171 *Philip Gamaghelyan* | Conflict Resolution Beyond the International Relations Paradigm. Evolving Designs as a Transformative Practice in Nagorno-Karabakh and Syria | With a foreword by Susan Allen | ISBN 978-3-8382-1057-5

172 *Maria Shagina* | Joining a Prestigious Club. Cooperation with Europarties and Its Impact on Party Development in Georgia, Moldova, and Ukraine 2004–2015 | With a foreword by Kataryna Wolczuk | ISBN 978-3-8382-1084-1

173 *Alexandra Cotofana, James M. Nyce (Eds.)* | Religion and Magic in Socialist and Post-Socialist Contexts II. Baltic, Eastern European, and Post-USSR Case Studies | With a foreword by Anita Stasulane | ISBN 978-3-8382-0990-6

174 *Barbara Kunz* | Kind Words, Cruise Missiles, and Everything in Between. The Use of Power Resources in U.S. Policies towards Poland, Ukraine, and Belarus 1989–2008 | With a foreword by William Hill | ISBN 978-3-8382-1065-0

175 *Eduard Klein* | Bildungskorruption in Russland und der Ukraine. Eine komparative Analyse der Performanz staatlicher Antikorruptionsmaßnahmen im Hochschulsektor am Beispiel universitärer Aufnahmeprüfungen | Mit einem Vorwort von Heiko Pleines | ISBN 978-3-8382-0995-1

176 *Markus Soldner* | Politischer Kapitalismus im postsowjetischen Russland. Die politische, wirtschaftliche und mediale Transformation in den 1990er Jahren | Mit einem Vorwort von Wolfgang Ismayr | ISBN 978-3-8382-1222-7

177 *Anton Oleinik* | Building Ukraine from Within. A Sociological, Institutional, and Economic Analysis of a Nation-State in the Making | ISBN 978-3-8382-1150-3

178 *Peter Rollberg, Marlene Laruelle (Eds.)* | Mass Media in the Post-Soviet World. Market Forces, State Actors, and Political Manipulation in the Informational Environment after Communism | ISBN 978-3-8382-1116-9

179 *Mikhail Minakov* | Development and Dystopia. Studies in Post-Soviet Ukraine and Eastern Europe | With a foreword by Alexander Etkind | ISBN 978-3-8382-1112-1

180 *Aijan Sharshenova* | The European Union's Democracy Promotion in Central Asia. A Study of Political Interests, Influence, and Development in Kazakhstan and Kyrgyzstan in 2007–2013 | With a foreword by Gordon Crawford | ISBN 978-3-8382-1151-0

181 *Andrey Makarychev, Alexandra Yatsyk (Eds.)* | Boris Nemtsov and Russian Politics. Power and Resistance | With a foreword by Zhanna Nemtsova | ISBN 978-3-8382-1122-0

182 *Sophie Falsini* | The Euromaidan's Effect on Civil Society. Why and How Ukrainian Social Capital Increased after the Revolution of Dignity | With a foreword by Susann Worschech | ISBN 978-3-8382-1131-2

183 *Valentyna Romanova, Andreas Umland (Eds.)* | Ukraine's Decentralization. Challenges and Implications of the Local Governance Reform after the Euromaidan Revolution | ISBN 978-3-8382-1162-6

184 *Leonid Luks* | A Fateful Triangle. Essays on Contemporary Russian, German and Polish History | ISBN 978-3-8382-1143-5

185 *John B. Dunlop* | The February 2015 Assassination of Boris Nemtsov and the Flawed Trial of his Alleged Killers. An Exploration of Russia's "Crime of the 21st Century" | ISBN 978-3-8382-1188-6

186 *Vasile Rotaru* | Russia, the EU, and the Eastern Partnership. Building Bridges or Digging Trenches? | ISBN 978-3-8382-1134-3

187 *Marina Lebedeva* | Russian Studies of International Relations. From the Soviet Past to the Post-Cold-War Present | With a foreword by Andrei P. Tsygankov | ISBN 978-3-8382-0851-0

188 *Tomasz Stępniewski, George Soroka (Eds.)* | Ukraine after Maidan. Revisiting Domestic and Regional Security | ISBN 978-3-8382-1075-9

189 *Petar Cholakov* | Ethnic Entrepreneurs Unmasked. Political Institutions and Ethnic Conflicts in Contemporary Bulgaria | ISBN 978-3-8382-1189-3

190 *A. Salem, G. Hazeldine, D. Morgan (Eds.)* | Higher Education in Post-Communist States. Comparative and Sociological Perspectives | ISBN 978-3-8382-1183-1

191 *Igor Torbakov* | After Empire. Nationalist Imagination and Symbolic Politics in Russia and Eurasia in the Twentieth and Twenty-First Century | With a foreword by Serhii Plokhy | ISBN 978-3-8382-1217-3

192 *Aleksandr Burakovskiy* | Jewish-Ukrainian Relations in Late and Post-Soviet Ukraine. Articles, Lectures and Essays from 1986 to 2016 | ISBN 978-3-8382-1210-4

193 *Natalia Shapovalova, Olga Burlyuk (Eds.)* | Civil Society in Post-Euromaidan Ukraine. From Revolution to Consolidation | With a foreword by Richard Youngs | ISBN 978-3-8382-1216-6

194 *Franz Preissler* | Positionsverteidigung, Imperialismus oder Irredentismus? Russland und die „Russischsprachigen", 1991–2015 | ISBN 978-3-8382-1262-3

195 *Marian Madeła* | Der Reformprozess in der Ukraine 2014-2017. Eine Fallstudie zur Reform der öffentlichen Verwaltung | Mit einem Vorwort von Martin Malek | ISBN 978-3-8382-1266-1

196 *Anke Giesen* | „Wie kann denn der Sieger ein Verbrecher sein?" Eine diskursanalytische Untersuchung der russlandweiten Debatte über Konzept und Verstaatlichungsprozess der Lagergedenkstätte „Perm'-36" im Ural | ISBN 978-3-8382-1284-5

197 *Victoria Leukavets* | The Integration Policies of Belarus and Ukraine vis-à-vis the EU and Russia. A Comparative Analysis Through the Prism of a Two-Level Game Approach | ISBN 978-3-8382-1247-0

198 *Oksana Kim* | The Development and Challenges of Russian Corporate Governance I. The Roles and Functions of Boards of Directors | With a foreword by Sheila M. Puffer | ISBN 978-3-8382-1287-6

199 *Thomas D. Grant* | International Law and the Post-Soviet Space I. Essays on Chechnya and the Baltic States | With a foreword by Stephen M. Schwebel | ISBN 978-3-8382-1279-1

200 *Thomas D. Grant* | International Law and the Post-Soviet Space II. Essays on Ukraine, Intervention, and Non-Proliferation | ISBN 978-3-8382-1280-7

201 *Slavomír Michálek, Michal Štefansky* | The Age of Fear. The Cold War and Its Influence on Czechoslovakia 1945–1968 | ISBN 978-3-8382-1285-2

202 *Iulia-Sabina Joja* | Romania's Strategic Culture 1990–2014. Continuity and Change in a Post-Communist Country's Evolution of National Interests and Security Policies | With a foreword by Heiko Biehl | ISBN 978-3-8382-1286-9

203 *Andrei Rogatchevski, Yngvar B. Steinholt, Arve Hansen, David-Emil Wickström* | War of Songs. Popular Music and Recent Russia-Ukraine Relations | With a foreword by Artemy Troitsky | ISBN 978-3-8382-1173-2

204 *Maria Lipman (Ed.)* | Russian Voices on Post-Crimea Russia. An Almanac of Counterpoint Essays from 2015–2018 | ISBN 978-3-8382-1251-7

205 *Ksenia Maksimovtsova* | Language Conflicts in Contemporary Estonia, Latvia, and Ukraine. A Comparative Exploration of Discourses in Post-Soviet Russian-Language Digital Media | With a foreword by Ammon Cheskin | ISBN 978-3-8382-1282-1

206 *Michal Vít* | The EU's Impact on Identity Formation in East-Central Europe between 2004 and 2013. Perceptions of the Nation and Europe in Political Parties of the Czech Republic, Poland, and Slovakia | With a foreword by Andrea Pető | ISBN 978-3-8382-1275-3

207 *Per A. Rudling* | Tarnished Heroes. The Organization of Ukrainian Nationalists in the Memory Politics of Post-Soviet Ukraine | ISBN 978-3-8382-0999-9

208 *Kaja Gadowska, Peter Solomon (Eds.)* | Legal Change in Post-Communist States. Progress, Reversions, Explanations | ISBN 978-3-8382-1312-5

209 *Paweł Kowal, Georges Mink, Iwona Reichardt (Eds.)* | Three Revolutions: Mobilization and Change in Contemporary Ukraine I. Theoretical Aspects and Analyses on Religion, Memory, and Identity | ISBN 978-3-8382-1321-7

210 *Paweł Kowal, Georges Mink, Adam Reichardt, Iwona Reichardt (Eds.)* | Three Revolutions: Mobilization and Change in Contemporary Ukraine II. An Oral History of the Revolution on Granite, Orange Revolution, and Revolution of Dignity | ISBN 978-3-8382-1323-1

211 *Li Bennich-Björkman, Sergiy Kurbatov (Eds.)* | When the Future Came. The Collapse of the USSR and the Emergence of National Memory in Post-Soviet History Textbooks | ISBN 978-3-8382-1335-4

212 *Olga R. Gulina* | Migration as a (Geo-)Political Challenge in the Post-Soviet Space. Border Regimes, Policy Choices, Visa Agendas | With a foreword by Nils Muižnieks | ISBN 978-3-8382-1338-5

213 *Sanna Turoma, Kaarina Aitamurto, Slobodanka Vladiv-Glover (Eds.)* | Religion, Expression, and Patriotism in Russia. Essays on Post-Soviet Society and the State. ISBN 978-3-8382-1346-0

214 *Vasif Huseynov* | Geopolitical Rivalries in the "Common Neighborhood". Russia's Conflict with the West, Soft Power, and Neoclassical Realism | With a foreword by Nicholas Ross Smith | ISBN 978-3-8382-1277-7

215 *Mikhail Suslov* | Geopolitical Imagination. Ideology and Utopia in Post-Soviet Russia | With a foreword by Mark Bassin | ISBN 978-3-8382-1361-3

216 *Alexander Etkind, Mikhail Minakov (Eds.)* | Ideology after Union. Political Doctrines, Discourses, and Debates in Post-Soviet Societies | ISBN 978-3-8382-1388-0

217 *Jakob Mischke, Oleksandr Zabirko (Hgg.)* | Protestbewegungen im langen Schatten des Kreml. Aufbruch und Resignation in Russland und der Ukraine | ISBN 978-3-8382-0926-5

218 *Oksana Huss* | How Corruption and Anti-Corruption Policies Sustain Hybrid Regimes. Strategies of Political Domination under Ukraine's Presidents in 1994-2014 | With a foreword by Tobias Debiel and Andrea Gawrich | ISBN 978-3-8382-1430-6

219 *Dmitry Travin, Vladimir Gel'man, Otar Marganiya* | The Russian Path. Ideas, Interests, Institutions, Illusions | With a foreword by Vladimir Ryzhkov | ISBN 978-3-8382-1421-4

220 *Gergana Dimova* | Political Uncertainty. A Comparative Exploration | With a foreword by Todor Yalamov and Rumena Filipova | ISBN 978-3-8382-1389-5

221 *Torben Waschke* | Russland in Transition. Geopolitik zwischen Raum, Identität und Machtinteressen | Mit einem Vorwort von Andreas Dittmann | ISBN 978-3-8382-1480-1

222 *Steven Jobbitt, Zsolt Bottlik, Marton Berki (Eds.)* | Power and Identity in the Post-Soviet Realm. Geographies of Ethnicity and Nationality after 1991 | ISBN 978-3-8382-1399-6

223 *Daria Buteiko* | Erinnerungsort. Ort des Gedenkens, der Erholung oder der Einkehr? Kommunismus-Erinnerung am Beispiel der Gedenkstätte Berliner Mauer sowie des Soloveckij-Klosters und -Museumsparks | ISBN 978-3-8382-1367-5

224 *Olga Bertelsen (Ed.)* | Russian Active Measures. Yesterday, Today, Tomorrow | With a foreword by Jan Goldman | ISBN 978-3-8382-1529-7

225 *David Mandel* | "Optimizing" Higher Education in Russia. University Teachers and their Union "Universitetskaya solidarnost'" | ISBN 978-3-8382-1519-8

226 *Mikhail Minakov, Gwendolyn Sasse, Daria Isachenko (Eds.)* | Post-Soviet Secessionism. Nation-Building and State-Failure after Communism | ISBN 978-3-8382-1538-9

227 *Jakob Hauter (Ed.)* | Civil War? Interstate War? Hybrid War? Dimensions and Interpretations of the Donbas Conflict in 2014–2020 | With a foreword by Andrew Wilson | ISBN 978-3-8382-1383-5

228 *Tima T. Moldogaziev, Gene A. Brewer, J. Edward Kellough (Eds.)* | Public Policy and Politics in Georgia. Lessons from Post-Soviet Transition | With a foreword by Dan Durning | ISBN 978-3-8382-1535-8

229 *Oxana Schmies (Ed.)* | NATO's Enlargement and Russia. A Strategic Challenge in the Past and Future | With a foreword by Vladimir Kara-Murza | ISBN 978-3-8382-1478-8

230 *Christopher Ford* | Ukapisme – Une Gauche perdue. Le marxisme anti-colonial dans la révolution ukrainienne 1917-1925 | Avec une préface de Vincent Présumey | ISBN 978-3-8382-0899-2

231 *Anna Kutkina* | Between Lenin and Bandera. Decommunization and Multivocality in Post-Euromaidan Ukraine | With a foreword by Juri Mykkänen | ISBN 978-3-8382-1506-8

232 *Lincoln E. Flake* | Defending the Faith. The Russian Orthodox Church and the Demise of Religious Pluralism | With a foreword by Peter Martland | ISBN 978-3-8382-1378-1

233 *Nikoloz Samkharadze* | Russia's Recognition of the Independence of Abkhazia and South Ossetia. Analysis of a Deviant Case in Moscow's Foreign Policy | With a foreword by Neil MacFarlane | ISBN 978-3-8382-1414-6

234 *Arve Hansen* | Urban Protest. A Spatial Perspective on Kyiv, Minsk, and Moscow | With a foreword by Julie Wilhelmsen | ISBN 978-3-8382-1495-5

235 *Eleonora Narvselius, Julie Fedor (Eds.)* | Diversity in the East-Central European Borderlands. Memories, Cityscapes, People | ISBN 978-3-8382-1523-5

236 *Regina Elsner* | The Russian Orthodox Church and Modernity. A Historical and Theological Investigation into Eastern Christianity between Unity and Plurality | With a foreword by Mikhail Suslov | ISBN 978-3-8382-1568-6

237 *Bo Petersson* | The Putin Predicament. Problems of Legitimacy and Succession in Russia | With a foreword by J. Paul Goode | ISBN 978-3-8382-1050-6

238 *Jonathan Otto Pohl* | The Years of Great Silence. The Deportation, Special Settlement, and Mobilization into the Labor Army of Ethnic Germans in the USSR, 1941–1955 | ISBN 978-3-8382-1630-0

239 *Mikhail Minakov (Ed.)* | Inventing Majorities. Ideological Creativity in Post-Soviet Societies | ISBN 978-3-8382-1641-6

240 *Robert M. Cutler* | Soviet and Post-Soviet Foreign Policies I. East-South Relations and the Political Economy of the Communist Bloc, 1971–1991 | With a foreword by Roger E. Kanet | ISBN 978-3-8382-1654-6

241 *Izabella Agardi* | On the Verge of History. Life Stories of Rural Women from Serbia, Romania, and Hungary, 1920–2020 | With a foreword by Andrea Pető | ISBN 978-3-8382-1602-7

242 *Sebastian Schäffer (Ed.)* | Ukraine in Central and Eastern Europe. Kyiv's Foreign Affairs and the International Relations of the Post-Communist Region | With a foreword by Pavlo Klimkin and Andreas Umland| ISBN 978-3-8382-1615-7

243 *Volodymyr Dubrovskyi, Kalman Mizsei, Mychailo Wynnyckyj (Eds.)* | Eight Years after the Revolution of Dignity. What Has Changed in Ukraine during 2013–2021? | With a foreword by Yaroslav Hrytsak | ISBN 978-3-8382-1560-0

244 *Rumena Filipova* | Constructing the Limits of Europe Identity and Foreign Policy in Poland, Bulgaria, and Russia since 1989 | With forewords by Harald Wydra and Gergana Yankova-Dimova | ISBN 978-3-8382-1649-2

245 *Oleksandra Keudel* | How Patronal Networks Shape Opportunities for Local Citizen Participation in a Hybrid Regime A Comparative Analysis of Five Cities in Ukraine | With a foreword by Sabine Kropp | ISBN 978-3-8382-1671-3

246 *Jan Claas Behrends, Thomas Lindenberger, Pavel Kolar (Eds.)* | Violence after Stalin Institutions, Practices, and Everyday Life in the Soviet Bloc 1953–1989 | ISBN 978-3-8382-1637-9

247 *Leonid Luks* | Macht und Ohnmacht der Utopien Essays zur Geschichte Russlands im 20. und 21. Jahrhundert | ISBN 978-3-8382-1677-5

248 *Iuliia Barshadska* | Brüssel zwischen Kyjiw und Moskau Das auswärtige Handeln der Europäischen Union im ukrainisch-russischen Konflikt 2014-2019 | Mit einem Vorwort von Olaf Leiße | ISBN 978-3-8382-1667-6

249 *Valentyna Romanova* | Decentralisation and Multilevel Elections in Ukraine Reform Dynamics and Party Politics in 2010–2021 | With a foreword by Kimitaka Matsuzato | ISBN 978-3-8382-1700-0

250 *Alexander Motyl* | National Questions. Theoretical Reflections on Nations and Nationalism in Eastern Europe | ISBN 978-3-8382-1675-1

251 *Marc Dietrich* | A Cosmopolitan Model for Peacebuilding. The Ukrainian Cases of Crimea and the Donbas | With a foreword by Rémi Baudouï | ISBN 978-3-8382-1687-4

252 *Eduard Baidaus* | An Unsettled Nation. Moldova in the Geopolitics of Russia, Romania, and Ukraine | With forewords by John-Paul Himka and David R. Marples | ISBN 978-3-8382-1582-2

253 *Igor Okunev, Petr Oskolkov (Eds.)* | Transforming the Administrative Matryoshka. The Reform of Autonomous Okrugs in the Russian Federation, 2003–2008 | With a foreword by Vladimir Zorin | ISBN 978-3-8382-1721-5

254 *Winfried Schneider-Deters* | Ukraine's Fateful Years 2013–2019. Vol. I: The Popular Uprising in Winter 2013/2014 | ISBN 978-3-8382-1725-3

255 *Winfried Schneider-Deters* | Ukraine's Fateful Years 2013–2019. Vol. II: The Annexation of Crimea and the War in Donbas | ISBN 978-3-8382-1726-0

256 *Robert M. Cutler* | Soviet and Post-Soviet Russian Foreign Policies II. East-West Relations in Europe and the Political Economy of the Communist Bloc, 1971–1991 | With a foreword by Roger E. Kanet | ISBN 978-3-8382-1727-7

257 *Robert M. Cutler* | Soviet and Post-Soviet Russian Foreign Policies III. East-West Relations in Europe and Eurasia in the Post-Cold War Transition, 1991–2001 | With a foreword by Roger E. Kanet | ISBN 978-3-8382-1728-4

258 *Paweł Kowal, Iwona Reichardt, Kateryna Pryshchepa (Eds.)* | Three Revolutions: Mobilization and Change in Contemporary Ukraine III. Archival Records and Historical Sources on the 1990 Revolution on Granite | ISBN 978-3-8382-1376-7

259 *Mikhail Minakov (Ed.)* | Philosophy Unchained. Developments in Post-Soviet Philosophical Thought. | With a foreword by Christopher Donohue | ISBN 978-3-8382-1768-0

260 *David Dalton* | The Ukrainian Oligarchy After the Euromaidan. How Ukraine's Political Economy Regime Survived the Crisis | With a foreword by Andrew Wilson | ISBN 978-3-8382-1740-6

261 *Andreas Heinemann-Grüder (Ed.)* | Who are the Fighters? Irregular Armed Groups in the Russian-Ukrainian War in 2014–2015 | ISBN 978-3-8382-1777-2

262 *Taras Kuzio (Ed.)* | Russian Disinformation and Western Scholarship. Bias and Prejudice in Journalistic, Expert, and Academic Analyses of East European, Russian and Eurasian Affairs | ISBN 978-3-8382-1685-0

263 *Darius Furmonavicius* | LithuaniaTransforms the West. Lithuania's Liberation from Soviet Occupation and the Enlargement of NATO (1988–2022) | With a foreword by Vytautas Landsbergis | ISBN 978-3-8382-1779-6

264 *Dirk Dalberg* | Politisches Denken im tschechoslowakischen Dissens. Egon Bondy, Miroslav Kusý, Milan Šimečka und Petr Uhl (1968-1989) | ISBN 978-3-8382-1318-7

265 *Леонид Люкс* | К столетию «философского парохода». Мыслители «первой» русской эмиграции о русской революции и о тоталитарных соблазнах XX века | ISBN 978-3-8382-1775-8

266 *Daviti Mtchedlishvili* | The EU and the South Caucasus. European Neighborhood Policies between Eclecticism and Pragmatism, 1991-2021 | With a foreword by Nicholas Ross Smith | ISBN 978-3-8382-1735-2

267 *Bohdan Harasymiw* | Post-Euromaidan Ukraine. Domestic Power Struggles and War of National Survival in 2014–2022 | ISBN 978-3-8382-1798-7

268 *Nadiia Koval, Denys Tereshchenko (Eds.)* | Russian Cultural Diplomacy under Putin. Rossotrudnichestvo, the "Russkiy Mir" Foundation, and the Gorchakov Fund in 2007–2022 | ISBN 978-3-8382-1801-4

269 *Izabela Kazejak* | Jews in Post-War Wrocław and L'viv. Official Policies and Local Responses in Comparative Perspective, 1945-1970s | ISBN 978-3-8382-1802-1

270 *Jakob Hauter* | Russia's Overlooked Invasion. The Causes of the 2014 Outbreak of War in Ukraine's Donbas | With a foreword by Hiroaki Kuromiya | ISBN 978-3-8382-1803-8

271 *Anton Shekhovtsov* | Russian Political Warfare. Essays on Kremlin Propaganda in Europe and the Neighbourhood, 2020-2023 | With a foreword by Nathalie Loiseau | ISBN 978-3-8382-1821-2

272 *Андреа Пето* | Насилие и Молчание. Красная армия в Венгрии во Второй Мировой войне | ISBN 978-3-8382-1636-2

ibidem.eu